D0090436

NO LONGER PROPERTY OF
SEATTLE PUBLIC LIBRARY

THE SAUDI TERROR MACHINE

THE TRUTH ABOUT RADICAL ISLAM AND SAUDI ARABIA REVEALED

PIERRE CONESA

Skyhorse Publishing

Copyright © 2016 by Pierre Conesa

All rights reserved. No part of this book may be reproduced in any manner without the express written consent of the publisher, except in the case of brief excerpts in critical reviews or articles. All inquiries should be addressed to Skyhorse Publishing, 307 West 36th Street, 11th Floor, New York, NY 10018.

First North American Edition 2018.
First Published 2016 in France by Robert Laffont.

Skyhorse Publishing books may be purchased in bulk at special discounts for sales promotion, corporate gifts, fund-raising, or educational purposes. Special editions can also be created to specifications. For details, contact the Special Sales Department, Skyhorse Publishing, 307 West 36th Street, 11th Floor, New York, NY 10018 or info@skyhorsepublishing.com.

Skyhorse® and Skyhorse Publishing® are registered trademarks of Skyhorse Publishing, Inc.®, a Delaware corporation.

Visit our website at www.skyhorsepublishing.com.

10 9 8 7 6 5 4 3 2 1

Library of Congress Cataloging-in-Publication Data is available on file.

Cover design by Rain Saukas

ISBN: 978-1-5107-3663-4
Ebook ISBN: 978-1-5107-3664-1

Printed in the United States of America

CONTENTS

"I think that one of the tragedies of this story is that the Saudi Arabians exported their problem by financing schools—the madrassas—all through the Islamic world. The Saudi Arabian government had two wings. The mainland Saudi leadership went into financial issues and defense issues, and controlled the elite establishment in order to purchase support. From the more fundamentalist religious groups, they gave certain other ministries, the religious ministries, education ministries, to more fundamentalist Islam leaders. And that's how the split occurred.

So the Saudi government was, to a certain extent, pursuing internally inconsistent policies throughout this period—reaching out to the West with sophisticated, well educated, internationally minded leaders like its foreign minister, like its ambassador in Washington and others. At the same time, it was funding with this vast oil revenue a different set of efforts: education, which was narrowly based on the Koran . . ."

—RICHARD HOLBROOKE,
former US Ambassador to the UN,
who did not mince his words, during an
interview granted in 2014.[1]

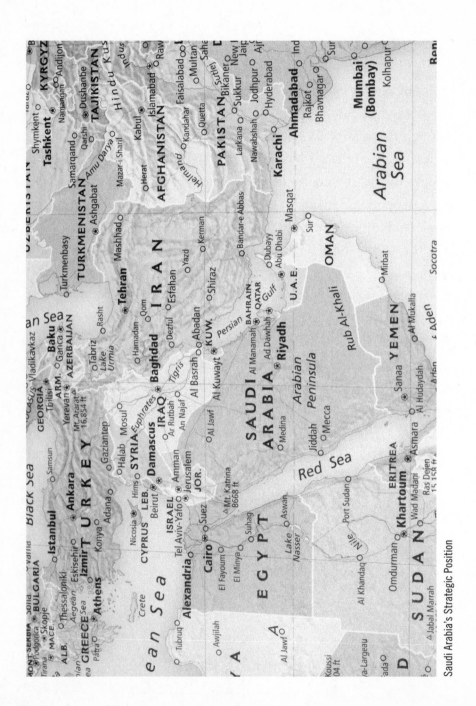

Saudi Arabia's Strategic Position

THE SAUD DYNASTY

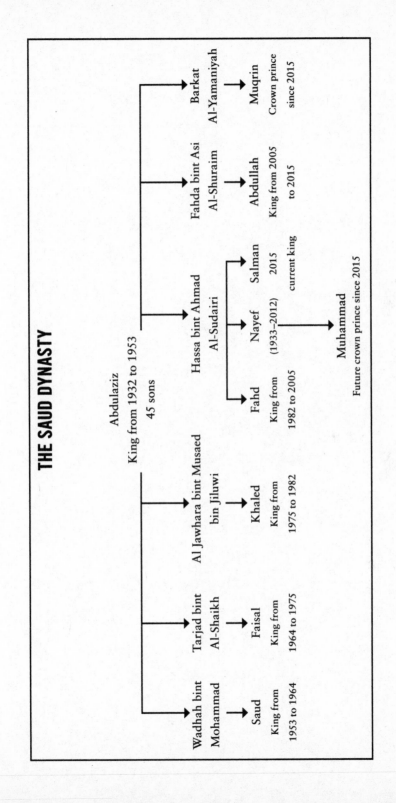

Abdulaziz
King from 1932 to 1953
45 sons

Wadhah bint Mohammad

Saud
King from 1953 to 1964

Tarjad bint Al-Shaikh

Faisal
King from 1964 to 1975

Al Jawhara bint Musaed bin Jiluwi

Khaled
King from 1975 to 1982

Hassa bint Ahmad Al-Sudairi

Fahd
King from 1982 to 2005

Nayef
(1933–2012)

Salman
2015
current king

Muhammad
Future crown prince since 2015

Fahda bint Asi Al-Shuraim

Abdullah
King from 2005 to 2015

Barkat Al-Yamaniyah

Muqrin
Crown prince since 2015

FOREWORD

by Hubert Védrine

Considering the major position Saudi Arabia has enjoyed in the oil economy and global geopolitics since the famous encounter between King Abdulaziz and President Roosevelt on the American cruiser, *Le Quincy*, on his return from Yalta, over seventy years ago, Pierre Conesa's book is essential in order to better decipher this country, as well as the Saudi regime, its vision of the world, and its policies.

Seven sovereigns down the line, under the reign of King Salman, who succeeded King Abdullah on January 23, 2015, the need to understand is even more acute because new questions are being raised—questions that had not been explicitly formulated earlier, in particular with regard to Saudi Arabia's role in recent decades in the propagation of a fundamentalist sect of Islam known as Wahhabism. At the same time, Saudi Arabia is facing the internal consequences of its oil policy, as well as Iran's inevitable return to the international arena. It is important to try to understand, beyond any immediate reactions, how Saudi Arabia will react to all this in the long term.

In particular, it is Saudi Arabia's "religious diplomacy" that Pierre Conesa has undertaken to analyze in this book. It is posited that this kind of proselytism is embedded in the "Saudi regime's DNA" and encompasses both the teaching and propagation of the faith, Conesa does not hide the fact that his approach is very critical. In fact, he analyzes Wahhabism, and Salafism—which, according to the author, go hand in hand—as a "totalitarian" political ideology deployed against Arab nationalism, Shiism, Iran, and the Western ideology of democracy and human rights.

He analyzes the history of this "religious diplomacy," always critically, before and after the Soviet invasion of Afghanistan and its various areas of action: countries in the first circle, countries with a Muslim minority, the former Yugoslavia, the former USSR, European countries, North America and Australia. The upheavals and convulsions of the last twenty years and the rising power of Salafism in many parts of the world have led him to describe Saudi Arabia as a Dr. Jekyll, surpassed by its alter-ego, Mr. Hyde.

Pierre Conesa has, of course, studied the internal workings of "Saudi-Wahhabism," but it is its outer dimension of a "soft worldwide ideological power" that interests him the most. In this respect, how can we dispute the legitimacy of such an approach, since it is true that the world today would be incomprehensible without taking into account the conventional power relations between states, global enterprises and financial powerhouses, but also soft power in all its forms? To begin with there is, of course, the global soft power of the United States (indeed, the American professor, Joseph Nye, used this concept to recommend a more sophisticated use of American power).

Nor can we fail to think of the soft power of Israel as well; the one the European Union hoped to exert, precisely because of its rejection of the balance of power, before it started doubting itself; the one that France reckons it has held on to through multiple levers, including Francophony; the one that Putin's Russia wishes to develop by allying itself with the Orthodox Church (moreover, when Putin goes to Mount Athos, we speak of "religious diplomacy"); the Vatican's soft power– which is obvious; that of the Dalai Lama; of NGOs as well as diasporas (Chinese, Iranian, African, etc.) and the countless lobbies . . . So there is nothing unusual about analyzing Saudi Arabia from this point of view, not just from the perspective of the oil industry.

In so doing, Pierre Conesa fills a gap in the political analysis of a mode of action that has profoundly changed international relations, since to our knowledge there is no book in English or French on this subject.

It is especially useful for France, which has become—among other things, due to its long-standing, strict secularism—the country least able to understand the deep-seated persistence of religious phenomena and has long been content with superficial generalities about Islam, Sunnis and Shiites, the dialogue of cultures, and so on.[2]

This rigorous but well-argued work, which will evidently arouse strong reactions, makes us want to go even further with the analysis—something the author himself calls for.

Further work is needed on the sources and drivers of today's Islamism and its extreme forms. Should such a study be limited only to Saudi Arabia and Wahhabi sources? Shouldn't it be extended to other countries, some of the Emirates, for example? To Muslim religious institutions, not necessarily linked to Saudi Arabia?

But also, more broadly speaking, what should one think of the way Erdoğan's Turkey has evolved from this point of view? How far can the re-Islamization of the country go? Why have other Muslim countries—in the Middle East, the Maghreb, Africa, and so on, which are often proponents of a very different, less extremist Islam—allowed themselves to be so strongly influenced? Is it a question of resources? Ideology? Resignation on the part of political authorities?

On the other hand, why are some Muslim states better off than others in defending moderate Islam? Morocco is one that comes to mind—it has managed to maintain close relations with Saudi Arabia while preserving its tolerant Maliki rites and is now happily training imams for West Africa.

Last but not least, is it possible to foresee where history will take us and what will be the future of Saudi Arabia's religious strategy? Is this critical study—one of great interest and the outcome of enormous work over the past several decades—still tenable for the future? Faced with

Daesh, those who have—and will—take charge of Saudi Arabia's fate in so different and so confused a Middle Eastern context, especially given the upheaval in the oil situation, cannot possibly fail toraise questions and consider heartbreaking revisions in their policy. Only time will tell. In the meantime, this book helps us to measure the stakes involved.

INTRODUCTION

The Saudis constituted the largest contingent of foreign combatants fighting the Red Army in Afghanistan (5,000 people), the largest contingent of the September 11 terrorists (15 of the 19 members), and the largest number of the Guantánamo prisoners (115 out of 611). Saudis also make up the second-largest contingency of foreign members of the Islamic State (Daesh) in Syria and Iraq today with 2,500 members enlisted because of their "extraordinary empathy for jihad." There must be some reason for this overwhelming appetite for jihad! After the first attack on the World Trade Center in 1993, the White House decided to conduct a strike against Sudan on the pretext that there had been 5 Sudanese among the 15 terrorists. However, after the September 11, 2001 attack, the White House pointed the finger at . . . Iran, Iraq, and North Korea, before going on to invade Afghanistan and Iraq although there had been no Iranian, no Iraqi, no Afghan, nor any North Korean among them. A real Saudi enigma!

There are about 50–60 million Salafists worldwide, with 20–30 million in India, 5–6 million in Egypt, 27.5 million in Bangladesh and 1.6 million in Sudan. Salafist communities are smaller elsewhere: about 10,000 in Tunisia, 17,000 in Morocco, 7,000 in Jordan, 17,000 in France, and 4,000–5,000 in Germany. According to German intelligence, Salafism is the fastest growing Islamic movement in the world. So the question is: Is there a correlation between Saudi religious diplomacy and the spread of Salafism? That is what we will try to analyze here.

This book is not a work of theology. There are many excellent works that help understand the differences between Wahhabism and the other practices of Islam; between Quietist Salafism and Jihadist Salafism or between Tablighis and Salafists. But that is not our intention here, for in our view, limiting the analysis to theological aspects seems as vain an exercise as was the thought—in other times—that it was necessary to differentiate between Kim Il-Sung's communism and that of Enver Hoxha. Similarly, there are excellent analyses on the internal convolutions within the royal family of Saudi Arabia—if you want to know whether the nonagenarian candidate will succeed in winning rather than the centenarian candidate, or if a "young" 40-year-old surprise candidate could change tribal power politics.

This book is an analysis from the viewpoint of political science and international relations, which attempts to demonstrate that in this theocratic-tribal regime, state diplomacy, aimed at safeguarding the reign of the Sauds, and religious diplomacy, devoted to propagating Wahhabism (very early on called Salafism), are dialectically linked. The Saudi regime has to reconcile its dynastic interests, which lead it to resort more than is reasonable to its Western protectors, with the ever-orbiting missionary ambitions of the Wahhabi hierarchy. Whenever the regime has called for help from the "infidels"—the worst enemies of its ulemas (clerics), doctors of the Koranic faith responsible for ensuring "compliance" with theological texts and principles—it has solicited theological support from the latter, which has been granted through a learned casuistry worthy of the best Jesuits. But in exchange, the king has conceded increasingly extensive powers to his clergy to govern society and develop his religious diplomacy. The clearer and bolder the ulemas' support of the regime, the greater the king's munificence. The sovereign could therefore promise Westerners that the financial aid given to radical groups would be restricted, but would certainly not change the nature of his international proselytism, always backed by almost unlimited financial manna.

It seemed unnecessary for the West to differentiate between the Saudi regime—a very wealthy client, but a geopolitical dwarf—and its religious diplomacy, as long as the latter did not create any problems while hindering communism or Arab socialism. But is that still possible? Radicalization is spreading its rot in all major religions today (American neo-evangelism around George W. Bush, radical Judaism in the Occupied Territories, Hinduism with the rise to power of the nationalist Bharatiya Janata Party (BJP) in India and even violent Buddhism in Myanmar), but the originality of Muslim radicalism is that it has been constantly supported ideologically and financially by a country with colossal resources and indisputable religious legitimacy. Saudi Arabia is not the first, nor the only country to cultivate Islamic solidarity—Hassan al-Turabi's Sudan, which established the International Organization for the Dawah (in Islamic theology, the purpose of "dawah" or "da'wah" is to invite people, Muslims and non-Muslims, to understand the worship of Allah as expressed in the Koran and the "Sunnah" of Prophet Muhammad and to inform them about Muhammad), was once called the "Mecca of terrorism." More recently, Qatar has financed the Salafists widely and with equal offhandedness. Khomeini's Iran or Colonel Gaddafi's Libya ordered Islamist groups to conduct attacks abroad. Today, Turkey is playing the religious card in Central Asia and the Middle East among Turkish-speaking groups. But very few of these policies have been as consistent and availed of resources as vast as those of Saudi Arabia, for decades together.

The key question regarding contemporary Islam is to understand how Wahhabism—denounced as a sectarian deviation by various religious authorities right from the time it emerged and as the Saudi regime was gradually established—became the quasi-dominant form of Islam, as Hamadi Redissi said in the title of his book, *Le Pacte de Nadjd ou comment l'islam sectaire est devenu l'islam* (*The Nadjd Pact or How Sectarian Islam Became Islam*).[3]

One of the answers lies in the originality of Saudi Arabia's international approach, which, from its inception, systematically developed a religious diplomacy that was favorably welcomed by the West since it seemed anti-Nasser and anti-Soviet. Contrary to Nasser's pan-Arabism, the West's chancelleries viewed pan-Islamism as the perfect barrier against "socialism." It was, and still is, almost unimaginable for many Western leaders to believe that this country could have its own strategy, which has ultimately proved deeply detrimental to democratic regimes. However, Saudi aid, conceived as an enterprise for the Wahhabization of Pakistan and Afghanistan, gave birth to the Taliban (religious students from Pakistan's Wahhabi madrassas, among others)—who were, in a way, pre-production models of the Salafi Jihadists. After 9/11, American neoconservatives managed to avoid accusing Riyadh. And Europe simply nodded in agreement! A worthy lesson in soft power, indeed!

Above all, the total similarity between Salafism and Wahhabism in terms of political ideas must be noted: sectarianism against other Sunni practices, legal violence against Shiism, racism against "non-believers," anti-Semitism, obscurantism, denial of human law as compared to divine law, hatred of the other (any "other," misogyny, homophobia, intolerance and so on). These are therefore totalitarian religious ideas. The kind of Salafism that does not explicitly call for war is called "Quietist Salafism." In all forms of violent radicalization there is always a certain ideological radicalization. Believing that there could be a tolerable, "quietist" Salafism would mean being almost as blind as to believe that Nazism could have a pacifist and tolerant form, or that democratic communism could exist. Simply identifying sources of funding of the Islamic State or terrorist groups will not suffice to ensure the dwindling of their numbers. The Salafism taught in the world's Wahhabi universities and madrassas is the ideological driving force that will continue to thrive even after the disappearance of the Islamic State, if it is not stopped.

What are the internal mechanisms of religious diplomacy?

Over time, an "ideological industry" to use Kamel Daoud's expression—a hybrid between the American type of powerful soft power and the propagandist machinery of the communist system—seems to have gained ground in Saudi Arabia.4 Saudi religious diplomacy, supported at the State's highest level without total governmental oversight, combines public action with private foundations, determining who should be helped, sanctioned, or excluded. Because of its diversity and complexity, the Saudi propaganda system can be comparable to the American system: personal actions of the royal gens, international organizations, funding and establishment of free Koranic schools (madrassas) for children and salaried imams all across the world, private foundations with immense resources, "humanitarian" NGOs, institution of a scholarship policy to attract the best students from foreign madrassas to the Kingdom's Islamic universities, investments in mass media, and so on. However, in many ways the Saudi system is also an heir to the Communist system given its stainless totalitarian ideology and its political commissars, corps of missionaries of all origins trained at its Islamic universities, mainly the one in Medina, which in another place would have been called "Lumumba University."5 The 25,000 foreign scholarship holders from 160 different nationalities who have passed through Saudi Islamic universities over the last 30 years or so are the new apparatchiks in charge of propagating the dogma. Riyadh continues to pay salaries to some who have set out to preach in their own country.

How does the system work? The publication by WikiLeaks of more than 60,000 Saudi diplomatic documents has provided access to this very opaque organization. The Muslim World League (MWL), a UN-recognized NGO, has been the key enforcer of the kingdom's religious diplomacy and has been able to adapt to local contexts. By claiming an Islamic identity with its Islamic courts and its Koranic schools in communitarian countries or by denouncing the "Islamophobic" legislation of secular countries like France, the League has used differentiated strategies in support of Saudi Arabia's religious diplomacy. The world's most intolerant regime pays for the luxury of playing an active role in interreligious dialogue by creating the King Abdullah Bin Abdulaziz International Center for Interreligious and Intercultural Dialogue (KAICIID), an NGO also registered with the UN. This is a kind of faceless diplomacy: no Sheikh Yamani with a smiling face in conferences on international issues, no elegant prince in his traditional costume—so attractive to journalists.

Religious diplomacy in Saudi Arabia is a mechanism supported by the political system, driven by a religious group with planetary ambitions—the Wahhabi ulemas—and endowed with a rigid but always adaptable ideology when it comes to rescuing the regime. This may be why it has been so little studied as a system. Yet it is clear from our estimations that Riyadh has spent as much money on its external religious activities as on its arms purchases in recent decades.

We will also examine the establishment of the multi-layered structures of the country's international religious diplomacy, right from its inception, but especially in the 1960s, primarily aimed at fighting against Arab socialism. As much as an overview of Riyadh's state diplomacy may reveal all kinds of reversals depending on what was required for the Al-Saud family's survival, its religious diplomacy is characterized by its constancy and explains the spread of Salafism and the pinnacle of conversions or of the switch to Jihadism. However, while it may not be realistic to imagine a totally organized and coordinated religious diplomacy, it is nonetheless true that the means employed, in particular financial resources, finally led to worldwide activities that have proved extremely effective in the long term, their impact initially destabilizing for Muslim countries but also for Muslim communities in Western countries. The system was taken over only when the monarchy was threatened either by attacks on its soil or by religious protests. Only then did the regime begin to control funding and modes of action more harshly, but never when its "non-believing" allies requested it to do so. Responding to such an injunction would have meant giving in to the infidels or "kafirs"—an intolerable idea for the ulemas.

The year 1979 was like an earthquake for the country. While Arab socialism's death certificate had been written since the Six-Day War, the regime was struck by a triple shockwave. In February, with the revolution in Tehran, Shiism took over political Islam's leadership and challenged the Sauds' legitimacy with regard to managing the religion's Holy Shrines. In November, the Great Mosque of Mecca was occupied for eighteen days by the ultra-conservative descendants of the Ikhwans who had helped the Sauds to take power; and last but not least, in December, the Soviet invasion of Afghanistan gave the regime the opportunity to launch the call for jihad outside the country and to dispatch its turbulent protesters there. Confronted with an internal or external crisis, the regime reacted as it has always done—with "more religion." Some of the modalities of Saudi diplomacy will be analyzed here, with regard to the first circle countries (Pakistan, Yemen, Egypt, etc.), those with strong Shiite minorities (Bulgaria, India), countries with a Muslim minority facing a crisis (Kosovo, Bosnia, etc.), Sub-Saharan African countries (Mali), those in the former USSR and, finally, Western countries. These few regional explorations have been touched upon to demonstrate the global nature of Saudi diplomacy. It would be impossible for a single researcher to conduct an exhaustive study, given the wealth of material to be examined. But a team made up of specialists from each of the regional spaces would be able to draft out a complete synthesis of this worldwide system.

Was the era of contradictions finally approaching? The divorce had been consummated in 1991, when the Sauds called for American troops against Saddam Hussein. The various crises that struck or have been striking the Arab–Muslim world in recent decades have profoundly changed the balance of power. Today, the Wahhabi regime is challenged both by the Muslim Brotherhood that it had protected against persecution by Arab nationalists, and by Salafist Jihadism and the Islamic State, to whose birth it had largely contributed. The attraction of Salafist Jihadism and its proto-state in Syria and Iraq has proved to be unparalleled at the international level (25,000 foreign fighters from a hundred nationalities), while Riyadh grants naturalization with the kind of parsimony worthy of a tax haven. More so than Riyadh, the Caliphate symbolizes the Ummah (the whole community of Muslims bound together by ties of religion) and, above all, the Sunni cause. Al-Baghdadi has placed himself above the Sauds and designated the regime as a future target. Riyadh, aware of this deadly challenge, is not seeking to destroy the Salafist Jihadism that so resembles its own society—rather, it rivals it by targeting Shiites, just asthe former does.

There are a number of critical works in English on the danger Saudi Arabia represents—indeed, there are all kinds of works on the subject (academic studies, reports by the US Congress, by NGOs, by associations for the defense of religious freedom, journalistic articles, etc.). With a few exceptions, academics have been very cautious on this specific subject for various reasons, ranging from the difficulty of finding sources to the fear of being denied visas and therefore losing access to their research areas. The two Arabic-speaking specialists who worked on this book preferred to remain anonymous. Similarly, interviews conducted in France, Switzerland, the Middle East and Central Asia with Imams, Muslim Brotherhood members, chairpersons of different associations, managers of mosques or Muslim World League (MWL) officials remain anonymous at the common request of my interlocutors.

In order not to be accused of Islamophobia—an accusation triggered with the same celerity as that of anti-Semitism when criticizing Israeli policy—I have used Muslim websites as far as possible in order to source the facts quoted.

CHAPTER 1

A RELIGIOUS DIPLOMACY INSCRIBED IN THE SAUDI REGIME'S DNA

The Saud family's interests were linked to those of the Al-Shaikh family of Abd al-Wahhab, the founder of Wahhabism, with the aim of undertaking a joint project that would lead to the establishment of the regime. Religious diplomacy was born at the same time as the Kingdom.

FROM BEDOUIN CHIEF TO KING

Saudi Arabia has never been fully colonized and the tribes living at the heart of the Najd desert have remained virtually isolated for centuries. For these Bedouins, time somehow stopped with the Prophet. The conquest of the peninsula was a family enterprise, based on the matrimonial alliance between a tribal chief, Ibn Saud, and a religious leader, Muhammad ibn Abd al-Wahhab. As soon as the Najd Pact was adopted in 1744, the commitment became reciprocal: the ulemas of Abd al-Wahhab's tribe, the Al-Shaikh, supported the regime, which promised to spread Wahhabi Islam in exchange. The definition given by Dominique Chevallier, professor emeritus at Paris-Sorbonne University, explained its essence: "[Wahhabism], both a religious and political, Arab and Muslim movement, set itself the primary goal [. . .] of building a Sunni state extending not only to the Najd Desert, but to all Arab countries, of restoring Islam to its initial purity by fighting all suspect (bida'ah) innovations or popular superstitions and by allowing itself

extensive opportunities for expansion, as in the time of the Companions [of the Prophet]."[6] Henri Laoust, a French orientalist specializing
in Hanbalism, added that Wahhabis liked to believe that they were the
"vangaurd of resistance to Shiism and any other suspicious sect."[7] In its
time, this worldwide program, propounded very early on, appeared
unrealizable in this country whose unification itself had taken more
than two centuries. Finally, on September 23, 1932, King Abdulaziz
decided by royal decree that the new State would be called the "Kingdom of Saudi Arabia." For their part, Abd al-Wahhab's disciples rejected
the name "Wahhabis" very early on, preferring to be called the "Ahl
al-Tawhid" or "People for Oneness" (of God) or Salafists (those who
live like the Companions of the Prophet). According to Hamadi Redissi,[8]
Wahhabism is the "last medieval sect given its strong immersion in the
medieval imagination, its linguistic universe, its obsessions and its
caprices. But it is also the first of the modern heresies [. . .]—it antici-
pates the crisis of tradition [. . .] unmasks despots, rebels against the
authority of the ulemas. . . ." This theological school advocates a return
to "true Islam," purged of all theological or legal contributions subsequent to the generation of the Prophet and his Companions (Salafs).[9]

THE (ORAL) NAJD PACT

It all began in 1744, when Ibn Saud hosted Abd al-Wahhab.The Imam, a member of the Al-Shaikh tribe who was seeking protection, preached a return to the roots of the Islamic religion, deeming that the original Islam had debased itself through its contact with sedentary and super- stitious urban populations and the refined aristocracies of the Middle East. Abd al-Wahhab countered these changes with a sermon based on the doctrinal purity of the theologian Ahmad Ibn Hanbal (who died in 855), the last and most rigorist of four great founding Imams of Sunni legal schools. Around 1739, Abd al-Wahhab began to preach and com- pose the "Kitab al-Tawhid" or "Treatise on (Divine) Unity," in which he emphasized the absolute requirement of direct submission to God, the prohibition of any other form of worship or idolatry, and the complete assimilation of orthodoxy and orthopraxy, which he considered had to be those of the Prophet's first companions. The marriage of Ibn Saud's son with the daughter of Muhammad Abd al-Wahhab sealed the efforts of both tribes to establish their political and religious power.

Abd al-Wahhab and his descendants described the war against the Ottomans as a "jihad,"[10] then applied it against other Muslims: "You are a wise man—I want you to promise to start a jihad against the infidels. In return, you will be Imam, head of the religious community, and I will deal with religious affairs."[11] In 1744, Muhammad Ibn Saud became the Imam of the first Saudi state.

The military force that supported the project was the Ikhwan Confraternity ("Brethren of Purity")—young Bedouins abducted from their families whom Ibn Saud settled in dedicated oases to educate them about "true" Islam and prepare them for war. An observer of the time described them in terms that resonate with very contemporary images: "They form a *sui generis* group . . . By becoming a Brother . . . he [the Ikhwan] becomes taciturn, his only pleasure being women—young women—that he takes, in excess . . . He no longer deigns to even return the traditional greeting and prefers to cover his face rather than to come across the face of the devil . . . He has the impression that he has left the false religion for the true . . . He does not accept anyone blessing his deceased parents because they died in paganism . . . He does not understand why anyone can refuse the unparalleled joy of becoming a Muslim . . . in which case, the death of impious recalcitrants is a meritorious act."[12]

Hostile to "modernization" of any kind, which they see as a perversion, the Ikhwans destroyed much of the religious and historical heritage of Hejaz (a region of present-day Saudi Arabia), which according to them was contrary to the dogma of Oneness, attacked Muslims who were practitioners of others rites, attacked pilgrims (violent incident in 1926 against Egyptian pilgrims because of their music) and later condemned Muslims who worked with foreign diplomatic representations. The Ikhwans held Ibn Saud's cooperation with the British against him, along with the kingdom's technological modernization (cars, planes, telephone, electricity, radio), the halting of raids on Iraq and Transjordan which deprived them of their main resources and, finally, they did not accept their exclusion from the government. They openly defied Abdulaziz ibn Saud by attacking Iraq on the pretext that its inhabitants were Shiites, making things difficult for the king vis-à-vis his British protectors.

When a second revolt broke out, Ibn Saud defeated the Ikhwan in October 1929 at the Battle of Sabilah. Their leader, Faisal al-Duwaish, died in Riyadh Jail on October 3, 1931, but in order to consolidate the new regime, Ibn Saud initiated a policy that re-emerges during every crisis in Saudi history: more religion! He decided to integrate them into a "white army" which would become the future National Guard, directly under the Crown Prince's authority. Ibn Saud pioneered a technique often used later—he radicalized his domestic religious policy as strictly as possible in order to calm down religion-based opposition. He had set up the "Jama'a" (Al-Jama'a Al-Islamiyya) in 1926, whose role was to "decree what was right and forbid the blameworthy," under the supervision of the Al-Shaikh family's ulemas.

After the fall of Hejaz came the creation of the Muttawa, a religious police authorized to control people's daily lives, enter private homes, seize music and alcohol, monitor women and, later, foreign embassies celebrating non-Muslim festivals. The experiment, initially defined in Hejaz, was applied to Riyadh from 1929 onwards, with the task of denouncing all breaches of Islamic law. The destruction of statues or objects considered as pagan took place immediately, in the aftermath of the seizure of Mecca. The sphere of social control exerted by the religious police therefore grew perpetually, through continuous harassment, following the practice of the Salafists who strived to control and punish, no matter where they were. At its foundation, the Kingdom was far less prudish and austere than it is today—proof of the pressure exerted by religious morality. For instance, in 1929, photographers could take pictures and men could smoke. In 1930, gramophones played music in Jeddah and, until the 1950s, Western women were not obliged to veil themselves. Religious control has been a long struggle aimed at opposing any kind of modernity.[13] The conflict between the regime and the ultra-conservatives, the Ikhwan, ulemas or their followers, was to break out again on different occasions in the Kingdom's history (1929, 1979, 1991, and 2001).

The country was ruled by just seven monarchs (Abdulaziz, Saud, Faisal, Khaled, Fahd, Abdallah, and Salman) in its seventy-eight years of existence, none of whom had any university degree, all having been shaped by Koranic schools. Saudi Arabia is the only country to bear the name of the family that conquered it. It is also the only family-run enterprise to have a seat in the United Nations, a privilege that no dynasty, no matter how prestigious, no multinational, no matter how wealthy, has ever enjoyed. Political quarrels are above all the affair of a large family, which in any case does not intend to be deprived of power in any way. The regime's diplomacy has therefore been aimed first and foremost at preserving the family's heritage: it did not matter that the monarch (Fahd) was a hemiplegic for a decade, from 1995 until his death in 2005, that his mobility was reduced, that he was only randomly lucid, that he was permanently under medical care and surrounded by a cohort of doctors. Similarly in 2009, Crown Prince Sultan Ibn Abdulaziz deserted the Kingdom for more than a year for a prolonged convalescence in Morocco, only fantasmically fulfilling his heavy responsibilities as Deputy Prime Minister, Minister of Defense and Inspector General of the Royal Armed Forces in an area tormented by the Iranian nuclear issue. The swarms of princes surrounding the hierarchs are props for a rickety regime, rather than real decision-makers. This dynastic paralysis contrasts with the constancy of the religious activities carried out by the Wahhabi authorities, whose reins the regime has left loose.

For its part, the Al-Shaikh family took control of education, the promulgation of "fatwas" or legal notices, justice, the management of religious affairs and the media, as shown in the following diagram with regard to the case of Ibrahim al-Shaikh, the "St. Paul" of Wahhabism.

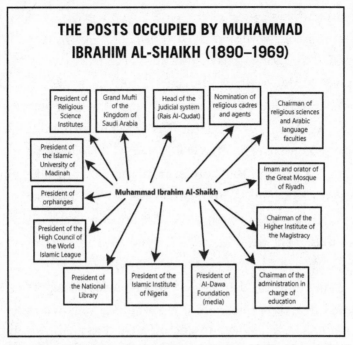

THE POSTS OCCUPIED BY MUHAMMAD IBRAHIM AL-SHAIKH (1890–1969)

Source Extract from *Circles of Islam: Religious Authority and Political Power in Saudi Arabia (18th-21st Century)* by Nabil Mouline

Understandably, with the exception of a short slump from 1969 to 1993, which was limited to not designating a member of the Al-Shaikhs as the head of the Senior Council of Ulemas for a few years, the interests of the two families have been mutually linked in order to ensure their power. Any reform of Saudi society could only take the form of even more religion.

A WORLDWIDE PROJECT

The Wahhabis consider the mission of the new authority is to spread their version of Islam all over the world.[14] Until the clever use of the term, "Salafist," Abd al-Wahhab's doctrine, strongly opposed by the major Sunni ulemas of the nineteenth and early twentieth centuries,[15] had little effect on the rest of the Arab–Muslim world. The sequel was more interesting. It was a political decision taken by Abdulaziz ibn

Saud that removed the use of the term "Wahhabism," replacing it in official terminology with that of "Salafism."[16] As early as in 1956, the prince and future king, Faisal, officially declared that "Islam [in its exclusive Wahhabite variable, of course] must be at the center of the Kingdom's foreign policy." Fifty years later, this principle was confirmed by Article 23 of the Basic Law promulgated in 1992 which maintained the principle of "Dawah," that is, the obligation to propagate Islam: "The State shall protect the Islamic faith and apply the Islamic Sharia. The State shall impose what is good and combat evil; it shall fulfill the duties to which it is called upon by Islam." And Article 34 states that: "The defense of the Islamic religion, of society, and of the fatherland is the duty of every citizen."

But at that time, the country was still a harmless geopolitical dwarf that needed imperial protection. It grew quickly only with the manna of oil and the repercussions of the Cold War. The country, which had never been colonized, was not a British creation—something fairly original in this region of the world, which was the playground of colonial diplomacy. The British in the Middle East wanted to protect the Suez Canal, control the Gulf and the mouths of the Tigris and Euphrates in order to secure the oil fields. To this end, on December 26, 1915, London signed a treaty with Abdulaziz ibn Saud, assuring the protection of his territories against his promise of neutrality. The King only responded on receiving news of the outbreak of Sharif Hussein's revolt against the Ottoman Empire, organized by Lawrence of Arabia. When Sharif Hussein proclaimed himself King of the Arabs, Abdulaziz demanded that the boundaries between their two kingdoms and the bonds of allegiance between the border tribes be clearly demarcated, not hesitating to send his forces against those of Hussein. In the five "independent" princely states that emerged from the ruins of the Ottoman Empire, the Hashemite family—the dynasty that was heir to the title of Sharif (i.e. direct descendants of the Prophet)—triumphed. In 1920, the British placed Faisal's father on Iraq's throne and Abdullah, his brother, on that of Transjordan. But it was the Hejaz region that was the strategic issue due to the presence of the Holy Shrines there.

In 1924, when Mustafa Kemal abolished the Ottoman caliphate, Hussein immediately proclaimed himself Caliph with the support of his brothers. The rest of the Muslim world and England opposed this. Abdulaziz Al-Saud then organized the conquest of Hejaz with the Ikhwan and finally took it over the same year, forcing Hussein to withdraw. When the future King entered Mecca on December 5, 1924, he pledged to purify the holy cities of all the practices that had defiled them. The wave of destruction that struck the city was similar to the ones unleashed by the Afghan Taliban, the Algerian Armed Islamic Group (GIA) or the Malian Salafists. The first "Mihrab" [a semicircular niche in the wall of a mosque that indicates the "qibla," i.e., the direction of the Kaaba in Mecca and hence the direction that Muslims should face when praying] of the Al-Qiblatayn mosque in Medina— used when those praying turned towards Jerusalem—was destroyed, followed by the Dar al-Arqam—the meeting place of the first Muslims in Mecca; then came the turn of the house of the Prophet's companion, Abu Ayyub Al-Ansari, who had sheltered the Prophet when he had taken refuge in Medina; then the tomb of Hamza, Mohammad's uncle, who fell during the Battle of Uhud; then the mausoleums sheltering the remains of the companions of the Prophet and other illustrious martyrs, inside al-Baqi cemetery . . . The Second World War changed the local strategic situation. The oil exploration concession ceded to a dormant English holding company went to Standard Oil of California (Chevron) in 1933, for a period of sixty years. In 1944, ARAMCO was founded around the four American companies that were the kingpins of the country's oil development, until 1973. Hence, the defining moment of World War II for Saudi Arabia was the signing of the legendary "Quincy Pact" in February 1945 with President Roosevelt, who, in exchange for access to oil, guaranteed the dynasty's military protection. It was a legendary pact because the two heads of state did not discuss any strategic alliance or oil guarantee, but rather Palestine and the advent of the Jews,[17] the Kingdom's encirclement by the Arab Unity projects of the Hashemite monarchies of Transjordan and Iraq, and the presence of the British. However, history will only remember that on February 14, 1945, the sixty-year Quincy Pact was based on two important items: the guarantee of the Kingdom's security, described as being of "vital interest" for the United States against any possible external threat, in exchange for guaranteed oil supplies to the USA. To satisfy the ulemas' criticism, it was asserted that no part of Saudi territory would be granted to concessionary companies and that they were mere "tenants" of the land being used. Of course, there was no provision for any renewal of concessions! But a renewal in 2005 by G. W. Bush for media and diplomatic reasons, four years after the September 11 attacks, was part of the State lies used to exonerate the old ally. In June 1926, Abdulaziz had convened an Islamic Congress that was to decide on the type of government to be set up, with sixty-nine delegates from India, Egypt, USSR, Java, Palestine, Lebanon, Syria, Sudan, Najd, Hejaz, Assir, Afghanistan, Yemen and others. But the participants could only take cognizance of it, because, in January of the same year, their host had already proclaimed himself the "Protector of the Holy Shrines." The acquisition of Hejaz gave him a certain religious aura and also brought in revenue for his Treasury: nearly 2 million pounds sterling per year. Hence, there was a continuum between the regime's stability, social control and religious diplomacy. As much as state diplomacy suffered from disappointments and uncertainties, religious diplomacy remained constant until the crises of the 1990s.

CHAPTER 2

THE ESTABLISHMENT OF THE SYSTEM: FROM PAN-ISLAMISM TO THE FIGHT AGAINST NASSERIST PAN-ARABISM UNTIL THE 1979 CRISIS

THE NASSERIST THREAT

The US–Saudi alliance proved useful in the face of rising Arab nationalism supported by the Soviet Union. Thus, the country became an important ally—but not yet the major ally. Apart from promoting Arab nationalism, Nasserism was also very anti-monarchist. "Arabs should start by liberating Riyadh before liberating Jerusalem," Nasser said as the leader of the pan-Arab movement that took power in 1952. In a speech on June 26, 1966, he even challenged the Saudi regime's diplomatic honesty, declaring, "I cannot imagine even for a single second that the Saudi Kingdom will one day be able to fight in Palestine, with American and British bases on its soil. Saudi Arabia should already dispose of its US and British military bases." Nassar believed in exporting the revolution through the Middle East monarchy, from Baghdad to Sana'a. Several events gave him hope: in 1956, the Kingdom of Jordan almost fell; in 1958, the Iraqi monarchy collapsed; in the same year, he announced the union between Egypt and Syria—the premise for a unified pan-Arab area into which he hoped to incorporate other countries; in 1965,

Boumédiène came to power in Algeria; in 1966, the military coup d'état took place in Damascus and in 1967, Colonel Gaddafi took power in Tripoli. This was to be the last surge of the nationalist tidal wave.

Surrounded on all sides, Riyadh felt increasingly threatened by the civil war in Yemen, which began in 1962. For beyond tribal divisions, a proxy war was taking place between Cairo and Riyadh. The Egyptians, heavily engaged militarily, were destabilizing the peninsula, but no territory had been won by 1965, despite the 60,000 soldiers deployed by Cairo. The defeat in the Six-Day War in 1967 finally tempered Nasser's ambitions and an agreement was reached in 1970.

King Faisal then countered Nasser's pan-Arabism with pan-Islamism. He developed his religious diplomacy with the help of the Muslim Brotherhood among the Egyptian refugees, creating national and international structures mirroring those Nasser had wanted. "I am not an Arab leader, I am a Muslim leader," replied the king to the journalist, Jean Lacouture.[18] The West saw it as much less malicious, blinded as it was by east-west rivalry, viewing Saudi Arabia with a certain condescension, above all as a cheap oil supplier, rather than as a strategic partner. The work of religious diplomacy began with a number of objectives. The Six-Day War and the Camp David agreements of September 1978 marked the diplomatic demise of Nasserist Egypt and Arab nationalism. The Arab League left Cairo and settled in Tunis. The 1973 oil crisis brought the kingdom unexpected revenues. International news coverage seemed to be smiling upon Riyadh.

But 1979 was, in fact, an annus horribilis, truly a multiple trauma for Riyadh: in February, Ayatollah Khomeini ensured the success of the Shiite revolution in Tehran; the Ikhwan attacked and occupied the Great Mosque of Mecca in November; and in December, the Communists, supported by the Red Army, moved into Kabul.

ANTI-IMPERIALISM AND ANTI-AMERICANISM: KHOMEINI TAKES HOLD OF POLITICAL ISLAM

The Iranian revolution awakened the specter of Shiite Iran as a rival regional and religious power.

The Iranian revolution marked the resurgence of Shiites in history, with a crash that sent shock waves all around the world. The anti-Semitic attack in Buenos Aires in July 1994 (84 dead, 230 wounded) brought Iran and Shia Islam to the forefront of the international stage when Shiite extremists claimed responsibility for the attack and the subsequent investigation pointed at possible Iranian backing of these terrorists. The Shah had never focused on the religious dimension of his diplomacy, especially since Riyadh and Tehran were in the same camp.

On the other hand, the Khomeinist revolution, based totally upon this issue, durably destabilized the region. As of 1979, Tehran launched a number of international initiatives to compete with the Saudi system: Conference on Islamic Thought, World Congress of Friday Imams and Prayer Leaders—a kind of alternative to the Muslim World League; a conference aimed at demonstrating solidarity with the Muslim people of Palestine and to criticize organizations and states, such as Saudi Arabia, which had approved of the Madrid conference. Tehran also established an international news agency, the Islamic News Agency, which was supposed to "serve the interests of all Muslim peoples," in principle, but was in fact competing with the International Islamic News Agency, which fell under the Organization of Islamic Conference (OIC—now Organization of Islamic Cooperation), dominated by the Saudis. Moreover, Tehran's development of the Arabic language was intended to break Saudi Arabia's monopoly on the airwaves and to provide Shiite people in the Arab States of the Gulf with information designed and produced to meet their needs. The project, aimed at creating a common Islamic market, was simply an initiative to replicate the Islamic Center for the Development of Trade (ICDT), another specialized body of the OIC. Khomeini in no way concealed his desire to drive out the corrupt monarchies of the Gulf, an appeal that found favor among the Shiite minorities of these countries. In 1981, a Shiite dignitary attempted a coup in Bahrain, but failed and took refuge in Iran. On the occasion of the violent and severely repressed demonstrations during the Hajj (400 deaths on July 31, 1987), as a supreme insult, Khomeini demanded that the management of the holy shrines be withdrawn from the Sauds and entrusted to an independent Islamic body. Riyadh broke diplomatic ties with Tehran and made the OIC vote for a restriction on the number of Iranian pilgrims.

Tehran granted asylum to Sunni Islamist movements and organizations to which Saudi officials were no longer able or willing to give any moral or financial support. Finally, Tehran supported opposition movements among the Shiite Arabs of the Gulf through the intermediary of the Lebanese Hezbollah. The most radical Shiites took the lead in the anti-imperialist struggle, denouncing the Great American Satan. Third-World ideology gradually shifted, with the war against Saddam Hussein's Iraq, supported by all powers. On November 26, 1978, the French philosopher, Michel Foucault, speaking of the revolution in Tehran, lyrically wrote in the Italian daily, *Corriere della Sera*: "It is an insurrection of bare-handed men who want to lift up the formidable burden weighing down on each of us, but especially on them—oil workers and peasants along the borders of empires: the weight of the whole world order. It was perhaps the first great insurrection against worldwide systems—the most modern and craziest form of revolt."[19]

The clergy in power in Tehran wanted to propagate a "revolutionary" Islam among "oppressed Muslims" to incite them not to submit to tyranny, not to accept injustice, but to stand up against the enemies of God and against their own leaders, if necessary. Saudi Arabia did not view this kind of discourse approvingly, as neither was its leaders' personal behavior nor their political management particularly exemplary. Shiism gradually became the designated enemy of Saudi religious diplomacy in place of Arab nationalism. Local demonstrations in eastern Saudi Arabia then fueled the new fear of Shiism.

THE ATTACK ON THE GREAT MOSQUE OF MECCA: THE IKHWANS AGAINST THE "GUCCI BEDOUINS"

"Progress without change"—that was the promise displayed as a slogan on the walls of major cities, with the Kingdom reaping an oil boom windfall as of 1973. However, this accelerated material modernization was overwhelming for the common man and shocking for the most radical. It is important to understand the trauma experienced by the Ikhwans' descendants, isolated from all civilization for thirteen centuries, when the country—taking advantage of the oil crisis—became rich practically overnight and was transformed in every respect, except religiously. Within less than a decade, the Saudis went from tents to elevators and vast air-conditioned shopping centers, from camels to four-wheel drives, from frugality to consumerist obesity. As early as in 1965, women's ready-to-wear shops or photography stalls had been vandalized.

On November 20, 1979, when Juhayman al-Otaybi snatched the microphone after the call to Friday's Great Prayers at the Great Mosque of Mecca, he denounced the same injustices the Ikhwans had when they revolted in 1929. He went on to announce the advent of the "Mahdi" or Messiah—in the person of his cousin, Muhammad Abdullah Qahtani—who would bring Justice and Truth on earth and put an end to the regime's corruption and the crapulence of Mecca's governor. The two hundred armed men who accompanied him made a large number of the pilgrims move out of the mosque, which was then transformed into a fortress. Juhayman al-Otaybi and his companions were pure Wahhabis who followed the lessons of the Grand Mufti (the highest religious authority according to the Ottoman classification), Ibn Baz. The crisis dragged on because the official discourse forbade the use of any violence in the Holy Shrines. Even the Great Sheikh of Al-Azhar University called for the end of the occupation. For three days, King Khaled brought together thirty-six great ulemas, to obtain the security of a fatwa from them on November 24, before the use of force in this sacred shrine. The fatwa, validated by Ibn Baz, admitted the hypothesis of the return of the Messiah, but specified that the authentic Messiah would fight "impious or corrupt regimes" above all, which was not, of course, the case of the Saud dynasty.

The first attacks triggered on the orders of the minister—a member of the royal family—failed. Finally, called upon to provide backup, the French gendarmes of the National Gendarmerie Intervention Group (GIGN)—lucky beneficiaries of a one-minute conversion (although it is not known whether it was accompanied by the ritual circumcisions)—finally took the Great Mosque back on the night of December 4.

On January 9, sixty-three mutineers, forty-three of them Saudis, were publicly beheaded without a trial in eight different cities of the Kingdom; the sessions were broadcast on radio and live on television. For eighteen days, the dynasty had been threatened by a group that was more radical than itself and proved incapable of solving the problem by itself. Shaken, the regime began by accusing Shiites; and the unrest that took place in the Shiite provinces in the east of the country, in Qatif and Hofuf, at the end of 1979, only revived its concerns. It then started accusing the Americans and, finally, the Israelis. In Islamabad, the influence of Wahhabi madrassas was so strong that a demonstration took the American Embassy by storm. Similar demonstrations took place in Turkey, Bangladesh, and India.

In fact, the attack carried out by a descendant of the Ikhwans revealed the weight of the ultra-conservative, millenarian, and messianic community, which wished to condemn the corruption of the princes, in particular. Like the Salafists today, it announced the end of the world and the advent of the self-appointed Messiah, Otaibah, a

National Guard officer and disciple of Sheikh Abdulaziz Ibn Baz. The mutineers were also all theology students and had taken his courses.

The regime, destabilized, reacted as it often did to crises—with "more religion." To calm down the pressure from fundamentalists and the religious hierarchy that had rendered great service to the regime, a vice squad, a Committee for the Prevention of Vice and the Propagation of Virtue and the Muttawa (Islamic religious police), falling under the King since 1976, were finally institutionalized by royal decree in 1980. Their leader was given the rank of a minister and a series of prohibition measures were taken in quick succession. New technologies were brought under surveillance; the four cinemas in Jeddah were closed down. It was forbidden to celebrate Christmas, Valentine's Day, or Halloween throughout the territory. The Islamization of teachings was entrusted to the ulemas. The closure of shops during the hours of prayer was severely controlled by the religious police and, finally, songs by the popular Lebanese singer, Fairuz, were banned from television. Video stores were closed down and, later, even mobile phones with cameras were banned. Satellite TV was filtered. In this conservative resurgence, women were specially targeted: they were prohibited from driving, the wearing of the Islamic veil became compulsory—even for Westerners, and segregation in banks and restaurants was instituted as early as 1980. In addition, funding for 241 new mosques and the restoration of 37 others was announced. Foreigners were now bound to abide by Saudi laws. And above all, endowments for the propagation of Wahhabism abroad were redirected and increased. The budget for the Committee for the Promotion of Virtue and the Prevention of Vice was tripled in spite of the economic crisis. The polemic between Ayatollah Khomeini and King Khaled had strengthened suspicions against Iranian pilgrims. The following year, a prohibited demonstration by Iranians, marked by a stampede and police violence, led to 402 deaths among the pilgrims, including 275 Iranians. As regards the modernization of Saudi institutions, a committee chaired by Prince Nayef was charged with drafting a Constitutional Charter, which finally came out only twelve years later.

Sheikh Ibn Baz, who had become the doyen of the Senior Council of Ulemas, accused the "fitna" (unrest or rebellion, especially against a rightful ruler) on rebels, in this case a division of the community of believers, but refused to condemn them, since many of his students were members of the Great Mosque's commandos . . . For the first time, a crack emerged between the Saudi clergy and their disciples.

THE SOVIET INVASION OF AFGHANISTAN: A GOOD JIHAD TO GET RID OF ITS RADICALS

The "jihad's" warrior version had always been a part of the national Saudi narrative. Mohammed Abd al-Wahhab had decreed it himself to mobilize the Ikhwans against tribes hostile to the Sauds or to go and raze Karbala to the ground. Juhayman, who had instigated the capture of the Great Mosque, a purist among the purists, had described to those close to him their revolt against Ibn Saud, who had allied with the disbelievers, using the tone of jihad, thereby more than crossing the red line of criticism against the regime.[20]

On December 27, 1979, the invasion by the Soviet troops came right on cue for the monarchy, undermined by the capture of the Great Mosque and criticism of its management of the crisis. It brought back the idea of the "good jihad" as armed solidarity to defend invaded lands of Islam. Largely encouraged by the authorities in order to relieve themselves of their turbulent youth, fueled by the early Ikhwan achievements,[21] nearly 15,000 young Saudis wanted to go to Afghanistan, about 5,000 joined Pakistan's training camps and about 2,500 crossed the border. The United States was so enthusiastic about this mobilization that it used its own charitable enterprises to support these "freedom fighters." An American NGO, Friends of the American University of Afghanistan, actually run by the US administration, even subsidized a magazine called "Afghan Jihad."

Yet, their cause was not very clear. The leader of the Arab volunteers, Abdullah Azzam—a Palestinian Sheikh and Osama bin Laden's mentor—had personally taught at the University of Jeddah. In the early 1980s, he had moved to Islamabad International Islamic University, built with Saudi funds.[22] In 1984, he moved to Peshawar, near the Afghan border, to establish the recruitment office to welcome the successive waves of Arab volunteers. According to him, jihad had become the sixth pillar of Islam—an individual moral obligation for all Muslims that no longer presupposed validation by religious authorities. He even asserted that Afghanistan was only the beginning: "This duty will not end with the victory in Afghanistan, but will remain an individual obligation until all other, once Muslim, lands return, in Palestine, Bukhara, Lebanon, Chad, Eritrea, Somalia, the Philippines, Burma, South Yemen, Tashkent, and Andalusia."[23] The Saudi intelligence services managing US aid directed it to the most radical Afghan movements (Abdul Rasul Sayyaf, Gulbuddin Hekmatyar), which had already been pointed out by the French intelligence.

Hence, the country was deemed to have spent more than $4 billion to support the Mujahideen, but also to implant Wahhabi madrassas for young Afghan refugees in Pakistan's tribal areas. The madrassas of the Deobandi school of thought,[24] emerging originally in the Indian subcontinent in reaction to colonization and advocating a "just Islam, respecting Islamic principles," had to make room for Saudi Arabia's madrassas. They led to the birth of the Taliban (students of Islamic theology), whose new regime was immediately recognized by Riyadh at the same time as Pakistan and the United Arab Emirates. The most famous of these foreign fighters, Bin Laden, proposed mobilizing his fighters in 1990 to defend his country, threatened by the Iraqi invasion. Disappointed by the regime's refusal, he took refuge in the Sudan from 1991 to 1996, protected by Hassan Al-Turabi. At the time, he was still the head of 5,000 Jordanian, Yemeni, Egyptian and Algerian veterans. He ultimately found refuge with the Taliban, and Riyadh only withdrew his Saudi nationality in 1994. For a young Saudi, trained in this highly religious educational system in a society suffering from a deep ennui, in which the national narrative presented jihad as the founding epic, there were just two options to escape from it all: alcohol and,[25] if possible, drugs,[26] or else the great adventure of jihad. And jihad had become the mythological horizon of the Salafists all over the planet. But against what enemy? Riyadh faced a dual challenge: the war against the Soviets and the Shiites. But the rapid increase in oil revenues in the early 1970s, from $65 billion to nearly $135 billion in 1981, allowed for a dual religious diplomacy in support of the many Islamic organizations around the world, such as the Algerian Islamic Salvation Front (FIS) and, at the same time, activities aimed at countering the Shiite influence.

CHAPTER 3

WAHHABISM AND SALAFISM: THE SAME BATTLE?

Although the Kingdom had decided to use the term "Salafism" instead of "Wahhabism," the question of the distinction between the two ideologies remained relevant. The internal debate has taken place in the West on whether to use the term Salafism (whether jihadist or not) more readily than Wahhabism. This was syntactically legitimate, because Salafism meant orthodoxy and orthopraxy. But it was less so politically. Making the connection between the two religious practices would mean holding Saudi Arabia responsible for the spread of Salafism, which Western leaders have always proscribed. However, the two are ideologically identical, as we shall try to demonstrate.

According to some authors,[27] Wahhabism is the strictest Saudi form of Salafism, supported by active and diligent leaders who use their considerable financial resources to promote this conception of Islam throughout the world.[28] Other scholars, like Stéphane Lacroix, differentiate between the old form of Salafism (called Wahhabism) and the new Salafism, called neo-fundamentalism: "As opposed to Wahhabism, Salafism refers [. . .] to all the hybridization that has taken place since the 1960s between the teachings of Muhammad ibn Abd al-Wahhab and other schools of Islamic thought." Hamid Algar and Khaled Abu El Fadl affirmed that during the 1960s and 1970s,[29] Wahhabists knew that they could not "spread in the modern Muslim world" in the repellant form propounded by the Saudi regime and, therefore, that a new qualifier was necessary.[30] Ahmad Moussalli categorized Wahhabism as a subset of Salafism,[31] declaring that "As a general rule, all Wahhabis are Salafists, but not all Salafists are Wahhabis."

In the one-step-forward one-step-backward competition between these two schools based on a nostalgic return to the dreamt of golden age of the Prophet, one can say that Salafism is the most modern form as it has managed to disseminate itself in countries and categories that Wahhabism had never managed to reach. Gilles Kepel observed that the European Salafists he had met in the 1980s were totally apolitical.[32] Then, in the mid-1990s, he noted that some were beginning to think that violent jihad was "justified in order to achieve their political goals" and concluded that the "combination of alienation practiced by the Salafists against everything non-Muslim in European society and violent jihad had created a volatile and explosive mixture that was more attractive than the propaganda of the old-generation Salafists, who were content with praying and fasting without taking action." According to him, Jihadist Salafism combined "respect for the sacred texts in their most literal form . . . with an absolute monomania for jihad, whose primary target was America, perceived as the greatest enemy of the faith." But in recent years, taking up the Wahhabist refrain once again, especially since the war in Syria and Iraq, jihad has been increasingly directed against the Shiites, bad Muslim rulers, Sufis and so on. Today, the term refers to a composite set of movements consisting of, in particular, quietist movements, activists advocating political action, jihadists, and former Muslim Brotherhood members who have shifted towards violence. "The theses of millenarian, misanthropic, untamed, warlike, anti-Christian, anti-Semitic, and misogynist Islam are found in the raw state in Wahhabism," wrote Hamadi Redissi.[33] The theological proximity of foreign Salafist preachers trained in Saudi Arabia who continue to maintain their ties with their masters, often cited as references, is not surprising: Abdulaziz Ibn Baz, Muhammad Nasiruddin al-Albani, Safar al-Hawali and so on. If a fracture did take place, it was the one that emerged during the Gulf War around the issue of the call to Western armed forces to defend the land of the Holy Shrines. This issue will be discussed in greater detail in the following chapters. However, it did mark the end of a long process of crises between the ultra-legitimist tradition of the ulemas loyal to the regime, along with some of its dissident members, with or without a jihadist past, and foreign scholarship students returning to their country.

The most lucid of the ulemas now recognize that ISIS or Daesh is a local by-product. The former Imam of the Great Mosque of Mecca, Al-Kalbani, stated in the *New York Times* in November 2015, that "Daesh adopted the Salafist ideology. It is not the ideology of the Muslim Brotherhood, Qutbism, or Asharis . . . Daesh drew its ideology from our books, our principles . . . We follow the same road, but take a different path."[34] If the semantics used in the countries concerned by Saudi religious foreign policy were to be analyzed, it would emerge that the terms used do not seek to differentiate between Salafism and Wahhabism on religious grounds, but rather in diplomatic terms, depending on the concerned country's relations of dependence vis-à-vis the Saudi regime. Hence, in Russia, it is Wahhabism, while in Kyrgyzstan, it is Salafism and definitely not Wahhabism. Therefore, it is the Salafist conception that is examined here, which Olivier Roy called "neo-fundamentalism" in his various works, including *Globalized Islam*.[35] The two characteristic elements are theological scripturalism and hatred of the West's cultural values, to which must be added a delegitimization denouncing all other forms of religious thought.

The Wahhabi and Salafist ideologies are impossible to distinguish today, which does not prevent them from rivaling or even battling each other. More than religious formalism, social control, anti-Occidentalism and the explicit legitimization of violence are quite similar in the texts of both movements, but there are two radical political and religious differences that fundamentally oppose them. First of all is the idea of the restoration of the Caliphate, inaccessible to the Sauds, which would delegitimize their position as "Custodians of the Holy Shrines." Secondly, the establishment of a real Islamic territory, different from the existing Muslim states, whose national identities the Salafists refuse to recognize.

POLITICAL IDEOLOGY: ACCORDING TO A FRENCH MUSLIM IMAM

A Literalist Sect

"Wahhabism is the Muslim form of religious totalitarianism," as one French Muslim theologian, who wished to remain anonymous, told me.

Like all sects that accuse other religions of being "sects," Wahhabi–Salafism describes other expressions of Islam as sectarian practices: "I call myself a Salafist to distinguish myself from all misguided sects who call themselves Muslims," said one of the interlocutors to Samir Amghar.[36] The Sacred Book is read and commented to the exclusion of any later contribution, in particular Islam's legal schools. It is conceived as a collection of social codes providing an answer for everything. Theological principles are simplified to the extreme: the oneness of God; the rejection of any other legal school and of ecumenism of any kind. In both camps, attacks against other practices of Islam are constant. Wahhabism rejected the influences of Sufism, which dominated in the Balkans, Turkey, Central Asia, India, Malaysia and Indonesia. The same behavior can be seen in the Salafist Jihadists, for example in Nigeria, Mali, and Senegal. Where violence has spread, Salafists have targeted traditional religious leaders first. Proof of this can be found in the assassination of Imam Sahraoui by the GIA in Algeria, or the attacks against the Sayyeds in Yemen, despite their being descendants of the Prophet.

The highly ritualistic Salafists are very anxious to differentiate themselves through their daily gestures: always use three fingers to eat, drink water in three stages with the right hand during meals, do not blow on tea to cool it, use the right hand while sitting down.[37] The quarrel over "crossed arms" during prayers, which, for a time, tore Côte d'Ivoire's Muslim community apart, illustrates this kind of rigorism. It set those who prayed with crossed arms on their breasts against those who prayed with outstretched arms, each claiming that they knew the Prophet's habits better. But, like the quarrel over the sex of angels that tore the Byzantine Empire apart, the debate remains open to this day.

As with any proper radicalism (secular or religious), theological quarrels include a competition for leadership. Since the Wahhabis refused to be challenged by the "Tablighi" (a traditionalist religious conception of Islam from India), Grand Mufti Ibn Baz declared that "The Tablighi Jamaat, which is of Indian origin, is full of fables, innovations, and forms of polytheism . . . following them is not allowed."

Detestation of Shiites

What about Shiites, then? They were seen as the internal enemy, the "fifth column," the subject of a real legal segregation with regular feverish outbreaks that were violently repressed in Saudi Arabia or outright enemies to be massacred for the Islamic State. It is true that it is easy to feel somewhat lost, what with the sixty-six or so registered branches of Shiism. But the Saudi ulemas were ready to go and flush them out everywhere. From the first pan-Islamic congress convened by Ibn Saud in 1928, 800 Wahhabi ulemas issued an unambiguous statement: "We asked Imam Ibn Saud to demand that Shiites pledge allegiance to Islam and forbid the public observation of their falsified rituals . . . to practice the five daily prayers in mosques under the presidency of Sunni imams . . ."[38] The Shiites, for their part, had murdered Abdulaziz ibn Saud in 1803 to take revenge on the Ikhwans who had destroyed the holy city of Karbala in Iraq and massacred more than 5,000 people.

Some Wahhabi scholars have published anti-Shiite pamphlets that are close to the Nazis' major anti-Semitic writings or those of Rwanda's

Hutu regime in preparation for genocide. Nasir al-Umar, in his essay, "Situation of those who reject in the land of monotheism," explained how to identify a Shiite in the spheres of business, education or administration, explaining that they took control of key sectors and that they were a danger to the Saudi nation![39]

Under the provisions of the Sharia as it is practiced in the country, Saudi judges are not required to record the testimonies of persons who are not practicing Muslims—in other words, those who do not abide by the official interpretation of Islam. So a judge can refuse the testimony of a Shiite citizen. Their works are forbidden, as is religious education beyond primary school. The great Ashura festival, commemorating the martyrdom of Hussein at the battle of Karbala, is tolerated only on the condition that it should not be too demonstrative: self-flagellation is forbidden. Indeed, one may well believe that that is not because of any respect for human dignity, given that this is a country that practices flogging, decapitation and mutilation . . . [40]

Daesh is no exception. Article 10 of the Islamic State's "Charter," circulated at the end of June 2014, prohibited all public demonstrations, namely Shiite ceremonies, claiming that they would be contrary to Islam.

While the Islamic State is content to massacre any Shiites they find, since the 1979 revolution the Kingdom has become increasingly concerned about the influence of Shiism in the world and about countries affected by Arab revolutions, notably in Egypt.[41] According to the *New York Times*, which has researched and studied thousands of Saudi diplomatic documents revealed by the WikiLeaks website, " . . . the Saudis fear that the lifting of international sanctions against Iran after the signing of the nuclear agreement offers Tehran even more ways of supporting groups (Shiites and Pro-Iranians)." These documents reveal a rivalry that goes well beyond everything else, with deep-seated ideological and religious roots . . . There is a "system of influence that the Saudi authorities have set up and funded through petrodollars."

Totalitarian Social Control

As early as in 1926, the monarch instituted the Committee for the Promotion of Virtue and the Prevention of Vice, later placed under the authority of the Grand Mufti, a mechanism of totalitarian social control delivered into the hands of the clergy, which can be found in all Salafist power structures. The Wahhabi Brotherhood's main activity was the promulgation of religious opinions on all subjects—the "fatwas" (legal notices). A pitched battle began in Saudi Arabia over the power to issue fatwas, after the promulgation of sometimes wacky religious opinions. Some even went so far as to denounce the "chaos of the fatwas," which were intended to govern the tiniest aspects of everyday life. For instance, there was a fatwa by one ulema, Sheikh Adil al-Kalbani, who announced that "There is no clear text in Islam prohibiting music," whereas concerts were and are forbidden in the Kingdom. His website was inundated with messages expressing contrary opinions. Another well-known ulema, Sheikh Abdul Mohsen al-Obeikan, also made quite a stir by decreeing that a woman could circumvent the strict law imposing the segregation of the sexes by breastfeeding the man. This opinion triggered a wave of protests, particularly by women's rights activists. The same ulema, a counselor at King Abdullah's court, drew the conservatives' wrath for suggesting that two of the five Muslim daily prayers, during which all businesses in the Kingdom are closed, could be grouped together when the weather was very hot in order to make the life of believers easier.

The highest religious dignitaries had to intervene to try to put an end to these polemics. On June 25, Sheikh Abdul Rahman Al-Sudais, in his Friday sermon at the Great Mosque of Mecca, spoke out against the "fraud" in fatwas, comparing those who promulgated them to traders who sold adulterated merchandise. The Kingdom's Grand Mufti, Sheikh Abdulaziz al-Shaikh, said in a televised interview that "those who promulgate fatwas without being qualified must be arrested." When asked about the fatwa on breastfeeding, he considered that it was an ancient Islamic text, relating to the "specific case" of an orphan who had to be raised by a particular family and could not be applied generally. Hamad Al-Qaed, a member of the advisory Shura Council, called for limiting the enactment of such edicts to the State Fatwa Council.

As for Sheikh Adil al-Kalbani, he said in a statement on the www.sabq.org website that he had not authorized all songs, but only those that were "decent": "I obviously did not mean Nancy Ajram's or Haifa Wehbe's songs," taking the names of Lebanese stars, which seemed to prove that he knew them. Music was officially banned. At least, that was what the Salafist Imam of Brest (France), Rashid Abu Hudeyfa, wanted, denouncing music lovers as "dogs or pigs" shortly after the Bataclan concert hall massacre in November 2015 in Paris. The same justification was given by the jihadist, Fabien Clain, the Islamic State's French voice, to justify the massacres in Paris: "A blessed attack whose causes Allah has facilitated, a group of believers, soldiers of the Caliphate—May Allah give them power and victory—[who] targeted the capital of abominations and perversion."[42]

To this must be added the Muttawa or religious police, with three to four thousand agents, plus volunteers. They ensure the application of the precepts of Islam and the Sharia in all areas of society: sexuality and homosexuality, prostitution, Islamic dress codes, store closures during prayer times, seizures of consumer goods and of prohibited media. The Islamic State has the same type of politico–religious police. Algeria too had similar groups during the dark years, with the GIA then the GSPC (Salafist Group for Preaching and Combat).

Legal Intolerance

In early February 2014, a royal Saudi decree sentenced all those "belonging to religious or intellectual currents, groups or formations defined as terrorists nationally, regionally or internationally; and all support of any kind whatsoever of their ideology or vision, any expression of any sympathy with them" to prison for three to twenty years. It declared that "terrorism" included atheism and any questioning of the fundamental principles of the Muslim religion.

The key theological concept—in a way, Wahhabi–Salafism's disintegrating gun in the hierarchy of enemies—was "takfir": the power of excommunication, designating a Muslim as being outside the true faith, thus enabling the right to his execution. The medieval thinker, Ibn Taymiyya, the concept's true creator, is constantly cited as a moral guide in Saudi schoolbooks, but also in the books used by the Islamic Saudi Academy, a Koranic school in Fairfax County, Virginia, sponsored by the Embassy of Saudi Arabia. Students are encouraged to consult the writings of this great thinker of intolerance. The West Point Counter-Terrorism Center found that Ibn Taymiyya's texts were "by far the most popular for modern jihadists." Needless to say, relapsed Muslims could be murdered without any notice. According to Saudi law, no disbeliever can be buried in Saudi territory. An example of the absolute nature of state intolerance in this matter is the fact that the red crosses of military ambulances during Operation Desert Storm were concealed. On the other hand, the attempts in December 1994 to have the white cross removed from Swissair airplanes or Scandinavian airlines proved totally unsuccessful.[43]

WHAT ABOUT HUMAN RIGHTS?

Would the religious system allow change? That may seem doubtful if you read Sheikh Muqbil's sermon: "Why do we forbid elections? We forbid them because they give Yemeni non-believers the same rights as Muslims." Saudi Arabia has formally acceded to the major international conventions on the protection of human rights: The Rights of the Child (1996); Against Torture (1997); Women's Rights (2000); Trafficking of Migrants (2002), etcetera. But it considers it its right to apply them only if these texts are not considered contrary to the Sharia— needless to say, none of them is complied with. As for slavery, has it been abolished—or rather, modernized? According to the CIA's *World Factbook:* "Saudi Arabia is a destination country for men and women subjected to forced labor and, to a lesser extent, forced prostitution; men and women from South and South-East Asia, [. . .] who voluntarily travel to Saudi Arabia as domestic servants or low-skilled laborers subsequently face conditions of involuntary servitude, including nonpayment and withholding of passports. Saudi Arabia does not fully comply with the minimum standards for the elimination of trafficking and is not making efforts to do so."[44] The most basic rights of Saudi citizens are flouted. For instance, Raif Badawi, a young Saudi blogger, was sentenced to one thousand lashes and ten years in prison for criticizing the role played by the religious police. Ali Mohammed al-Nimr was sentenced to be beheaded and crucified and finally publicly exposed "until his flesh rotted."[45] In 2012, when he was only seventeen years old, he had taken part in a protest against the regime in the Shiite region of Qatif. The Saudi authorities also accused him of being a "terrorist" and alleged that he had thrown Molotov cocktails at the police. The young man was also unlucky enough to be the nephew of the Shiite dignitary, Al-Nimr, who was himself sentenced to death and executed on January 3, 2016.

THE BEST PERFORMANCES OF THE
SAUDI RELIGIOUS POLICE

On the morning of March 11, 2002, in front of a girls' school that was on fire in Mecca, religious police banned students from leaving the building because their clothes did not conform to the Islamic dress code. Fourteen of them died in the panic caused by the fire.[46] On May 19, 2005, the Muttawa arrested forty Pakistani Christians for practicing their religion in Saudi Arabia. Barbie dolls and Pokémon games are forbidden because they do not conform to the country's good morals of the country. A Lebanese man named Ali Hussain Sibat, the father of several children, was arrested in 2008 during the pilgrimage, and sentenced to death in November 2009 for "witchcraft" because he used to give future predictions on a Lebanese channel widely broadcast in the Gulf States. The Medina Court of Appeal upheld the sentence on March 10, 2010, but it has not yet been enforced.

Saudi laws and regulations do provide that the accused must be treated equally, but in reality, when crimes are committed against Muslims, the penalties incurred are far more severe than for crimes committed by Muslims against non-Muslims.

As far as women are concerned, a major crisis for the regime was the one following Faisal's decision to institute women's education in 1960. The ulemas did not accept this revolution, except at the cost of severe modifications: school walls had to be raised in height, female teachers were imposed (who were almost non-existent), or male teachers were allowed only if they were blind or placed behind smoked glass. Showing great concern about being indulgent towards women, they also alerted public opinion that educated women would end up as spinsters.

WIPING OUT ALL SIGNS OF THE PAST—EVEN MUSLIM SIGNS

Most non-Wahhabi Muslims were attached to the holy shrines and mausoleums associated with ancient Islam. Some had long remained places of pilgrimage, especially Prophet Muhammad's tomb. The Wahhabi doctrine disapproved of this interest and the destruction of these monuments began as soon as the Wahhabis took power, particularly Al-Baqi, the cemetery in which some of the Prophet's companions were buried. Ziauddin Sardar, in his book, *History of Mecca* recorded the demolition of a large part of the historical and archaeological heritage of the holy cities.[47]

WAHHABI DESTRUCTION

Mosques: The mosque housing the tomb of Hamza ibn Abdul Muttalib, the Prophet's uncle; the mosque of Fatima Zahra, the Prophet's daughter; Manartain Mosque; Ali al-Uraidhi ibn Ja'far as-Sadiq's mosque and tomb; four mosques of the Battle of the Trench in Medina; the Abu Rashid Mosque; the Salman al-Farsi mosque; and the Raj'at ash-Shams Mosque.

Tombs and cemeteries: Medina's Jannat al-Baqi razed to the ground; also destroyed were Jannat al Mualla, Mecca's former cemetery; the tomb of Hamida Al-Barbariyya, the mother of Imam Musa al-Kazim; the tomb of Amina bint Wahb, the mother of Muhammad, was destroyed and burned in 1998; Banu Hashim's tomb in Mecca; the tombs of Hamza and other martyrs of the Battle of Uhud; Eve's tomb in Jeddah, sealed with concrete in 1975; and the tomb of Abdullah ibn Abdul Muttalib, Muhammad's father, in Medina.

A building was erected in the twenty-first century on top of the house where Muhammad was born in 570. After its rediscovery during Mecca's extension works in 1989, the house of Khadija, Muhammad's first wife, suffered the same fate; Muhammad's house in Medina, where he had lived after his departure from Mecca, was also brought down; the first Islamic school (Dar al-Arqam), where Muhammad taught has disappeared today under the extensions of the Masjid Al-Haram Mosque. In 1994, Mufti Abdulaziz ibn Baz, the highest religious authority in the Wahhabi regime, issued a fatwa stating that "glorifying historic buildings and sites is not allowed." Such rites are considered "chirk" (filthy) because, as Abdul Wahhab claimed, they lead to polytheism. Five to six hundred mausoleums and other monuments from the origins of Islam were demolished. Ninety-five percent of buildings dating back more than a thousand years are said to have been razed to the ground over the last twenty eight years.[48]

Salafists from different parts of the world have been more hard-working, but more dispersed: the Bamiyan Buddhas in Afghanistan were destroyed with canons; miner's bars and purifying fire put an end to Mali's centuries-old libraries; the statues in Iraqi museums were destroyed by the masses and Palmyra's iconic sites with dynamite . . . The Islamic State went even further in its provocation, questioning whether the "Kaaba" or black stone dating back to the time of Adam and Eve, according to tradition, was a manifestation of polytheism. Through the voice of a certain Abu Turab Al-Mugaddasi, the Islamic State went so far as to advocate its destruction and to "kill those who worship it" on the grounds that its veneration was a form of pre-Islamic worship and therefore an after-effect of polytheism. In his words, "If Allah wills it, we will kill those who worship stones in Mecca and destroy the Kaaba. People go to Mecca to touch the stones, not for Allah."

THE QUIETIST LIMITATION OF VIOLENCE: HANDS OFF MY PRINCE![49]

Ulemas pronounced executory sentences in the form of fatwas that directly legitimized violence as an "open" right to assassinate apostates. Racist expressions were used against non-believers: "Whoever supports infidels against Muslims is himself an infidel," said Sheikh Hamoud al-Uqla in a fatwa issued in October 2001. Calls for public support for armed struggle (for Muslims against Christians in the Moluccas or Indonesia's Spice Islands) were issued by the same author. Whether in Saudi Arabia or Egypt, re-Islamization resulted in a series of religion-based convictions: Faraj Foda was murdered because he was considered an apostate by Abdul Azhar; Abu Zeyd's marriage was forcibly dissolved in Egypt for the same reason; Christians were assaulted and even sentenced to death for blasphemy in Pakistan and Egypt; or there was Ashraf Fayadh, a Palestinian poet, sentenced to 800 lashes and the death penalty. In the 1990s, both the Muslim Brotherhood and the Salafists legitimized violence in their terrorist activities to counter repression by various regimes. Egypt's

Al-Jamaa Al-Islamiyya group attacked tourists (sixty-two people killed or wounded in Luxor in 1997) and Algerian GIAs were responsible for mass massacres, such as in Bentalha, a village razed to the ground in September 1997 to punish its inhabitants for having gone out to vote despite a fatwa prohibiting it. The result: between 85 and 400 dead. Saudi ulemas never challenged the use of "takfir" (excommunication) on the basis of which the GIA massacred so many civilians. This did not prevent the Senior Council of Ulemas from denouncing Al-Qaeda's deviation by issuing a fatwa in June 1998, dubbing it "takfirist" (secessionist) and proclaiming the illegitimacy of the revolt against authority and the right to proclaim jihad by itself and, finally, terrorism.[50]

Even earlier, Abd al-Wahhab had described the raids by the tribes supporting Ibn Saud's assumption of power as jihad, when those serving the cult obviously inherited part of the booty.[51] On the other hand, jihad had been officially banned from Saudi territory since 1930, as a pure Islamic state had been born then. It was still taught in the Kingdom's schools as an epic fresco of the national Saudi narrative, just as movies of the "Western" genre had been, in another part of the world. Hence, the ulemas could develop arguments to legitimize "good jihad," just as others could legitimize "preventive war" or "just wars." Al-Madkhali criticized the Algerian GSPC's excesses against villagers and the authorities, explaining that the real jihad had to be fought against European countries like France or Italy. In fact, since the attacks in May 2003, the Saudis had been fighting against Al-Qaeda within the Kingdom, just as they had fought against extremism until then.[52] But the same did not apply to global jihad, which they continued to hold in affection. Supreme Court President Saleh ibn Mohammed Al-Luhaidan was unknowingly recorded as he explained to young Saudis how to join Iraq and the anti-American insurgency. And in November 2004, thirty-six Wahhabi clerics, most of whom were Saudi government employees, called for suicide bombings against Iraqi (Shiite) and American forces in Iraq.[53]

A Saudi book, *The Foundations of the Legality of the Destruction That Befell America*, using the Internet, justified the assassination of thousands of Americans. The introduction was written on November 16, 2001 by an eminent religious leader, Sheikh Hamud bin Uqla Al-Shuaybi, who was relying on Allah's help to strike the United States with further destruction. Al-Shuaybi's name also appeared in a book entitled *The Great Book: Compilation of Fatwas*, discovered in Kabul in a Taliban office, as well as on the Hamas website as a source of religious legitimacy for suicide bombings. The Wahhabi group, Al-Jama'a Al-Salafiyya— among other Saudi clerics—dedicated attacks perpetrated against US soldiers in western Iraq to it. Al-Shuaybi's thoughts spread across the world. Born in 1925 in Bouraydah, a bastion of Wahhabism, he was the disciple of King Faisal's Grand Mufti, Sheikh Muhammad ibn Ibrahim Al-Shaikh. The list of his own students reads like a who's who from Saudi Arabia and includes the current Grand Mufti, former Islamic Affairs Minister and Secretary General of the Muslim World League, Abdullah Al-Turki. The same arguments were given about the New York attacks by Sheikh Abdullah ibn Abdul Rahman Jibrin, currently a member of the Directorate of Theological Research, Islamic Jurisprudence, Islamic Propagation and Guidance—an official ramification of the government.

Other declarations by ulemas also deserve to be quoted: in a May 2003 publication, Nasser ibn Hamed Al-Fahd, a renowned Wahhabi theologian, justified the use of weapons of mass destruction against America on the basis of the law of retaliation and affirmed the right to kill ten million Americans in response to the US government's crimes against the Islamic nation.[54] Al-Fahd, more prudent later, has since disavowed some of his radical theses, probably in the same way as Galileo did when he emerged from the tribunal of the Inquisition.

While some analysts call the Wahhabi ulemas "quietists," their "pacifism" is limited to forbidding violent action against the reigning dynasty and Saudi territory—a sort of "Hands off my prince!" (to take inspiration from the anti-racism French SOS Racisme slogan, "Hands off my friend!"). In short, while it may not be "soft jihadism," it strangely resembles it. The Wahhabi ulemas have therefore been the most violent of the Quietist Salafists, willing to justify jihad in the "Dar al-Harb" ("world of war") as a counterpoint to their legitimist submission to the ruling powers within the "Dar al-Islam" ("world of Islam"). Elsewhere, Saudi leaders gave themselves the liberty to declare Arab heads of state as being impious or relapsed Muslims. The Egyptian, Sheikh Al-Qaradawi, was not officially a "quietist" Salafist established in Qatar, but a well-known Muslim Brotherhood member (the difference in the Sharia's prescriptions are not clear). He had issued an appeal on Al Jazeera to rebel against Gaddafi, believing it "lawful to kill him." And in February 2012, the Saudi religious dignitary, Sheikh Raed Al-Karani, decreed a fatwa legitimizing the assassination of Bashar al-Assad.[55]

Consequently, the declared support along official diplomatic lines then made it possible to take considerable liberties. In a communiqué dated October 5, 2015 from the International Union of Muslim Scholars, some fifty Saudi clergy called upon Arab and Muslim countries to support those taking part in the jihad in Syria against Bashar al-Assad's regime and his Russian and Iranian allies: "We call on the Ummah [nation] to reject Russia's intervention in Syria by providing moral, political, and military support to the Syrian people's revolution."[56] The appeal was signed by Saudi religious leaders, including figures from the Islamist movement, who compared Russia's intervention in Syria with the Soviet invasion of Afghanistan in 1979. It also echoed the diplomatic stand taken by Riyadh on September 30, 2015, when it described the Russian offensive as an "Orthodox Christian crusade in the land of Islam." However, due to a certain legitimist restraint, the official Saudi clergy always "officially" prohibited nationals from participating in the fighting. Moreover, the program for the "de-radicalization of jihadists," Saudi fashion, consisted in transforming a Salafist jihadist into a Wahhabi full of hatred of the "other," but a legitimist. The results were magical—a 95 percent success rate, according to official figures.[57]

The ulemas therefore played an essential role in protecting the regime, which returned the favor manyfold.

NO, NOT QUITE THE SAME!

If you do not understand the differences between Salafism and Wahhabism, do not worry. The same difficulty was faced in the 1960s and 1970s in understanding the ideological nuances between Castroism, Trotskyism, Maoism, and Stalinism; or if you are better-versed in theological issues, the difference between the "transubstantiation" laid down in around 1079 by Hildebert of Tours—a dogma confirmed by that of Trent (1545–1563)—and the "consubstantiation" upheld by others like Occam or Duns Scotus, which would later be taken up by Protestant Lutherans in the debates on Reformation in the West. But the essential divergences between Wahhabis and Salafists were more significant in political and religious terms.

THE UMMAH AND PASSPORTS

The Salafists regard nationality as a sin: "I am neither French, nor Arab. I am a Muslim," declared Khaled Kelkal, the person mainly responsible for the 1995 Paris attacks. This explains the Islamic State's global appeal. On the other hand, Saudi Arabia is extremely strict about its own passports. Briefly, according to the Saudi Arabian Citizenship System: "Individuals born inside or outside the Kingdom from a Saudi father, or Saudi mother and unknown father, or born inside the Kingdom from unknown parents (foundling) are considered Saudis. Individuals born inside the Kingdom from Non-Saudi father and Saudi mother may be granted Saudi Citizenship. . . . Individuals born outside the Kingdom from a non-Saudi father with a known nationality and a Saudi mother shall also be regarded as foreign; nevertheless, at the legal age, the child has the right to apply for Saudi nationality . . ."

GENEROUS CYNICISM AS A MEANS OF COMMUNICATION

"The Kingdom of Arabia has once again drawn the world's attention to racist and inhuman rhetoric against Muslim refugees (in the West). It has called on all countries and humanitarian organizations, civil society organizations and the media to abandon racist rhetoric in order to strengthen the protection of refugees fleeing brutal regimes and terrorist groups. "We are facing a humanitarian catastrophe unprecedented since the Second World War. The High Commissioner for Refugees (UNHCR) has confirmed that there are nearly 20 million refugees and 40 million internally displaced persons, with figures rising every day due to the lack of funding and lack of appropriate protrection mechanisms," said Saad ibn Abdullah al-Saad, Deputy Permanent Representative of the Saudi delegation, at a meeting of the UN General Assembly. "The Syrian crisis is the greatest humanitarian tragedy of the twentieth century," he said. The diplomat said that Saudi Arabia has taken in 2.5 million Syrian refugees since the beginning of the crisis. The country did not want to treat them as refugees and put them in camps, in order to preserve their dignity and safety. It has granted them freedom of movement and gives those who want to stay in the Kingdom a residence permit, like other expatriates, with all the rights flowing from it, that is, free health care and access to work and education. The number of Syrian students receiving free education probably exceeds 100,000. Saudi efforts extend to providing support and care in neighboring countries namely, Jordan, Lebanon and others. The humanitarian aid provided by Saudi Arabia amounted to an estimated $700 million, according to statistics from the Third International Donor Conference held in Kuwait on March 31 . . . "We must not allow fear of the risk of terrorist attacks and the escalation of racist rhetoric to make us lose the spirit of solidarity with the refugees."[58]

Comment

These figures are disputed by Amnesty International, which reports no Syrian "refugees" in Saudi Arabia. Undoubtedly, they are just a mirage in the desert![59] The concept of asylum does not exist anywhere in the Gulf. None of the countries has ratified the Geneva Convention on the Status of Refugees. According to international law, an asylum application cannot be made from abroad. There is therefore no obligation for any State to accept these applicants if the latter are outside their borders. Human Rights Watch's Nicholas McGeehan believes that "if there is an obligation for the Arab countries, it is more of a moral obligation. In the sense that, for example, if the United Arab Emirates or Saudi Arabia are directly involved in conflicts like in Yemen or Syria, their responsibility is at stake. However, they do not show much concern for the effects of their actions."

There was and is no question of "hijrah" (returning to the land of Islam) on Saudi soil! The Kingdom never contemplated transforming Muslims into "Saudis." A passport divides them. The Salafists, for their part, have no territorial conception of a State, but promise a mythical "Ummah" (community or peoples), which would finally unite all Muslims. With the re-Islamization movement, "a new identity-based approach seeks to recreate a community that cannot be embodied in a given territory, except in a virtual and fantastical form," observed Olivier Roy in 2002.[60] The first practical translation of the disappearance of the state among Salafists was the Afghan Taliban regime, which used only the vague term "emirate." This deconstruction was reflected in the absence of a constitution, the exclusive reference to the Sharia and in the position of supreme judge, taken by Mullah Omar, as "commander of the believers." The most powerful ministry was that of "the Promotion of Virtue and the Prevention of Vice."[61] Mullah Omar, refusing to exercise the functions of head of state, did not govern the country from the capital—he only governed through prohibitions. Urgent needs were delegated to foreign NGOs on the express condition that they abide by the Sharia. This model began to appeal to foreign Salafists and other emirates started flourishing elsewhere, as intermediate steps before the establishment of the Caliphate. One such was the Kano Emirate in Nigeria, run by the Boko Haram sect. The Hizb ut Tahrir, born in Amman, Jordan, following a split within the Muslim Brotherhood in the 1950s, gradually began to advocate the caliphate through its chief, Sheikh Zalum (prudently settled in Beirut). But as the party took refuge in Great Britain, it was careful not to speak of jihad.

THE CALIPHATE

When Ataturk abolished the Caliphate in March 1924, it had not been Arab for a very long time. The Sharif (descendant of Prophet Muhammed) of Mecca, Hussein bin Ali (who had helped Lawrence of Arabia), had proclaimed himself the Caliph and was immediately challenged by Ibn Saud, as we discussed previously.

But the latter never dared to compete for the title, having no affiliation with the Prophet's tribe. He preferred to call himself the "Protector" and then the "Custodian of the Holy Shrines." Even Bin Laden, at the height of his notoriety, never thought of proclaiming himself Caliph. Al-Baghdadi, the head of the Islamic State, has been the first to attempt to do so by taking up the ambitious and high-flown title of "Ibrahim (Abraham) Al-Muminim (Commander of the Believers—an Abbassid era title), Abu Bakr (name of the first caliph) al-Baghdadi al-Husseini al-Qurashi (name of the Prophet's tribe)." To date, the IS project continues to attract foreigners from around a hundred countries—a new concept of the state that covers both the need of Muslim communities for an identity in different countries and, at the same time, the crisis faced by the Saudi model. Today, Baghdadi's caliphate is expanding through annexation, whenever local jihadists rally together. The new Caliph's battle seems strategically well thought out, with the first anti-Shiite attacks taking place on Saudi soil, claimed in November 2014.

The Saudi dynasty is now doubly threatened: geographically and theologically, internally and externally.

TRIFLING DIFFERENCES BETWEEN WAHHABIS AND SALAFISTS

There are also some non-theological differences.

The princely families do not live like the Companions of the Prophet. A symbol of this caste, Prince Alwaleed bin Talal, often described as the most influential businessman in the region, filed a lawsuit against the US magazine, *Forbes*, in 2013, upset that his wealth had been underestimated—at about $30 billion. "For a Saudi, holidays abroad mean enjoying forbidden pleasures. For Saudi women, they mean getting rid of the veil . . . and living in the absolute opposite way as compared to their austere existence in the Kingdom," explained Amal Zaher in *Al-Watan*.[62] He went on to say, "Most Saudis go abroad to escape the cumbersomeness and flee the restrictions of our society, in which we have to justify our every gesture and movement. They can be found in all places of pleasure and corruption, but very rarely in museums or on the trail of past cultures or present civilizations. Parents shut their eyes to all their sons' follies as long as they occur far from home." In the 1990s, for instance, large-scale drug trafficking was discovered in the royal entourage by the French police on board the monarchy's private fleet on its way to France.[63] But the trafficking had not been organized by the authorities, unlike the trafficking managed directly by Daesh.

The Kingdom has also demonstrated that it can be of service to Western countries in difficult times. During the Mitterrand years, faced with its three devaluations of 1981, '82 and '83, the Left succeeded in avoiding the crash thanks to a "secret" loan of $2 billion granted by Riyadh.[64] The country has also been adept at welcoming dictators, even those who have fought Islamists—whether it was Ben Ali, a strong opponent of the Salafists, or Idi Amin Dada, whose regime led to "only" 300,000 victims (but he converted to Islam); they both took refuge in Saudi Arabia. Riyadh is also rumored to have tried to negotiate with Egypt's Muslim Brotherhood for Mubarak's freedom for $10 billion.

But not a single bullet has been fired against Israel! The Wahhabi dynasty, which urges Arabs and Muslims to go to Palestine or Afghanistan, has never fired a shot at the Hebrew state, despite the fact that the two borders are just a few score kilometers apart in the Gulf of Aqaba. During the Six-Day War, Riyadh sent a brigade to join the Jordanian forces, which they reached . . . only when the war was over. It seems that in jihadist literature, the best Arab ally of the United States therefore seems to be an objective ally of Israel. Flying to the aid of the regime, the Grand Mufti Sheikh Abdulaziz Al-Shaikh replied in December 2015 that the members of the Islamic State were not "true Muslims," but that they were "descendants of the Kharijites who had (once) revolted against the caliphate." Referring to the recent threats made by Daesh against Israel, he went on to say, "This threat is simply a lie. Daesh is a party of Israeli soldiers."[65]

Finally, has Wahhabism "Salafized" itself, or has it simply mutated like the influenza virus does every year?[66] That is an excellent question, whose answer does not really matter, since the conjunction of religious diplomacy and the evolution of Third-World ideologies have created a planetary bomb whose cluster munitions can explode anywhere and at any time.

THE INNER WORKINGS OF SAUDI–WAHHABISM

The Power of the Clergy

On the death of Abdulaziz ibn Saud in 1953, the modernization sought by Faisal, the Saudi system's political head, implied a transformation in the role of the great ulemas into well paid bureaucrats loyal to the regime. Respected for his piety, he knew how to handle them. When he finally became king, he pampered them by giving them more power, but under his control. The Senior Council of Ulemas, established by Decree No. 1/137 of 1971, was a seventeen-member body (including the Minister of Justice) appointed by the monarch, in which the country's most eminent theologians took part, in theory. The Wahhabis obviously consolidated their monopoly by excluding other Sunni schools from official bodies. It was not until 2009 that non-Wahhabi dignitaries were admitted, while the demands of the Kingdom's Shiites, for their part, have always been rejected.[67]

The Council soon established itself as the regime's ideological shield. It was the country's main legislative body, alongside the Council of Ministers. It issued fatwas, directed justice, controlled its embassies abroad for a long time and, finally, coordinated activities with the rest of the Muslim world.68 The Saudi political authorities tried to control its access and functioning in order to avoid any insubordination. Similarly, the religious elite, through its formal and informal networks, ensured that it maintained its cohesion and homogeneity in order to perpetuate the hegemony of its discourse, by imposing more or less precise conditions on pretenders to official "clerical" offices. According to Nabil Mouline,69 no known document specifies the rules of access. He identified three broad categories of ulemas: self-made men, children of "middle-level religious cadres" and heirs of the great religious dynasties. The first category is composed of ulemas of foreign origin and Saudis from modest backgrounds. Education and access to high-level religious functions offer incalculable opportunities and guarantee social promotion, though generally limited. The second category (67 percent of the cases) are those of children of "middle-level religious cadres who have worked in the magistracy, teaching, imamat of a mosque or even preaching, without enjoying any significant prestige." The third is that of the country's greatest religious family, which has reigned supreme over the religious establishment since the eighteenth century—the Al-Shaikhs, the third great family of the kingdom, after the Al-Sauds and Sudairis. Direct descendants of Abd al-Wahhab, its successive members have occupied the highest religious posts. King Faisal is one of the children of the family union between Abdulaziz and the daughter of the kingdom's first Mufti.

However, this politico–religious alliance underwent a crisis in the 1960s after the death of Grand Mufti, Muhammad bin Ibrahim, when Faisal attempted to bureaucratize the ulema. The alliance lasted for less than thirty years and concluded with a power-sharing agreement. The Senior Council of Ulemas was restored, but it was Abdulaziz ibn Abdullah ibn Baz who took the lead. He was a citizen of non-tribal origin, from a family of "middle-class religious cadres," who occupied the post traditionally reserved for the Al Shaikh family, but he did enjoy a certain religious aura. He was anything but a Liberal—a true caricature. His statements about the flatness of the Earth ("As far as I can remember, when I saw it, it seemed flat," said the old blind man, very accurately), about the immorality of photography or the fact that women who studied alongside men were prostitutes, became milestones. But even this intransigent man was able to change his mind when he had to. He had criticized the presence of American companies in the Al-Kharj oil district in 1944, but justified the Washington army's intervention in 1991 to fight Saddam Hussein's forces.

In July 1993, King Fahd divided the Ministry of Pilgrimage and Religious Endowments by creating a Ministry of Islamic Affairs and Religious Endowments and a Council for Islamic Propagation and Guidance, chaired by the Minister, in order to defuse criticism by the religious authorities and the Islamist opposition, while consolidating his image as the "Protector of the Holy Shrines." It was an institutional translation of the "Dawah"—the constitutive principle of the Saudi state—which was obliged to propagate Wahhabism, in accordance with the spirit of the Najd Pact. The traditional alliance with the Al-Shaikhs was re-established in 1999 when Abdulaziz ibn Abdullah Al-Shaikh was appointed Grand Mufti of the Kingdom and chairman of the Senior Council of Ulemas on the death of Ibn Baz. Since then, the members of the dynasty have gradually taken over most of the functions they once occupied. In addition to the Grand Mufti, two members of the family were included in the Senior Council of Ulemas—one was the Minister of Islamic Affairs and the other, the Minister of Justice, who was also Chairman of the Consultative Assembly or the Shura Council.

Ulemas of foreign origin were admitted to the Senior Council of Ulemas (three of them) only at the time it was set up. More competent and qualified than the local clergy, they were devoted to the state and to Wahhabism, to which they owed everything. But in 1999, the Senior Council of Ulemas was closed to foreigners and even their children were no longer admitted. The return of the Al-Shaikhs resulted in increased radicalism. In fact, during the last episode in November 2015, the Grand Mufti decreed the destruction of "all the churches" in the Arabian Peninsula! According to him, "Islam is the only religion that can be practiced in the region." It should be noted, however, that between the total exclusion of the Jews and non-believers, which Ibn Baz had sought when he was a young imam in the 1940s, and the targeting of churches today, a certain realism has prevailed in countries where the entire economy was based on the active presence of non-Muslims.

According to Nabil Mouline, "None of the ulemas had any political past, manifested any opposition to the regime, or criticized the decisions of the Senior Council of Ulemas or any of its members, even if their own stands went against official decisions." Religious leaders have supported the regime—or at least, they have not dared to oppose it openly, issuing legitimist fatwas when necessary: for instance, in November 1979, in order to use the military to get rid of the insurgents occupying the Great Mosque of Mecca—a sacred shrine where all violence was prohibited by the religion; in 1994, to strengthen the peace process with Israel; to condemn Islamist "sedition"; and, even in 1990, when the king called upon American GIs to be sent to the Kingdom. Indeed, the politico–religious alliance may have broken, but it never disintegrated. The Grand Mufti did what the regime expected of him and strived to get the young hotheads to see reason. The counterpart for this exemplary discipline was the power granted to the religious authorities to regulate daily life as a whole or to oppose any modernization that could appear contrary to the Sharia. Hence, according to Sheikh Al-Bandar Khaibari, the Earth did not revolve around the Sun and the Muslim World League attempted to get Creationism recognized in its Koranic version . . . Regulating the daily life of the Saudis gave free rein to the ulemas' imaginations. It was therefore one of the aporias of the system that was incomprehensible to Westerners. Only religious criticism was allowed, within certain limits. The regime always reacted to the slightest perturbation by infusing more religion—there was no "liberal criticism." The ulemas occupied the religious, legislative and educational domains, regulating charitable associations, governmental and non-governmental organizations, and the economic and financial spheres. Three ulemas, Abdullah ibn Mani—Abdul Wahhab Abu Suleiman and Abdullah Al-Mutlaq—acted as experts and consultants in Saudi financial markets to validate the compliance of banking services with the Sharia. They were also members of several boards of directors of banks and companies within the framework of what were known in Saudi Arabia as "Al-lijan Al-sar'iyya" or Islamic Commissions. The name of a well-known "Alim" or Muslim learned in religious matters on the brochure of a company or firm was the best kind of advertisement. But the fatwa-based regulations sometimes generated rather surreal conflicts.

SETTLEMENT OF EDUCATIONAL
DISPUTES WITH LASHES[70]

After six hearings, Judge Suleiman Al-Fantookh sentenced Professor Hamza al-Mizeini to 275 lashes and four months' imprisonment, plus a ban on writing in the media. His opponent, Dr. Abdullah Al-Barrak, a professor at the same university—King Saud University—had filed a complaint accusing him of smearing the institution's image by claiming that the Islamic textbooks taught were radical. The debate began with an article in *Al-Watan* entitled "Highlights: King Saud University, an example," dated May 23, 2004. Dr. Al-Mizeini had written that the quality of university education had fallen due to Islamist political movements (the Muslim Brotherhood refugees in the 1960s and 1970s [Ed.]). According to him, the university had abrogated its role of open-mindedness by introducing new programs as compulsory subjects: thus, the subject of "Islamic culture" exactly portrayed the culture of the Muslim Brotherhood's members trained in Syria and Egypt in the 1960s.

The war between the two professors in Saudi newspapers lasted a few months, before Dr. Al-Barrak finally filed a case in a Sharia court to demand that his opponent be punished for religious reasons. The Crown Prince annulled the judgment on the grounds that a recent royal decree stipulated that all disputes concerning publications would be dealt with by the Ministry of Culture and Information.

The political quietism of candidates for membership of the Senior Council of Ulemas was a key criterion for selection. Religious challenges—the "Sahwa" movement, which emerged publicly in 1991 (see Chapter 5)—would, for a time, mark the dividing line which only partly disappeared when the dissidents paid penance. The leaders of the dissent who, in the 1990s, had criticized the authorities, agreed to no longer make their claims, because of their great political commitment at the time. One of them, Al-Hawali, said, "For the government, the senior ulemas must be apolitical men, men who are totally ignorant of politics." Another, Salman Al-Awda, added that "future members of the Council must be men with an uneventful background."

Ministry of Religious Affairs

The ministry was just a modernist adaptation of the ulemas' authority. It oversaw and funded both the construction and maintenance of almost all the country's mosques, although more than 30 percent were built and financed by private funds. The ministry also paid the salaries of the imams and all other staff working in them. In this country of 30,000 mosques and 100,000 inhabitants living off religion (with their families), the kingdom spent nearly a billion dollars in the 1980–90 decade on the upkeep of places of worship and of the ninety theological universities and faculties—an absolute world record in relation to the country's population density. The ministry ensured the ulemas' "quietism" in a very specific manner. Recently, a Saudi Imam issued a fatwa calling on Muslims to attack Israelis around the world in retaliation for the bombing of the Gaza Strip. "All interests and everything related to Israel are a legitimate target for Muslims, wherever they are," decreed the religious edict by Sheikh Awad al-Qarni. The Israelis "must become targets. Their blood must be shed, just as the blood of our brethren in Palestine has been shed," added the Imam.[71] He was not called to order. A truly strange definition of quietism!

The Political Management of the Hajj

The protection of Islam's holy shrines was entrusted to descendants of the Prophet's family who enjoyed the title of Sharif. The shameless exploitation of pilgrims, long the sole resource of the Hejaz region, was an almost constant rule during the Ottoman Empire, under a Turkish governor. The exploitation peaked under the dominion of the famous Sharif Hussein (1908–1925). It was in the name of safeguarding and ensuring the respect of pilgrims that Abdulaziz ibn Saud conquered the city in 1924. He immediately undertook expansion and embellishment work, the like of which the holy mosques had not seen for nearly ten centuries. In the absence of a legitimacy similar to that of the Hashemites that he had just dethroned, he would not have succeeded in ensuring that his seizure of the shrines by force would be accepted, unless he paid them special attention. As early as in 1926, pilgrimage conditions, taxes, and the activities of the many agents living off the event were reviewed. Today, income from the pilgrimage would be the equivalent of around $20 billion per year. And since October 28, 1986, Saudi protocol stipulated that King Fahd Ibn Abdulaziz Al-Saud was no longer to be addressed by using the traditional term "Majesty," but rather the title of "Servant (later Custodian) of the Two Holy Shrines," the name used for the first time by the Ayyubid Sultan, Saladin, in the twelfth century.

For several years, the stubborn determination of the Al-Sauds to impose the rites of a Wahhabi-inspired pilgrimage on all Muslims gave rise to strong criticism and even a radical reappraisal of their legitimacy. Since the establishment of the Islamic regime in Iran in 1979, the Hajj became an occasion for recurrent clashes between Iranian pilgrims and Saudi policemen.[72] The Shiite principle of "Velayat-e faqih" or the "principle of the Islamic Republic of Iran," which gave the Ayatollahs their power—was the basis for the power challenge within the Al-Saud family, which had never been acknowledged for its science and rarely its religiosity. On the religious level, Iranian officials denied them the right to claim any leadership of the Ummah. For them, Wahhabism was just an intolerant, minority sect, isolated and discredited within the Muslim world. In their doctrinal blindness, the Sauds had deliberately destroyed dozens of venerable religious buildings and historical monuments belonging to the heritage of all Muslims, preserved by all those who had previously exerted their authority over the holy shrines, or allowed them to be destroyed. Their ulemas were merely court savants—servants who, by means of honors and religious allowances, were in charge of promulgating all the fatwas necessary for the defense of their common interests and to justify their American protectors.

The occasion for confrontation was the manifestation of the ceremony called the "execration of the pagans," a Shiite ritual during the pilgrimage, which soon turned into a denunciation of the Al-Sauds and their American allies after the 1979 revolution. "The pilgrimage is no less a political than religious activity," said Tehran, which wanted to denounce both the usurping Zionist regime, the "enemies of Islam and Muslims" and the "growing dependence of Muslim states in the region with respect to the Great Satan [America], the Lesser Satan [the Soviet Union], and the Little Satan [Israel]." On the other hand, for the Saudi authorities, supported by its ulemas, the ritual had no theological basis and constituted no more or less than a "bida," that is, a heresy, containing the risk of division and anarchy. In fact, to the religious danger was added a political challenge and a competition to assert their leadership of the community of pilgrims. The situation degenerated in 1981, with violent clashes leading to the death of one of the Iranian pilgrims. This was proof of the "Al-Sauds' inability to manage the Holy Shrines," said Khomeini. The Hojatoleslam's Mousavi Khoeiniha, the Iranian Imam's personal representative on the pilgrimage, was arrested in Mecca the following year. After being released and arrested again in Medina for conducting unauthorized demonstrations at the Al-Baqi cemetery, he was eventually deported. Saudi officials adopted a quota system in the Organization of the Islamic Conference (OIC), justifying it due to the "renovation works in the holy mosques," agreeing to admit only 45,000 Iranians for the next five years, along with a formal prohibition of any demonstrations in the Holy Shrines. Tehran insisted on a figure of 150,000 pilgrims, explaining that the Iraqi sanctuaries of Najaf and

Karbala had been closed because of the war and refusing to renounce the Execration of the Pagans ritual, presented as "a right and a duty."

In 1986, the Iranian delegation withdrew, accusing Saudi Arabia of "forbidding Iranians from the pilgrimage." When bomb blasts struck petrochemical facilities in the eastern province with a large Shiite minority in 1988, Saudi Arabia broke off relations with Tehran while placing three conditions for their normalization: not disturbing the progress of the pilgrimage by renouncing the Execration ritual; accepting the limited quota of pilgrims set by the OIC during the period the renovation work would take; and finally, recognizing Saudi Arabia's rights to the holy shrines. Kuwait's occupation by Saddam Hussein in 1990 and then the Gulf War allowed the resumption of diplomatic relations and Iran then returned in great strength to the pilgrimage, with an exceptional quota, increased to 120,000 people per year during the years 1991 to 1993. Iranian officials bowed before the quota with more or less goodwill—there were no demonstrations, even in the camps—but a gathering took place in an external venue granted solely for the broadcasting of one of the mullahs' sermons. A fresh incident was triggered by relatives of the new guide, Ali Khamenei, who organized a noisy ceremony in 1993. In retaliation, the Saudis announced the cancellation of "compensatory measures that no longer have grounds to exist, since the double quota for three years made it possible to meet the accumulated demand."

In order to prevent risks, the Saudi authorities undertook a series of measures every year during the pilgrimage. In all Mecca's mosques, dozens of preachers and translators, assisted by students of religion, exhort the faithful to fulfill the pilgrimage in the spirit of and according to heavily Wahhabi inspired rites. The aim is to diminish the potential influence of Shiite clerics who might harangue the pilgrims. The authorities also mobilize the members of the Committee for the Promotion of Virtue and the Prevention of Vice to ensure that all pilgrims, including Iranians, undertake the pilgrimage rituals as defined by Wahhabi scholars, respect the time limit within which they can be present in the Holy Shrines and abide by the Kingdom's customs and traditions.

There were slightly more than one million foreign pilgrims in 1995 and 1.8 million in 2010. In 2012, for the first time, the number exceeded the 3 million mark. Many radical militant groups seized the opportunity the pilgrimage presented in order to raise funds by creating NGOs or shell companies to launder money. A broadcast of an American cable by WikiLeaks demonstrated the process.[73]

The Pakistani Lashkar-e-Taiba (LeT) and Jamaat-ud-Dawa (JUD) are part of the same organization, originally called Markaz-ud-Dawa-wal-Irshad (MDI). Founded by Hafiz Mohammed Saeed and professors at the University of Lahore in 1986, it was intended to prepare to fight the Soviets in Afghanistan. After 1989, the goal became combat in the Indian districts of Kashmir, while MDI remained focused on religious and humanitarian activities. When the United States dubbed the LeT a terrorist organization in December 2001, MDI reorganized its activities by changing its name to JUD. The Pakistani government always resisted American pressure to take action against this group. The activism of the JUD, which came to the rescue of the victims of the October 2005 earthquake in Pakistan, made it an almost untouchable organization. In December 2005, an official of the Idara Khidmat-e-Khalq Foundation made a donation for the JUD through a LeT shell company in Saudi Arabia. To justify the transfer, the JUD spoke about financing the construction of new schools or modernizing a madrassa's facilities. Saeed, the leader, and Lakhvi, the commander of LeT operations, continue to head the organization despite their acknowledged role in the Mumbai attacks of 2008 which left 164 dead. Lakhvi was still in charge of the PKR LeT's military budget in 2009, estimated at about US $5.2 million per year.

Teaching and Training of Minds

As mentioned, in the 1960s, many Muslim Brotherhood teachers, driven out by Nasser, took refuge in Saudi Arabia. The first arrived from Egypt, Iraq, and Syria, followed by a second wave in the 1970s, with Brotherhood members freed from prison by Anwar Sadat. For Faisal, then in power, modernization meant Islamization and, noting the lack of cadres, he entrusted the main teaching functions to them. They became the pillars King Khaled needed. Between 1975 and 1980, the numbers rose from 3,028 to 5,300 elementary schools, 649 to 1,377 secondary schools, and 182 to 456 universities. The document, "Educational Policy in the Kingdom of Saudi Arabia" specified the general principles, aims and objectives of education in 24 articles, including: "Promoting fidelity to Islamic Law; understanding the total harmony between science and religion in Islamic doctrine; encouraging and promoting the spirit of scientific research and reflection, strengthening the capacity for observation and meditation, and motivating students to perceive the signs of the presence of Allah in the Universe."[74]

Primary and Secondary Education [75]

Public education, from primary to university, is never completely separate from its Islamic roots. Among its objectives, it imposes the promotion of "belief in God," in Islam as a way of life and "in Muhammad as the Messenger of God." In primary school, an average of nine periods per week are devoted to religious matters; eight per week at the secondary level, nine periods for the Arabic language and twelve in total for geography, history, mathematics, science, arts, and physical education. At the secondary level, there are six periods per week for Arabic, nineteen for other disciplines.[76]

The US Center for Monitoring the Impact of Peace commissioned two reports. The first, published by the Center itself in collaboration with the American Jewish Committee, analyzed the contents of 119 Egyptian textbooks in terms of the references made to issues related to peace and "the other"—Christians, Jews, and the West in general. The book by Antoine Sfeir is the second report based on the contents of 93 Saudi school textbooks.[77] Christians and Jews are denounced as "infidels," the West is a "decaying society in the process of dying" and Jews are a "wicked nation characterized by corruption, malice, lies, treason, aggressiveness, and pride."

Here are some quotes:

"The religion of Islam is the true religion and all others are false. [It] is noble and prevails over all [other] religions. God has fulfilled his promise, for since the sun of Islam has risen on Earth, it is far above other religions. And this must remain so—as God promised—until God inherits the earth and all that lies therein" (Commentary on the Koran, Class 3, 2000, p. 88).

"The non-believers among the peoples of the Book and polytheists will burn eternally in the fires of hell. They are the vilest of creatures" (Commentary on the Koran, Class 5, 1998, p. 116).

"The Muslim nation is characterized by a specificity that makes it the best nation that has ever been created for humanity. This [specificity] consists in the exhortation to do good and the prohibition of evil" (Commentary on the Koran, Class 5, 1998, p. 94).

"There is no doubt that the power of the Muslims irritates the infidels and arouses envy in the hearts of the enemies of Islam—Christians, Jews and others—so that they plot, gather their strength, harass and seize the slightest opportunity to eliminate Muslims. Examples of this hostility are innumerable, starting with the Jewish conspiracy against the Messenger and against Muslims right from the beginning when the light of Islam spread and, finally, with what is happening to Muslims today—an alliance between cross-bearers and Jews, striving to

eliminate Islam from all continents. The massacres directed against the Muslims of Bosnia and Herzegovina, Myanmar, the Philippines and Africa are the best proof of the malevolence and hatred felt by the enemies of Islam towards this religion" (Geography of the Muslim World, Class 4, 1994, p.32).

"It is forbidden to make friends with infidels, to support them or to help them in any way. Whoever grants them their friendship departs from the path of truth" (Commentary on the Koran, Class 3, 2000, pp. 60–61).

"Jihad for the cause of God is the way to attain victory and strength in this world, as well as in paradise in the next world" (Commentary on the Koran, Class 3, 2000, p. 90).

"The religion's interests are above all other interests, for they constitute the pillar of that which is good, both in this world as well as in the one to come [. . .]. God, in his mercy, has decreed various ways of preserving religion. Among others: killing apostates and heretics; jihad for the cause of God, from the soul and with all one has" (Islamic Jurisprudence, Class 2, 2001, p.10).

A Grade 10 lesson contains a text recently posted on the Ministry of Education's website, teaching about killing homosexuals. It is permissible to kill an apostate, an adulterer and those who practice "one of the principal polytheisms." Shiites are counted among "polytheists," not to mention the Ahmadiyyas and Bahá'ís. Last year, the BBC was able to verify that these books were used by five thousand Muslim students in Britain, some even being used in Islamic schools in the United States.

In the 1960s, the monarchy was particularly concerned by the fact that Egypt's prestigious Islamic Al-Azhar University in Cairo taught a progressive "Nasserist" Islam that directly challenged monarchical systems and the obscurantism of Wahhabism. In 1961, with the Muslim Brotherhood's help, the Islamic University of Madinah was set up, and was considered the breeding ground for all the faith's religious cadres and technicians that the establishment needed. A real city within a city, it has its own infrastructure, a small hospital, a supermarket and residential areas for students, professors, and administrative staff. It has nine faculties and two higher studies' institutes, including faculties of Islamic law, theology, Arabic language, social sciences [Islamic], preaching and communication, etcetera. The great Saudi ulemas come exclusively from the Faculties of Law and Theology and the Higher Institute of Magistracy. The students of these three domains receive a scholarship and, at the end of their first year, are granted the rewarding title of Sheikh. In 1967, the King Abdulaziz University was founded in Jeddah, which then incorporated Mecca's Sharia College; it then became the Umm Al-Qura University. In 1970, the Mecca–Medina–Jeddah triangle had the highest concentration of Islamic institutions in the world. Three of the Kingdom's eight largest universities were Islamic in 1990. Ibn Saud University, founded in 1974, trained 5,000 graduates per year in 1980 and 27,000 in 2002. The Islamic University of Mecca, founded in 1981, had 15,000 students in 2002. Riyadh University developed two subsidiaries in Saudi Arabia and five abroad, in the United Arab Emirates, Japan, Indonesia and Djibouti. Some Saudi ulema apprentices go to the Egyptian Al-Azhar University to observe this reputable university's organization, structures and operating mechanisms and then import them into Saudi Arabia.

The curriculum is based on short textbooks focusing on applied law and rituals, with an emphasis on things leaning towards Hanbalism. The study courses have been shortened to three to five years, from the previous fifteen years that were formerly deemed indispensable for laying claim to the title of ulema. The theological lessons of the great Saudi masters have been limited to social codes and definitions of what is licit and illicit. Teaching the theories of Darwinism, Freud, Marx, music and Western philosophy is not allowed.

The overproduction of graduates from Islamic universities is a growing problem. Recruitment has become increasingly democratic and the new graduates have no princely relations. After having explored all possible fields, some are sent to facilitate Islamic centers abroad while others remain unemployed during economic recessions. The successive waves of all these graduates with no special know-how, apart from religious knowledge, lead them to exert constant pressure to re-Islamize the law, so that the Sharia may be mentioned in the Constitution; so that all judicial decisions can be challenged on the basis of Koranic texts and, therefore, so that the Muslim identity becomes a reference that stands above that of nationality, which many foreign states have agreed to do in order to calm their fervor.

THE "WAHHABI IDEOLOGICAL INDUSTRY": AMERICAN SOFT POWER IN ITS STRUCTURE, SOVIET IN ITS METHODS

As Nabil Mouline observed, "Unlike other Arab countries, Saudi Islamism is not a reaction to the marginalization of Islam in the public sphere, but the outcome of the strategy of national and international legitimization adopted by the monarchy in the 1960s, based on Islam and Islamic solidarity."[78] The advent of the Muslim Brotherhood brought its men to Saudi Arabia without cadres, but it also brought an ideology that the Salafist ulemas did not have the intellectual means to conceive of—in terms of organization, knowledge of the world, or major contemporary ideologies. As a result, the Saudi soft power system was primarily a "frerist" or confraternal (brotherhood-based) system that the authorities would only be able to control over time—especially depending on events. The churning between them gradually gave rise to a certain "Salafization" of the Brotherhood and to the "confraternalization" of the Wahhabis.

The pan-Islamist movement had begun in the 1960s around a group of religious institutions in Hejaz province.[79] It was based on the struggle against Nasserism and was built up and diversified to the point of constituting a full-fledged soft power in itself: public policy, major international organizations, NGOs, private foundations, universities and scholarships for foreign students, traditional and new media. It was a hybrid of the American system, given the multiplicity of mechanisms and the close cooperation between public and private actions, and the Soviet system, through its revolutionary and at the same time conservative totalitarian ideology promoted by a body of ideologically trained political commissioners. In response to Nasser's dynamism, the Sauds first created the World Islamic Congress (1949–52), the Jerusalem General Islamic Congress (1953), the High Council for Muslim Affairs (1960) and, above all, the Muslim World League (MWL) to counter Nasser's Arab League (1962), with the World Assembly of Muslim Youth (WAMY) as a subsidiary (1972). In 1969, after the fire at the Al-Aqsa mosque, the Saudi monarch launched the Organization of the Islamic Conference (now the Organization of Islamic Cooperation). The Six-Day War marked the death of Arab socialism and the oil embargo decided upon during the 1973 War gave Saudi Arabia both a strategic role in the energy market and, at the same time, the financial means for its religious diplomacy.

These different organizations seemed to enjoy a strong enough autonomy at their birth, especially when limited to international issues. Hence, the importance of the support the Saudi regime gave the world's Salafist organizations during this period needs to be qualified. At least, that is the opinion of Gilles Dorronsoro,[80] who had observed the activities of the MWL (Muslim World League) and the Red Crescent in Peshawar and noted that even during the years 1980 to 1990, most of the staff were Muslim Brotherhood members, concluding that the authorities in Riyadh probably enjoyed less control over them than the literature leads us to believe.

Since Nasser's accession to power in 1956, the Arab League had been a forum for pan-Arabism. The same year, Faisal responded using Islam as the main thrust of the Kingdom's foreign policy. Hence, the Muslim World League was established in Mecca in the midst of the

"Arab Cold War,"[81] with the status of an NGO that only admitted "acceptable" associations. Shiites were therefore excluded from this time on. This status means that, even today, nothing is known about its composition, its financing or its mode of operation, so that it is impossible to know how representative it actually is. At the time, rivalry also took place on theological grounds: Egypt's Al-Azhar University presented the Saudi regime as a supporter of the United States to the detriment of Arab interests and took the opportunity to broadcast a version of Islam that was highly critical of Wahhabism. The rivalry turned political when Riyadh welcomed the Muslim Brotherhood and funded attempts to assassinate the "Ra'īs" or head of state.

At its inception, twenty-two countries and organizations joined the MWL. It enjoyed observer status (category A) in the United Nations and a consultative status with the Economic and Social Committee of the United Nations (ECOSOC). It was accredited to UNICEF and an observer at all OIC conferences. It was a founding member of the International Supreme Council for Dawah and Relief. Its objectives, if the Geneva Mosque's website is consulted and according to the charter adopted on December 15, 1962, are: "To propagate Islam, to clarify uncertainties concerning the religion, to fight against false allegations aimed at undermining the unity of Muslims and to convince them of the need to obey God, while helping them to solve the problems they face, undertake projects in the field of Islamic propaganda, education and culture." In fact, the MWL's ultimate objective is more ambiguous than suggested by the documents presented to Western authorities. The MWL's Charter is more explicit: "We, the Members of the Muslim World League, also reaffirm our belief that there shall be no peace in the world without the application of the principles of Islam."

In 1962, when the MWL was founded, the Saudi government transferred a quarter of a million dollars to it. In 1980, this contribution had grown to $13 million,[82] not including private donations. The WML is present in 120 countries and controls about 50 major places of worship in Europe: Mantes-la-Jolie, Madrid, Grenada, Kensington, Copenhagen, Brussels, Geneva, Zurich, Rome and Sarajevo, among others. It plays a consular role in countries where Riyadh does not have an embassy, sometimes even replacing official diplomacy. For instance, it opened an office in Beijing before the Kingdom initiated diplomatic relations with China and called for Djibouti's independence when it was still a French overseas territory.

Based in Mecca, its Secretary General has to be Saudi. Abdallah bin Abdulmohsen Al-Turki, a prince of the blood, a former student of the Universities of Riyadh and Al-Azhar, a member of the Board of Directors of a number of Islamic universities across the world, then Minister of Religious Affairs, has been its Secretary General since 2001. He founded and then headed the Islamic University of Riyadh and was at the same time President of London's Islamic World Council and of the League of Islamic Universities. He presides over the Universities of Islamabad and Niger and is a member of the Board of Directors of the Centers of Islamic Studies in Oxford, Chicago, and Frankfurt.

The reorganization of the mosques controlled by the MWL in Europe has grown over time. Bernard Godard, mission in charge of France's Ministry of the Interior's office on worship, explained, "For decades, the Saudis, reputed to be wealthy, have responded to almost all requests without much discernment. They donated funds for the construction of Islamic Centers in Brussels, Madrid, Rome, Copenhagen, Evry, and Mantes-la-Jolie. But now, they have the very unpleasant impression of having been tricked, especially by certain people from the Maghreb who managed their places of worship."[83] Saudi diplomats now often perform executive functions in these centers (Paris, Geneva, etc.). The League, fearing that it may be suspected of favoring terrorism, has cleaned up its mosques in Belgium, France, Spain, and Switzerland, letting go of some employees. Although the regime boasts about the independence of the organization, a law was instituted in 1993 stipulating that all Muslim humanitarian funds had to be placed under the control of a prince. Saudi diplomatic staff stationed abroad exerts religious control over the mosques run by it. The MWL's boards and those of its subsidiaries are all headed by a Saudi official. The Grand Mufti, who is also a member of the King's cabinet, presides over the Muslim World League's representative Council. The Minister of Islamic Affairs chairs the World Muslim Youth Assembly's Executive Secretariat and the Al-Haramain Foundation's Board of Directors. Saudi periodicals regularly publish details about the royal family's gifts to these three organizations.

THE CASE OF GENEVA

Let's take the case of the Geneva Center: Yussuf Ibrahim, Imam of the Great Mosque, of Moroccan origin, who cannot claim to have studied at the prestigious Al-Azhar University due to his lack of resources, was very quickly recruited in Medinah thanks to a scholarship. After he finished his studies, his first post was a diplomatic position at the Saudi Embassy in Berne and then at Geneva's Islamic Cultural Foundation. Dismissed as a result of his opposition to the Gulf War, he was recruited by the Berne Mosque. Due to a second polemic about the right to beat one's wife, he was dismissed once again and recalled subsequently by the Islamic Foundation of Geneva. The only conclusion one can draw is that dismissals are dictated solely by the desire not to make waves in the country, but without any real disavowal. He eventually became Director of Geneva's Grand Mosque and finally resigned for health reasons.

The Geneva Cultural Foundation was successively headed by a Saudi general, an officer of the embassy, a diplomat working with international organizations and then by a diplomat from the embassy in Switzerland—all Saudis.

During his trial in Canada, Arafat Al-Asahi, the Canadian Director of the International Islamic Relief Organization (IIRO) and of the local MWL office, had said under oath, "The Muslim World League, IIRO's parent organization, is an organization that is fully funded by the government. In other words, I work for the Saudi Arabian government, of which I am an employee. Secondly, IIRO is the humanitarian branch of this organization, which means that all our activities and programs are controlled by the government . . . The office [IIRO]—like any other function in the world, here or in the Muslim World League—has to comply with the Saudi Arabian government's policies. If anyone were to depart from them, they would be dismissed."[84]

In August 2006, the US Treasury Department accused IIRO's Philippine and Indonesian branches and its Executive Director, Abdul Hamid Sulaiman Al-Mujil, nicknamed "Million Dollar Man," of having supported Islamic militant groups, provided donor funds directly to the Al-Qaeda, and collected funds for other entities, including the Abu Sayyaf group. On August 4, 2006, the United Nations included Al-Mujil's name on the Sanctions Committee's list. The Saudi authorities did not take him to court. He submitted a petition to the UN Ombudsman and his name was removed from the UN Security Council's Sanctions Committee in July 2013. But that was more than six years after he had ceased to be an IIRO employee.

The functions of the MWL's local missions vary. In Benin, North Korea, Guinea-Bissau, and Venezuela, the stranglehold of Saudi embassies and the IIRO's objectives are explicit:

"[. . .]Through local MWL offices, the local conditions of Muslims shall be analyzed and assistance provided in cooperation with local Saudi embassies

[. . .] Local offices in countries where there are no Saudi embassies receive instructions and are granted powers by the Ministry of Foreign Affairs to issue visas for the Hajj [. . .]."

Since 1984, some embassies have had religious attachés stemming directly from the Wahhabi brotherhood whose mission is to promote Islam. In the 1980s, the Saudi embassy office in Washington had an annual budget of $8 million and 35–40 staff to build mosques, distribute Korans and provide Salafist training to foreign imams for conducting congregations. Medinah's publishing center had already distributed 138 million copies of the Koran across the planet in 2000.[85]

The MWL was originally funded by the Arabian American Oil Company (ARAMCO)—the US–Saudi oil company. But the financing system gradually became increasingly complex and opaque: Al Baraka Bank, founded in 1982 and the supplier of funds to the MWL, was mainly supported by the Faisal Islamic Bank, set up in 1979. It is itself a subsidiary of DMI (Dar al-Maal al-Islami, the "Islamic Money House"), established on July 29, 1981 and long regarded as the central structure for the funding of international Islamism by the Saudis. It is based in Switzerland, at Cointrin.

MWL and IIRO are part of the Saudi Relief Committee, along with the Saudi Red Crescent and World Assembly of Muslim Youth (WAMY). The Al-Haramain Foundation was also a member before being declared persona non-grata by international organizations after the September 11, 2001 attacks.

Founded in Jeddah in 1972, WAMY aims to educate youth according to the precepts of the "authentic Islam." Like other Saudi NGOs depending on the association of Muslim charities, it too is suspected of facilitating the transit of funds for armed struggles or terrorism under the guise of humanitarian aid. Its literature, proselytizing in nature, is deemed to include documents inciting hatred, even armed jihad. The first document linking these organizations and terrorists was discovered in Bosnia: the handwritten report of a meeting in the late 1980s at which the MWL Secretary General and representatives of Bin Laden were present, and where IIRO declared it was ready to make its Pakistani services available to militants, specifying that "attacks could be launched from its premises."[86] IIRO is suspected of assisting armed jihad in the Philippines, Russia, East Africa, Bosnia, and India.

Al-Qaeda originally got used to obtaining support from IIRO. Abdullah Yusuf Azzam, Bin Laden's mentor, was the head of MWL services in Peshawar, Pakistan, when the country served as a backbone for resistance against the Soviet occupiers in Afghanistan. In the Philippines, Bin Laden's brother-in-law, Muhammed Jamal Khalifa, headed IIRO's services and was suspected of serving as a financial conduit for the Abu Sayyaf organization. Muhammad Al-Zawahiri, the brother of Bin Laden's Egyptian partner, Ayman Al-Zawahiri, worked for IIRO in Albania. A Bangladeshi IIRO employee, Sayed Abu Nasir, was in charge of the cell that intended to attack the US consulates in Madras and Calcutta. His superiors could have explained to him that 40–50 percent of the donations received had been diverted to finance training camps in Afghanistan and Kashmir.[87]

THE NEBULOUS AL-HARAMAIN

The Al-Haramain Islamic Charity Foundation (AHIF), a MWL partner based in Saudi Arabia, was active in Afghanistan, Albania, Bangladesh, Bosnia, Comoros, Ethiopia, Indonesia, Kenya, the Netherlands, Nigeria, Pakistan, Somalia, Tanzania, and the United States. Its funding enabled it to provide aid to the tune of $40–50 million per year, worldwide. Part of it went to the Al-Qaeda, proving that money from Islamic charities was a "major source of funding." Until 2004, the Saudi government's rather timid efforts to reduce the flow had failed. On June 7, 2004, on a special advisory opinion from the Security Council to Interpol and the United Nations, AHIF's founder and former leader, Aqeel Abdulaziz Aqeel Al-Aqeel, was reported for "his participation in the financing, organization, and preparation or execution of acts or activities in association with or in support of Al-Qaeda." In September 2004, an investigation by the US Treasury Department proved "direct links" between the foundation and Bin Laden. Between 2004 and 2010, fourteen branches of the charity were listed by the United Nations Security Council as being subject to "sanctions" (freezing of assets, travel ban and arms embargo). On June 2, 2004, the US Treasury Department referred to it as "one of the leading Islamic NGOs supporting Al-Qaeda and promoting Islamist militancy on the planet." The Russian Federation also accused the bank of transferring funds to the Chechens in 1999.

Finally, forced to denounce the foundation, Riyadh closed its eleven foreign offices in Indonesia, Pakistan, the Netherlands, Afghanistan, Albania, Kenya, Tanzania, Bangladesh, Ethiopia, Bosnia and Somalia, as well as 267 charitable organizations.

In each country where the League is present, a Muslim World League Organization Bureau (MWLOB) is established, with the authority to finance projects for the construction of mosques and Islamic centers. It is an actor that provides support to Saudi diplomatic initiatives by discreetly supporting dissident movements claiming to be Islamic. Algeria and Egypt have, in particular, denounced such incentives, but Riyadh continues to respond by declaring that it has no control over "private" funding. According to Michel Renard, a convert and former director of the magazine, *Islam de France*, the MWL "is convinced that in a hundred years, it will have converted a large part of the French population."

In a few decades, the MWL has financed the construction of over 7,000 mosques or places of worship, each with a library and a cultural center that manages associative activities, as the Muslim Brotherhood used to do in 37 countries in Asia and Africa.[88] By 1996, its funding had already been used to build some 210 Islamic Centers, more than 1,500 mosques, 202 colleges and nearly 2,000 Muslim schools around the world "to counter the caricature of Islam portrayed in articles by the Western media." Could there be any better advocate than Saudi Arabia to correct Islam's negative image?

Although the entire movement of developing Islamic schools cannot be wholly attributed to Saudi funding (for example, in Turkey under the Özal government), many private institutions received its aid. In 1975, there were 100,000 (Taliban) students in Pakistan, whereas by 1998 there were between 540,000 and 570,000, half of them in Punjab,[89] while the number of primary and secondary institutes under Egypt's Al-Azhar institution had only tripled between 1986 and 1995. In the early 1970s, the MWL followed the wave of Arab migration to Europe in order to provide immigrants with religious education and other services that were not available at that time. MWL opened offices in Copenhagen, London, Moscow, Paris, Rome, Vienna, New York and Washington, among others. To achieve its goals, between the 1970s and 1990s, it often teamed up with other internationally recognized Muslim movements—especially the Muslim Brotherhood, who did not necessarily share the Wahhabi worldview. Hence, senior officials—such as Kamal El Helbawy, of Egyptian origin, based in London—held senior leadership positions in the League and the Assembly.

Nasserism may have been practically wiped out, but the issue of Shiism remained. From the outset, the anti-Shiite dimension had been part of the Saudi diplomatic–religious doctrine, but it only took full form with the Khomeinist revolution of 1979 (a subject that will be discussed later). After September 11, the counter-shock suffered by the Saudi regime led to a reorientation of the MWL, which, without reducing its anti-Shiite activities—inscribed in its genes—would henceforth be mobilized for the defense and promotion of the Saudi regime abroad.

THE MUSLIM WORLD LEAGUE'S GEOPOLITICS OF ACTION

In democratic countries based on a communitarian model, the strategy was to establish a Muslim identity. The model the MWL preferred was "British-style" multiculturalism, which opened the door to "Islamic citizenship."

In August 1991, the MWL held a meeting in Washington,[90] with the participation of imams from the United States and Canada, the theme of which was, "Developing strategies to introduce the Sharia in Canada and the United States." The aim was to convince Muslims to withdraw from secular laws, considering that there was only one sovereignty—that of God. Arafat Al-Ashi, then a MWL director in Toronto, said, "No Muslim can claim to be one if he cannot apply this law [. . .], otherwise he is considered a non-believer." The three main avenues of action were: Islamic courts, Koranic schools and the training of imams.

Conservative re-Islamization was first carried out by schools: 100,000 Muslim children underwent Koranic education in 700 Islamic schools or madrassas in the United Kingdom, according to the *Times* of

January 1, 2009. More and more exclusively Muslim schools were set up and militants expanded their activities by demanding the application of Sharia rules in hospital canteens—they even set up "halal" hospitals in Germany, the United Kingdom and the Netherlands, which soon also witnessed the emergence of halal convalescent homes.

The second line of action was the claim made by the so-called Sharia-based Islamic courts, based on the principle of equal rights between the different communities. Canada was targeted as one of the countries in which the MWL believed it had the best chance of successfully completing this project, because of the constitutional guarantees minorities enjoyed in terms of multiculturalism. Sheikh Fawaz, a member of the first Sharia Council in Canada, which was established in the Al-Ummah mosque in Montreal, adjacent to the Muslim school, wrote: "Our role is to solve couples' problems, to help families and provide answers to religious questions."[91] The president of the Canadian Muslim Association called for the revision of a 1991 law so that it allowed the resolution of civil or commercial disputes through arbitration, in order to apply it to Muslims, by establishing a structured network of Islamic courts. In response to the first wave of shields raised in Ontario, home to more than one-third of Canada's 600,000 Muslims, the provincial government asked Attorney General Marion Boyd for a report on the issue. In December 2004, she said it was possible for resolving family disputes (childcare, division of property in case of separation, etc.) in the name of minority rights. A petition issued on the website www.nosharia.com by a resident of Iranian origin soon collected 10,000 signatures. The Muslim community was itself divided on the subject. Some imams and the Canadian Muslim Society were in favor of the proposal. "Jews already have such courts, why not us?" said Syed Mumtaz Ali, president of the Canadian Muslim Society at the time. On their part, orthodox Christians practiced arbitration, but above all to settle commercial disputes. As for the Canadian Muslim Women's Council and the Canadian Muslim Congress, they both rejected a "two-tier justice system," one for Muslims that would be harmful for women and one for all other Canadian women. In Quebec, the Minister of International Relations immediately stated that she categorically opposed the proposal. Ontario finally dropped the idea. Prime Minister Dalton McGuinty said his government would also ban all other existing religious tribunals, whether Christian or Jewish.

The approach adopted in Great Britain was more discreet. Islamic courts there were allowed to practice the Sharia and take decisions sanctioned by the High Court. They were headed by the Hijaz College Islamic University in Nuneaton, headquarters of the Muslim Arbitration Tribunal (MAT), headed by Faiz-ul-Aqtab Siddiqi, a rigorist jurist of Somali origin. This accreditation was made possible by the Alternative Dispute Resolution (ADR) facility resulting from recent reforms of the British legal system dealing with commercial, civil and matrimonial matters as well as cases of domestic violence and other neighborhood quarrels. Journalists listed only five courts: London, Manchester, Bradford, Birmingham and Nuneaton. But according to the study carried out by Denis MacEoin,[92] a scholar and specialist of Islam, there were probably at least eighty-five such courts—or seventeen times more than that number. These courts, based mainly in mosques, settled financial and family disputes on the basis of religious principles and rendered fully enforceable decisions. The MAT could draw from 38 arbitrators, half imams, half lawyers, judges and magistrates; 65 percent were men and 35 percent women. They could not issue criminal decisions: no floggings, amputations or stoning. The Somali jurist presented the Sharia as an "enrichment of British law."

But what about gender equality, given that the Sharia allowed the repudiation and inequitable treatment of women in matters of inheritance, with women receiving just half the share that sons received? A study by Civitas, an independent think tank, concluded: "Among the rulings . . . we find some that advise illegal actions and others that transgress human rights standards as they are applied by British courts."

The study cited the example of a court that had ruled that no Muslim woman could marry a non-Muslim man unless he converted to Islam and that the children of a woman who did so would be taken from her until she married a Muslim. Other decisions approved of polygamous marriages and endorsed a woman's duty to have forced sex with her husband. "The fact that so many Sharia rulings in Britain relate to cases concerning divorce and custody of children is of particular concern, as women are not equal in Sharia law, and Sharia contains no specific commitment to the best interests of the child that is fundamental to family law in the UK. Under Sharia, a male child belongs to the father after the age of seven, regardless of circumstances." The Civitas study recommended that the formal recognition of Islamic courts be terminated. According to its Director, David Green, "The reality is that for many Muslims, Sharia courts are part of the atmosphere of institutionalized intimidation established, backed by the ultimate sanction of a death threat." These courts operated out of sight of independent observers, were unfair to women and were based on intimidation. The law allowed recourse to religious precepts for arbitration, but excluded it "in criminal cases or in certain family law matters." But MAT went beyond the limits by treating criminal cases in civil law as domestic violence cases. Some Muslim lawyers insisted that this had resolved problems of violence while saving the marriages in question. In the six cases of spousal violence handled by MAT, the arbitrators ordered husbands to take anger management courses and undergo tutoring, supervised by elders in the community. All the women had then withdrawn their complaints and the police stopped its investigations. Informed of these decisions, the Department of Justice let it go at that. Receiving little media attention, the birth of this parallel arbitration system did not provoke any reactions in Great Britain. The controversy surrounding the spread of the Sharia was amplified as its application had been supported by the Archbishop of Canterbury, Dr. Rowan Williams, and Lord Phillips, the head of the magistracy, who then resigned. According to the former, the Sharia's role appeared to be "inevitable" and Lord Phillips thought there was no reason why Sharia-based decisions should not be recognized by national courts. The Muslim Council of Britain condemned the Civitas' study for its "incitement to hatred," stating, "The Sharia's advice is perfectly legitimate. There is no evidence that it is intimidating or discriminatory against women. The system is purely voluntary and if people do not like it, they can go elsewhere." Philip Davies, a Conservative MP, responded, "Everyone should be deeply concerned by the number of these courts. They divide society and do not favor integration or social cohesion. They lead to a segregationist society."

Two other Islamic courts opened in Glasgow and Edinburgh, with the consent of the Scottish Anglican Church, Reverend Ian Galloway having declared that Islamic courts had been unjustly depicted. The same held true for the Netherlands—for former Christian Democrat Prime Minister Jan Peter Balkenende, the establishment of the Sharia should be possible if voted in by a parliamentary majority, a majority being the essence of democracy. Minister Wouter Bos, a PvdA socialist, wished to authorize halal banks, applying the financial Sharia, which, according to him, would have a positive effect in the fight against terrorism. As for Minister Ella Vogelaar of the Labor Party, she was not against the wearing of the burqa or veil, but recognized that it was not advisable in cases where it was a professional hindrance, for example where considerable contact with the public was involved, etcetera.

However, this position is no longer acceptable, even in this country known for its tolerance. The former Minister of Immigration, Rita Verdonk, was not ready to accept any compromise. When an imam refused to shake her hand "for religious reasons," she immediately cancelled the meeting and concluded, "And when we meet again, I hope you will be speaking Dutch!" According to a survey, after the murder of the filmmaker, Theo van Gogh, by a Moroccan Islamist in November 2004, 47 percent of the Dutch had become less tolerant towards Muslims.

In secular countries like France, the League took advantage of the lack of any government policy in order to finance mosques, schools and cultural centers. Long headed by Daniel Youssof Leclerc, then by the Saudi, Abdulaziz Sarhan, the MWLB's headquarters meandered between Évry, Mantes-la-Jolie and Paris today. In 2002, its representative in Paris declared that in two years, he had received more than thirty requests for funding to build mosques or schools from all over the metropolitan territory. But MWL officials were quick to understand the diversity of the French Muslim population, often torn between the competing national interests of their countries of origin. Built in 1981 thanks to Libyan donations, the Mantes-la-Jolie Mosque was returned to the MWL in 1997 when Prince Abdulaziz inaugurated the adjoining Islamic Cultural Center and Libya, under embargo, could no longer follow in its footsteps. In September 2000, the MWL bought the entire facility for a symbolic sum and moved its headquarters there. The Évry Mosque was built thanks to collaboration between the MWL (about 9 million Euros) and the Moroccan Hassan II Foundation. The large mosque in Lyon, inaugurated in 1994, was financed by a personal donation by King Fahd (about 4 million Euros) and the MWL. The MWL's European Center was finally based in Belgium, a more peaceful and less secular country. At least in France, because of the resistance of other Muslim participants, some considered that it did not exert such a strong ideological influence on these institutions as its financial investments would suggest. The MWL was close to the Muslim Brotherhood of the Federation of Islamic Organizations in Europe (FIOE) and was the main patron of the Union of Islamic Organizations of France (UOIF). It was generally associated with complaints lodged by Muslim organizations about violations of Islam, such as during the trials against Houellebecq (2002) and against the caricatures published in the satirical weekly, *Charlie Hebdo*, in 2007.

This echoed the Salafists' attitude—they had a bottom-up strategy consisting, on the one hand, in challenging republican law on the grounds of religious freedom and, on the other, in dividing society by ghettoizing it into groups where collective peer pressure led to the enforcement of their standards. Here is an example of how issues were broached on the website, www.salafislam.fr: "Is it permissible to bury a child who is a non-believer in Muslim cemeteries if a Muslim adopted it and it died before reaching puberty? Answer: It is not permissible to bury a non-believer in Muslim cemeteries, regardless of whether he is adopted by a Muslim or not, and it does not matter whether he has reached puberty or not." This attitude refers to Saudi law, which prohibits the burial of non-Muslims anywhere within the Kingdom's territory.

ORGANIZATION OF THE ISLAMIC CONFERENCE (OIC)

This intergovernmental organization is the permanent interstate entity Riyadh wished to establish. On September 25, 1969, following the fire set by an Australian Christian fundamentalist at the Al-Aqsa Mosque, the leaders of several Muslim countries met in Rabat, Morocco. In March 1970, the first Islamic Conference of Foreign Ministers set up a General Secretariat to liaise and coordinate their activities. The OIC, which has had its headquarters in Jeddah pending the "liberation of Jerusalem," had a permanent delegation of fifty-seven member states to the United Nations. It was more akin to a discussion forum for defining joint diplomatic positions than an entity for providing support to Saudi religious diplomacy. It was the only denominational organization whose signatory members were states. It should be noted that the Declaration on Human Rights in Islam, adopted at the 19th Conference on August 5, 1990, subjected all legislation to the Sharia (Article 25) and effectively prohibited conversions (Article 10). In 1989, the forty-four member countries condemned the book, *The Satanic Verses*, demanded its prohibition and recommended the adoption of "legislation necessary for protection against the religious ideas of others." The declaration asserted that the author was "considered heretical," an obligatory diplomatic position, while acknowledging that Islamic law could not be applied in non-Muslim states. It therefore marked a certain distance from the fatwa or death sentence against Salman Rushdie. In 2004, it supported the UN project of an "alliance of civilizations" proposed by Spain and Turkey. In October 2006, the OIC drafted the "Mecca Document," co-signed by Iraqi Shiite and Sunni dignitaries, calling for the end to interfaith violence, the release of all hostages and Iraq's unity. Focusing more on diplomatic and economic issues, the organization changed its name and became the Organization of Islamic Cooperation in June 2011. It suspended Syria from its membership on August 16, 2012.

On the other hand, it has yet to denounce the murder of Imam Abdullah al-Ahdal, rector of the Brussels Center, killed in March 1989 along with his librarian, simply for his moderate attitude towards Salman Rushdie, and that of the Japanese translator, Hitoshi Igarashi, killed in July 1991, while the Italian translator, Ettore Capriolo, suffered a similar attack but survived. The Norwegian publisher, William Nygaard, also survived an attempted murder in Oslo in October 1991. In July 1993, radicals set fire to a hotel in Turkey where members of a cultural festival were staying, including the Turkish translator of *The Satanic Verses,* who managed to survive the attack, while thirty-seven people perished in the fire.

FOREIGN THEOLOGICAL STUDENTS

The Islamic University of Madinah trained foreign students attracted by scholarships that large institutes such as Egypt's Al-Azhar University were unable to offer to young people from the Third World. Since its inception, the university has graduated about 45,000 religious cadres from 167 different nationalities. This is the aggregate figure for Saudis, children of immigrant workers and foreign scholarship holders. To this must be added thousands of foreign students who passed through other

Saudi educational institutions, both inside and outside the country, and through informal education networks. According to the statements made by one of our interlocutors, the university had "almost 60–70 percent 'foreign' students." Other formal, informal and private organizations have been established since then to meet the demand for a constantly growing religious market. For instance, the Islamic University of Manama, established by Saudi Arabia, declared that it had sponsored 2,053 students from over 130 countries in the academic year 2012, including 168 students born of expatriates working in the Kingdom.

Muhammad Al-A'la, Dean of the University of Madinah, gave an explanation about the selection of foreigners in the Arab daily, *Al-Watan:* "Three committees in the Admissions Department, one African, one Asian and one European, screen the qualifications and check whether the future students meet all the requirements." The allocation of scholarships is based on each country's needs in terms of helping promote Islam and its values. "Students receive an admission email along with visa numbers and an e-ticket. Upon arrival, a bonus of free accommodation, a monthly amount [Ed.: of around 500 to 900 USD] throughout their studies, and free bus rides for travel between the campus and the Mosque of the Prophet, discounted meals and annual tickets." Scholarship students commit to return to their country, sometimes with a salary guaranteed by the Kingdom. As stated in their contract, "Before doing anything, know that the Islamic University's goal is that you will go to do the 'Dawah' in your country once your studies are over. The country therefore does not tolerate having any people who wish to do 'hijrah' [migrate to a 'purer' Muslim land] and may [be tempted] staying on after their studies are over."[93]

As mentioned earlier, it is estimated that more than 25,000 foreign scholarship students passed through Saudi Islamic universities in about thirty years. This is a realistic figure in the light of UNESCO's data, which estimates an average of 700 foreign students per year in Saudi universities, presumably more in theological than technical faculties.

They are then distributed according to the strategy described above. In fact, a Saudi specialist, Anouar Abdallah,[94] has referred to 800 missionaries with their different assignments, including 13 in the United States, 8 in Pakistan and Bangladesh, 12 in Albania and even 3 in Japan with diplomatic status, which is theoretically prohibited by the Vienna Conventions. One of the WikiLeaks' telegrams mentioned the names of 14 preachers returning to Guinea and contracts with 12 others sent to Tajikistan (a Persian-speaking country, but mainly Sunni).

Further, their teachers' influence subsists even after they leave—the Saudi system's intellectuals are preachers, like Salman Al-Awdah who has about 1.3 million followers on Facebook. Joas Wagemakers of Radboud University Nijmegen (Netherlands), a specialist on Islamist groups, once said, "If we drew up a list of the 10 greatest Wahhabi preachers of all time, most are spontaneously quoted by radical Salafists around the world today."[95]

EXPENDITURE EQUAL TO ARMS PURCHASES?

It is extremely difficult to credibly estimate the expenditure (of any kind) that the Sauds or various public bodies or private foundations have devoted to religious diplomacy. According to various studies by the US Treasury Department, including that of Charles Allen, in the twenty-three years between 1979 and 2002, Saudi Arabia reportedly spent at least $70 billion in various type of aid—probably even more if private donations are taken into account. It is impossible to determine exactly how much of this manna was diverted towards funding the jihad movement.[96]

The MWL does not publish data on its budget, which seems to be funded mainly by Saudi royal funds and therefore likely to be subject to the vagaries of the oil market. For instance, in 1997, the *New York Times* reported that the MWL Secretary General thanked King Fahd for his donations of $1.3 billion since the founding of the League.

The OIC is sometimes credited with what seems to have been something the MWL did. Yahya Birt attributed the construction of "1,500 mosques, 210 Islamic Centers and dozens of Muslim academies and schools"[97] to the OIC, at a cost of between $2 billion and $3 billion each year, since 1975. According to him, OIC activities may have funded about "90 percent of the expenses of the faith as a whole in the Muslim world." Others estimate an expenditure of $200 billion over thirty years (or $7 billion a year) in terms of all Saudi Arabia's financial assistance to create madrassas, mosques and other facilities in Belgium, France, the Netherlands, Great Britain, Germany, Bosnia, Kosovo, and the Arab world.[98] Former CIA Director, James Woolsey, in a speech on "Saudi Government Propaganda in the United States: Avowed Ally or Secret Enemy?"[99] at the American Enterprise Institute in 2005, estimated that since the mid-1970s, the Saudis had spent almost $90 billion to export Islamic ideology to the world. In 2003, the Center for Security Policy (CSP), a Washington think tank, produced the same figures as the US Treasury. Finally, the European Parliament, in its 2013 report, estimated that Saudi foundations had spent more than an estimated $10 billion on "charitable" activities.

One of our interlocutors confirmed that the annual amount spent by the MWL stood at $5 billion. Together with direct royal donations or private contributions, it may be concluded that the country spent as much on arms imports (smoothed annual average of $7–8 billion) as on support for Islam in the world (annual average of $5–7 billion on a decennial basis). That is between two to seven times what the USSR was spending for its propaganda at the height of its powers and, in 2011, the Vatican's annual budget was €245 million. Alex Alexiev, a researcher at the CSP, described this as "the biggest propaganda campaign ever mounted in the world." This expenditure has done much to overwhelm Islam's less obscurantist local Muslim sensitivities, according to observers like Dawood al-Shirian and even Lee Kuan Yew, the former Malaysian prime minister. It seems that this "pious money" not only led to a large number of conversions, but also attracted many swindlers, and resulted in numerous embezzlement cases, in Switzerland,[100] Bosnia, France and other countries. Control by the authorities seems to have grown, not after September 11, but rather after the attacks within the Saudi national territory in 2003 and 2004. The decision-making cell around the king, mentioned in the WikiLeaks telegrams, apparently resulted from this situation. However, the same problem seems to be arising in all democratic countries today—that of keeping a check on NGOs and associations receiving funds from abroad that are not subject to any examination by government authorities.

DIPLOMATIC–RELIGIOUS LOBBYING IN DEMOCRACIES: RICH CLIENTS COMMAND RESPECT

Here is an interesting little anecdote:[101] when Riyadh wanted to buy radar-equipped AWACS, the US Congress, orchestrated by different lobbies, blocked and deferred its vote. The Saudi ambassador had solicited his friends, but some promises were not kept. David Rockefeller, CEO of Chase Manhattan, in particular, did nothing to tip the vote. "You should order the Minister of Finance to transfer $200 million from Chase Manhattan to JP Morgan," said Ambassador Bandar to his uncle, the Crown Prince. No sooner said than done: the following day, David Rockefeller made a phone call to the ambassador at eight in the morning. "I was asleep," he recalled. "He called again at 9, I was busy. At 10, I was out. At 4 pm, the hotel's switchboard called me to tell me that D. R. was in the lobby and that he had come from New York specially to see me." Bandar made him wait till 6 in the evening, telling him that he would be going to Congress to attend the vote . . . "I'll stay in Washington too to vote," replied David Rockefeller. When the vote came in positive a few days later, the $200 million came back from where they had left.

The most powerful component of the "Arab lobby" in the United States consists almost exclusively of Saudi Arabia and the local industrial interests supporting it: oil, construction, luxury goods and armaments companies. As for the US, the Saudis' well-being is one of the fundamentals for the West's economy and security. No other Arab state has a similar influence, even marginally. The Saudis work "right from the top": direct relations with the President are established in order to short-circuit the State Department administration. Lobbying is done downstream of the elections, for example by contributing to presidency-related actions. Foundations (with the Clinton Foundation), libraries and study centers (with $23 million for the Center for Middle Eastern Studies, plus $10 million for the Clinton Library in Arkansas, the same amount as was given to George W. Bush, and $1 million for Nancy Reagan's anti-drug campaign), and so on. The US ambassador to Riyadh has traditionally been a close associate of the US President—G. W. Bush sent his personal attorney. Diplomats and US civil servants who had served locally most often become consultants to the Saudi government once they retire. Extremely well connected, they become advocates of the Saudi cause both in the political establishment and in the American media.

SAUDI PATRONAGE AND FOREIGN ELITE

Some of the most prestigious American, British, and Russian universities have yielded to Saudi patronage: the University of California, Santa Barbara under King Abdulaziz Al Saud; the Harvard Law School under King Fahd, the same for the University of London's School of Oriental Studies (SOAS); and finally, Prince Naif paid for the post of a resident professor at the University of Moscow. To these may be added the American University of Colorado, the University of Washington, North Carolina's Duke University, Washington's Howard University, Maryland's Johns Hopkins University, Washington's Middle East Institute, North Carolina's Shaw University and New York's University of Syracuse. Ten million dollars was donated to Yale University for a Center of Islamic Law and Civilization. The royal family gave Harvard and Georgetown $40 million. Muslim student associations and discussion sites encouraged by the leaders of these prestigious universities sometimes reveal a surprising abuse of youth: Mehdi K. Alhassani, Special Advisor to the Chief of Staff in the National Security Council was quite close to the Muslim Brotherhood in his youth, when he was studying at George Washington University from 2005 to 2006.

Often, the creation of student websites is encouraged by university administrations. Those of Saudi students in the 1980s to 2000 were highly Salafist (sorry, Wahhabi) in content.

Think tanks are important places of influence. The choice of studies there is free, but sometimes arouses interesting reactions regarding the Saudi case. In 2002, Laurent Murawiec, a researcher at the Rand Corporation, presented a paper entitled, "Expel Saudis from Arabia," describing the regime as absolute evil. The project may have been solicited by the US authorities, one year after 9/11. The author proposed a redefinition of the Middle East that was essentially designed to ensure Israel's security. The research scholar was dismissed after the report was leaked. But was it because he had described the country's true nature, or because the study coldly considered regional boundary changes for the sole purpose of Tel Aviv's security? In fact, the scholar was dismissed for both these reasons! Kissinger had also envisaged the hypothesis of invading the oil province in the east of the country during the 1973 embargo.

Obviously, the media and virtual world were not spared either by the Kingdom's political or religious authorities. By the 1990s, dozens of satellite channels and hundreds of websites were born. Social networks were also flooded. All kinds of services were offered, sometimes in several languages. The investment in new technologies was funded by the State, along with traditional means of disseminating information, such as "millions of pious pamphlets, cassettes, CDs and books throughout the world, at low prices if not free of charge, since the 1980s."[102] Saudi Arabia has a number of paper-based media. The 250,000-strong daily, *Asharq Al-Awsat* is part of a media group comprising fifteen other titles, belonging to the family of Prince Salman bin Abdulaziz, brother of the king and governor of Riyadh. *Al-Hayat* has a circulation of 120,000. It was bought-over at the beginning of the 1990s, along with the weekly, *Al-Wasat*, by one of the sons of Prince Sultan ibn Abdulaziz, brother of the king and Minister of Defense. In audiovisual media, the MBC channel, which broadcasts in Arabic from London, belongs to one of King Fahd's brothers-in-law. Its programs can be picked up in Europe, North Africa and the Middle East on FM (Gulf Music), Panorama FM (hit Arabic music), ART Zikr (recitations of the Koran and preaching), and ART Music. The "Al-Arabiya" news channel has one of the best ratings in the Middle East.

Through the Arabsat and Nilesat satellites and satellite dishes, these media reach Muslim minorities all over the world, including the United

States.[103] Private media play the same propagandist role: Iqraa, Al-Nas, Al-Majd, for instance. Saudi investments also financially support global audience channels such as Fox News or social networks like Twitter. Saudi diplomacy is constantly seeking to influence Western media (Canada, Australia, France, among others) and Arabic media (Egypt, Lebanon, etc.), in exchange for equity stakes and financial aid, or even by buying over managers in recalcitrant channels, or more directly by asking broadcasters to withdraw Iranian channels from their subscription offers (for example, in the case of the Lebanese Hezbollah's "Al-Manar" channel that was withdrawn from the Arabsat satellite). A WikiLeaks cable shows that the Kingdom had paid the Lebanese MTV channel $5 million (although it had asked for 20) to adopt an editorial line that was more favorable to the Kingdom.[104] A document on the renewal of subscriptions to different publications, dated January 1, 2010,[105] gave details about Saudi contributions to approximately thirty publications in Damascus, Abu Dhabi, Beirut, Kuwait, Amman and Nouakchott. These sometimes amounted to modest sums of less than $33,000, but the fate of these publications was clearly determined by the continuation or termination of Saudi subscriptions. According to the disclosed documents, contributions were inversely proportional to the profitability of the invested capital, since Riyadh received only political dividends from this mollifying and obedient press.

The history of the bilateral relationship between Riyadh and Washington is punctuated by multiple betrayals by the West that weakened the Saudi regime. During the legendary meeting on board the *Quincy*, Roosevelt's promise to King Ibn Saud to consult him before voting on the creation of the State of Israel at the UN was not kept, as his successor, Harry Truman, did not feel bound by his predecessor's word. In 1973, Johnson's promise to force Israel to negotiate against lifting the oil embargo was not honored either. In 1974, Gerald Ford recognized Jerusalem as the capital of the Hebrew state without consulting his great ally, and faced with Saudi threats, Kissinger and Schlessinger, the CIA's head at the time, came up with a secret plan envisaging an American landing in the oil-rich Eastern provinces. Washington's unwavering support for Israel in its various military actions (in Lebanon or in its repression of the Intifada) and the lack of support for King Fahd's plan—which promised to recognize Israel if the occupied territories were returned—was taken badly in the Kingdom. Finally, the invasion of Iraq in 2003 seemed to have petrified the king, alarmed by the disappearance of the last Sunni buffer against Iran. The deep anti-imperialism of Saudi society can therefore be better understood in the light of these betrayals.

Riyadh has been a member of the UN Human Rights Council since January 2016, despite criticism from several non-governmental organizations. WikiLeaks provided the key to understanding the undertones to this surprising election:[106] before the November 2013 vote in New York, a secret agreement had been reached between Britain and Saudi Arabia to ensure that both countries would be elected simultaneously to the Council. The chairman of the Saudi Arabian Commission for Human Rights defended himself, recalling that his country had made "real progress" over the past four years and had committed to "uphold human rights in accordance with the Sharia." Bandar bin Muhammad al-Aiban mentioned micro-reforms for women, such as the sale of lingerie and cosmetics, the recruitment of women cashiers in shops and the appointment of thirty women to the Shura Council, among others. On the other hand, fundamental rights had still not been guaranteed. Nothing was said about religious tolerance or the massive and regular expulsion of immigrants: in 2013, Riyadh gave 8 million immigrant workers six months to regularize their situation, then decided to expel only 4 million, mainly Africans, Indians and Yemenis. The lessons taught by Western countries were always discreet, as the Saudis hated them. A few years ago, a French Minister of Defense had a bitter experience when she dared to mention the deficiencies of Saudi Arabia's educational system before her counterpart, Prince Sultan. The meeting lasted just seven minutes.

Saudi Arabia is a country that knows how to remind its suppliers of their obligations. In 2014, Riyadh imposed trade restrictions on the Netherlands in protest against Geert Wilders, the far-right leader who had distributed anti-Muslim stickers in the colors of the Saudi flag. High-ranking diplomats traveled to Riyadh to try to defuse the situation, but no solution could be found. Trade between the Netherlands and Saudi Arabia amounted to some €3.7 billion in 2010, with almost 4 percent Foreign Direct Investment in the petromonarchy—a good lesson of tolerance delivered by the most intolerant state on the planet!

Saudi Arabia's capacity for lobbying was focused mainly on certain commercial contracts. Al-Yamamah was an enormous arms sales contract (over 100 combat aircraft) concluded between London and Riyadh from 1985 and renewed in 2006. All the contracts awarded under this heading shared one particularity: payments were made in kind on the basis of oil deliveries. Many allegations of corruption in favor of members of the royal family were made when the contract documents were declassified in Great Britain. However, many legal actions by the NGO, Corner House, or investigations by the Serious Fraud Office were suspended, the last time in 2006, following a letter from Tony Blair guaranteeing the termination of proceedings to the Saudi Arabian King (for "reasons of national interest").

Through its skillful diplomacy of influence, the regime succeeded in spreading its conception of Islam, without any direct recourse to violence: nothing but soft actions, no hard persuasion! Presented as a bulwark against communism, the Saudis' politico–religious diplomacy marked one success after another in the 1980–2000 period.

THE INCREDIBLE SUCCESS OF SAUDI ARABIA'S DIPLOMATIC AND RELIGIOUS STRATEGY: SEPTEMBER 11 AND THE "AXIS OF EVIL" COUNTRIES

There have been no accusations against the Saudis—how could such a sleight of hand take place?

The Intelligence Committee of the House of Representatives holds highly classified secret documents; one of them, twenty-eight pages long, entitled, "Finding, Discussion and Narrative Regarding Certain Sensitive National Security Matters," was been classified as a "Defense Secret" for fifteen years.[107] It raises the question of Saudi Arabia's role in the attacks on the World Trade Center. At the time the report was released, overseen by the Senate Intelligence Committee in 2002, Florida's Democratic Senator, Bob Graham, was amazed that the twenty-eight pages had been removed at the request of the Bush administration, for reasons of "national security." For all these years, the same argument had prevented its declassification. "This report reveals the Saudi government's direct involvement in the funding of September 11," said the former senator. "We know at least that many of the nineteen suicide bombers received financial support from several Saudi entities, including the government . . . The Saudis know what they did, and they know that we know. The real question is how they interpret our response. As for what I think, we have shown that whatever they do, there will be impunity. They have therefore continued to support Al-Qaeda and, more recently, they have provided economic and ideological support to the Islamic State. It is our refusal to face the truth that led to the new wave of extremism that struck Paris," the former senator said. In mid-January 2015, Graham held a press conference in the Senate with two representatives, Republican Walter Jones and Democrat Stephen Lynch, who presented Resolution HR 428 again, calling for the declassification of the twenty-eight pages. According to the *New Yorker*, two of the suicide bombers were reportedly financed and housed in San Diego by someone who was in permanent touch with the Ministry of Islamic Affairs' section based in Los

Angeles. Saudi Arabia denied any responsibility and called for the declassification in order to clear its reputation. Some of the people who worked on the document, such as Philip Zelikow, Director of the 9/11 commission, described the twenty-eight pages as "unconfirmed preliminary reports." For him, the answer was simple: "The Bushes are very close to the Saudis who feared for their reputation." Obama followed the same path, with the US–Saudi relationship still considered vital. He shortened his visit to India to attend the funeral of the deceased sovereign and greet the new king, along with thirty senior politicians, while no US official had bothered to travel to Paris after the terrorist attacks in January. That says a lot about Washington's priorities.

In July 2016, at the end of his reign, President Barack Obama decided to publish the missing twenty-eight pages.[108] They first of all revealed the inconsistencies of US policy, which had refrained from gathering intelligence on Saudi Arabia, considered an "ally." The first FBI-CIA working group was set up only on November 18, 2001. As one FBI official noted during a hearing before the Congressional Investigating Committee on the attacks, "it is the questions raised by members of Congress that made it possible to ask about the links between the group of nineteen terrorists and the Riyadh regime." As for the rest, the report highlighted the large number of official contacts and the support the terrorists received through two Saudis, Omar al-Bayoumi and Ossama Bassman (who probably had fake passports). These intermediaries probably belonged to the Saudi secret services; they had received erratic payments through various official channels without any counterpart provided, either directly or through one of their wives. Transfers of funds to Al-Barakaat, a subsidiary of the Bin Laden group, went through the Ibn Taymiyyah Mosque in Culver City, California. Finally, some of the interrogators testified to the FBI and CIA investigators' bitterness before the Saudis' unwillingness to face questions related to the attack, as well as concerning other individuals suspected of terrorist activities.

It is therefore understandable that, as early as in January 2002, G. W. Bush, highly attached to the Riyadh regime, so quickly decided to declare war against . . . Iran, Iraq and North Korea!

A document published by WikiLeaks described Saudi Arabia as the terrorists' cash machine, from a secret memo written by Hillary Clinton, dated December 2009, when she was Secretary of State.[109] It highlights the Gulf countries' inability to block funding for groups such as the Al-Qaeda, the Taliban, and the Pakistani LeT. The problem was particularly acute in Saudi Arabia, where all sorts of activists were concealed, disguised as pilgrims at the time of the Hajj, to receive money through government-certified charities in order to set up shell companies to launder funds. A cable details how the LeT—the architect of the Bombay attacks in 2008—used a Saudi-based shell company to finance its activities. The LeT charity branch, Jamaat-ud-Dawa, raised funds for new schools at considerably inflated costs and siphoned off excess money to finance militant activities. The LeT operated on a budget of $5.25 million per year, according to US estimates. Washington criticized the Saudi refusal to ban three charities within its territory that had been classified as terrorist entities in the United States. US diplomats reserved their criticism for closed-door talks, contrary to the public criticism often inflicted on other countries such as Pakistan and Afghanistan.

The antipathy of American opinion towards the Kingdom reached a peak of 66 percent in 2004 and, in 2010, 58 percent of Americans still had a rather unfavorable opinion of Saudi Arabia. The Saudis embarked on a public relations campaign, spending about $100 million on lobbying and consulting to convince Americans that they were allies in the war on terrorism. The same was done in France in recent times. Saudi Arabia's main concern has always been the survival of the House of Saud. All the rest—the weakening of Israel, the spread of radical Islam, (temporarily)—was secondary.

INTERRELIGIOUS DIALOGUE: AND WHY NOT?

The Wahhabi regime is the worst possible interlocutor on the subject, which does not prevent it from being extremely active thanks to its unparalleled financial resources. In the large family of Saudi international organizations, on October 13, 2011, the King Abdullah ibn Abdulaziz International Center for Interreligious and Intercultural Dialogue was set up, already mentioned earlier and better known in English under the acronym KAICIID—an independent international organization recognized by the United Nations. The Saudi monarchy thus embarked on an experiment in which it had strictly no competence: religious tolerance! It chose not to manage this international institution alone and appealed to three European states: Austria and Spain to join as founding members and the Holy See as an observer. The sovereign pontiff would have accepted for the sake of preserving the presence of the old Christian communities of Iraq, Syria, Egypt or elsewhere in the Orient.[110] Headquartered in Vienna's magnificent Sturany Palace, KAICIID's Secretary General was obviously Saudi: Faisal ibn Abdul Rahman ibn Mouammar, a very close advisor to King Abdullah ibn Abdulaziz before his accession to the throne. In addition to his post at KAICIID, he was Secretary General of the Abdulaziz Center for National Dialogue in Riyadh. The KAICIID organized prestigious events: expensive symposiums, VIP invitations and formal agreements. For instance, in February 2013, on the sidelines of the Fifth World summit of the Alliance of Civilizations, a convention was signed on cooperation with UNESCO, "for the greater respect of cultural and religious diversity and the promotion of mutual understanding between men [sic]." Opponents of this institution referred to the fact that the 1961 Geneva Convention on Diplomatic Relations applied to KAICIID, so no Austrian State official could enter it or exert any form of control.

CHAPTER 4

RELIGIOUS DIPLOMACY TRANSFORMED: ANTI-SHIISM AND ANTI-COMMUNISM

The system that had been set up in the 1960s was not very structured, seeming more akin to a worldwide extension of the "zakat" (a tax, comprising percentages of personal income of every kind, levied as almsgiving for the relief of the poor: the third of the Pillars of Islam). The Muslim Brotherhood's members were the only ones able to manage it by endowing it with a strategic vision, an international network and their unparalleled knowledge about local communities. It can therefore be said that this period's religious diplomacy was not totally "Saudi" or "Wahhabi." On the other hand, when the first international difficulties and crises threatened to destabilize royalty, it was taken strongly in hand. Control finally passed up to the highest level through the Senior Council of Ulemas, placed under the monarch, bringing together various ministers, including the Intelligence Minister, as can be seen in WikiLeaks' telegrams. The management of Saudi religious diplomacy finally evolved further to meet the challenges of internal stability rather than under international pressure.

It must be noted that in strategic thinking circles in the West, Tourabi's Sudan had been designated as "The Islamists' Mecca" in the 1980s and 1990s. What an example of strategic blindness!

As mentioned earlier, there are reportedly about 50–60 million Salafists in the world, including 20–30 million in India, 5–6 million in Egypt, 27.5 million in Bangladesh and 1.6 million in Sudan. Salafist communities are smaller elsewhere: about 10,000 in Tunisia, 17,000 in Morocco, 7,000 in Jordan, 17,000 in France and 4,000 to 5,000 in Germany. The Wahhabization of Islam was the subject of open criticism in Morocco, Indonesia and Pakistan . . . but not in France and not in Europe either.

Jihadist Islam became the new anti-imperialism—in Palestine, in the face of Western inertia, the Hamas ousted the Palestinian Liberation Organization (PLO) from Gaza and in Lebanon Hezbollah spearheaded the resistance against Israel. The Iranian revolution overthrew the Shah, a privileged ally of the West, and stood up to the coalition of all the Western countries. Anti-Soviet resistance in Afghanistan took the symbolic place of the Vietnam War. And the ultimate fall of atheist Soviet communism demonstrated the power of the united Muslim armies. The errors of the American invasion of Iraq (torture in Abu Ghraib prison, the Battle of Fallujah, etc.) widely expanded Al-Qaeda's popularity and international mobilization, which far exceeded the previous Third-Worldism circles. The first impetus occurred with the war against the Soviets in Afghanistan (5,000–10,000 foreign fighters); the Bosnian crisis drew 1,000–2,000 foreign fighters; NATO's invasion of Afghanistan 1,000–1,500; 4,000–5,000 foreign fighters joined against the Americans in Iraq and, finally, the Syrian crisis broke all records. The more than 40 left-wing groups trained in PLO camps turned into over 20,000 foreign fighters from some 100 countries fighting alongside the Islamic State in Syria and Iraq: 11,000 from the Middle East and Maghreb, 5,000–7,000 Saudis (2,500 according to official figures); 2,000–3,000 from Tunisia, 1,500–2,000 from Morocco, 1,300–2,500 from Jordan, 1,300 from Turkey and about 500 from Egypt. To these were added some 5,000–6,000 from the countries of the former Soviet Union, 500–700 from Indonesia; 4,000 from Western countries, including about 150 Americans and 150 Australians.[111] If those already present in the area, those who died there or were detained and those who were in transit to join are added to these numbers, France emerges as the main European supplier country, followed by the United Kingdom with 700 departures, Germany 600, and Belgium about 250.[112] These mobilization flows around the Syrian and Iraqi crisis increased since the Western military intervention. At the same time, and by way of comparison, probably 6,500 foreign fighters still remained in Afghanistan and a few hundred in Libya, Pakistan and Somalia.

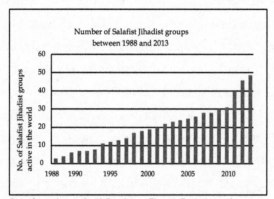

Data from the study: "A Persistent Threat: Evolutions of Al-Qaeda and Other Salafi Jihadis," Seth G. Jones, RAND, 2014.

THE RELATIONSHIP BETWEEN THE MAIN TENETS OF SAUDI RELIGIOUS DIPLOMACY AND THE JIHADIST MOBILIZATION

WikiLeaks Saudi Database:
Current Organization and Strategy Seen from the Inside

Stéphane Lacroix believes that the Saudi arena of power is likely divided into different sectors:[113] the "political sector" is exclusively the responsibility of the Al-Saud family, while the "religious sector" probably enjoys a certain autonomy; and the "intellectual sector," first promoted by the government in the 1970s, led to the emergence of a "body of modern era clerics." The economic and military sectors, more exclusively under the direct control of the political sector and the Al-Sauds, are also part of this arena of power. However, this segmentation may need to be re-assessed in the light of the WikiLeaks telegrams.

On Friday, June 19, 2015, WikiLeaks began publishing the Saudi cables that had reached its site: in all, more than half a million documents from the Saudi Foreign Ministry, including secret communications to various embassies. The publication included Top Secret reports from the Kingdom's Ministry of the Interior and Intelligence Services, as well as a large number of email communications between the Ministry of Foreign Affairs and offices abroad. To date, WikiLeaks has released approximately 70,000 miscellaneous administrative documents. These extraordinary documents give a precise idea of the Saudi strategy and methods in the world.

The Supreme Council for Islamic Affairs, composed of officials from the Ministry of Foreign Affairs, the Interior and Islamic Affairs, the Intelligence Service and the King's Office, devoted to missionary activities, meets directly with the monarch. The Ministry of Foreign Affairs submits applications for funding to officials in Riyadh. The Ministry of the Interior and the Intelligence Agency selects the potential beneficiaries and the World Muslim League helps coordinate action closely with Saudi diplomats around the world. Together, these officials have identified Muslim leaders and foreign associations, the funds to be distributed and the dissemination of religious literature produced in Saudi Arabia, the preachers trained in Saudi Arabia and the payment of their wages. After its inception, the process turned into a full-fledged public policy.

The Saudi regime, challenged from the inside by its most radical fringes, has always reacted by accentuating religious rigorism—a way of giving the Wahhabi authorities a voice—but never by political openness. Over the past eighty years, Saudi Arabia has delighted the hearts and minds of Muslims through the deployment of financial and human resources for the Hajj and Islamic funding agencies around the world. In the Third World, Saudi Arabia has succeeded in extending its influence in many countries, thanks to its humanitarian assistance, while at the same time Western countries in crisis witnessed a shrinking of their resources. Thus, in 2014, the Kingdom donated $500 million to Iraq, exceeding all European donors combined ($200 million).

This religious framework made democratization impossible and the country, under pressure from the West since 1991, became the country of "immobile reforms." According to Senator Jon Kyl, Chairman of the Senate Judiciary Committee's Subcommittee on Terrorism and Homeland Security, "In July 2006, the Saudi government confirmed its policy of reforming textbooks to eliminate all passages that denigrate or promote hatred towards a religion or religious group." The State Department said that the promise would be fulfilled "in time for the beginning of 2008." But a WikiLeaks cable from the US embassy reported that educational reforms had been "frozen." In its new version of the 2010 Annual Report on Religious Freedom, the State Department wrote, "Despite the government's revisions to primary and secondary textbooks, they retained language intolerant of other religious traditions, especially Jewish, Christian, and Shiite beliefs, and included commands to hate infidels for their 'kufr' (unbelief) and to kill apostates."

The Saudi Kingdom's Islamic identity gave it a level of credibility unparalleled in the world. Initial traces of democratization would appear to be a concession to the "kafirs." Hence, it was religious diplomacy that helped manage the regime's structural contradiction, making it possible to safeguard the regime's official image while continuing to conduct its diplomacy of intolerance—truly Dr. Saud and Mr. Jihad!

The geopolitics of Wahhabi-Salafist religious diplomacy developed from an initial circle comprising of Pakistan, Afghanistan and Yemen. Subsequently, the underdeveloped countries of the Sahelian zone benefited greatly since the 1960s from Nasserian Egypt's strategy of encirclement. With the dismantlement of the USSR, many new opportunities emerged, first in failed countries and in gray areas: Kashmir since 1990;

the Somalian crisis since 1991; Bosnia and Kosovo from 1992 to 1995; Afghanistan in 1994 with the Taliban, then in 2002 with NATO's invasion; the Moro insurgency in the Philippines since 1991, with extensions in Malaysia and Indonesia; the Uighurs of Chinese Xinjiang; the Salafization of the long Tuareg revolt which began in the 1990s; Boko Haram in Nigeria since 2001; and more recently, Iraq and Syria with Daesh, and so on.

The shrinking of the former Soviet region multiplied demand: the Chechen insurgency and its metastases in the North Caucasus since 1994; the poorly controlled area of the new Central Asian Soviet states after 1991, Uzbekistan, Turkmenistan, Kazakhstan (the Fergana Valley was divided into three states); Badakhshan and the Rasht Valley, with tentacles in Russia, Siberia and Tatarstan.

In almost all these insurrections, there were two recurring phenomena: first, an official policy on the construction of mosques and madrassas, with or without humanitarian assistance, and secondly the recruitment of young religious cadres trained in Saudi Arabia, with optional training in Pakistan, Yemen or Afghanistan.

The following pages offer a few examples, which, although only superficially covered, give an idea of the global scope of Saudi Arabia's religious diplomacy.

SAUDI ACTION IN THE COUNTRIES OF THE FIRST CIRCLE[114]

Pakistan: An Ideal Target

Described as a country of the "pure" ("pak" meaning "pure"—referring to Muslims) by its founding father, this country created the first Islamic republic in world history. The founder, Ali Jinnah, died a year after its independence, and it was the Jamaat-e-Islami of Abul A'la Maududi who drafted the constitution. Religion became an instrument for the political management of this composite country (75 percent

Sunnis, 15–20 percent Shiites and 5 percent other religions). At the time of its independence in 1947, there were about 137 madrassas. In 2000, they were estimated at 7,000, and by 2003 the number is estimated to have grown to 10,430.[115]

Under Ayub Khan (1958–1969), the first professional soldier in power, a ministry was set up to register and control madrassas in order to align their teaching with that of public schools. Opposition from all the religious parties hindered the attempt.[116] During this period, the number of madrassas seems to have stagnated. Ali Bhutto (1971–1977) used Islam to create a "national feeling" in the context of the secession of East Pakistan in 1971, led by the Awami League, which wanted to establish a secular regime. In 1979, Marshal Zia contradicted his predecessor and, from 1978 to 1988, envisaged the establishment of 5,000 madrassas and then set up a National Committee to transform the madrassas into "an integral part of our educational system."[117] He established a compulsory "zakat" system (legal alms in Islam), which led to the rapid growth of religious institutions at the local level. The system was further promoted by the recognition of their equivalence with university degrees for government jobs. The Zia government allowed students from foreign madrassas free entry and movement in the country, while simultaneously encouraging them to join the Jihad in Afghanistan. The madrassas along the border with Afghanistan received recruits from Central Asia, North Africa, Myanmar, Bangladesh and Chechnya, alongside Afghan refugees. Foreigners accounted for 10–50 percent of the students. Naturally, between 1979 and 1995, some 3,906 new madrassas mushroomed.[118]

Saudi Arabia's influence in Pakistan began in the late 1970s when Riyadh teamed up with General Zia ul-Haq and the United States against the Soviet occupation of neighboring Afghanistan. "Since the Iranian revolution, the Saudis had been trying to forge closer ties with certain political parties, particularly the Islamists, in order to expand their influence in Pakistan," a Western diplomat had said in Islamabad.

The Saudis welcomed Prime Minister Nawaz Sharif after the military coup in 1999. Seven years later, he resumed his political career after Saudi leaders intervened in his favor with General Pervez Musharraf, the Chief of Army Staff at the time. Riyadh had only to recall the generous Saudi rescue plan in the form of free oil during the three years of the West's boycott against the Pakistani nuclear tests of 1998. Saudi Arabia spent more than an estimated billion dollars a year to fund the madrassas responsible for mobilizing public opinion, recruiting and training jihadists and other forms of religious activism in Pakistan. The best known are those of the Jamaat-e-Islami's Rabita Trust and also those set up by Jamiat-Ulema (JUI), headed by Maulana Fazal-ur-Rehman. The pre-existing Deobandi and Wahhabi madrassas went on to produce the Taliban.

Some Pakistanis deplore what they call the "Arabianization of Pakistan" through the growing influence on schools in Pakistan. A senior Pakistani official estimated that 80 percent of the madrassas were Deobandi or Wahhabi and that "2,000 are involved in violent activities." Over the past thirty years, these institutions have been the main human resource providers for terrorist causes in Kashmir, Afghanistan and India. "It is a source of pride for Sunni teachers and students to study in Saudi Arabia," said Hasan Askari Rizvi, a political commentator. "We know that these students going to Saudi Arabia are generally entitled to a scholarship and are proud of it."[119] However, according to another survey, only 6 percent of the students in these schools were there for religious reasons, while the others were there for economic reasons.[120]

Today, Pakistan plays the role of a secondary training center, attracting students from Nigeria, Indonesia, Malaysia and elsewhere, who then return radicalized. "The ideology propagated by these schools is extremely important in shaping minds in the Muslim world," explained Vali Nasr, a political scientist of the Johns Hopkins School of Advanced International Studies. "If normal schooling does not fulfill its role of educating people, you don't need to be a brain surgeon to understand the impact of the schooling imparted by these schools that spread fanaticism." The influence of Pakistan's Islamic education became topical once again in December 2015, after the shooting in San Bernardino, California. A young man, Syed Rizwan Farook, of Pakistani origin, born and educated in the United States, and his wife Tashfeen Malik, a recent immigrant from Pakistan, killed fourteen people. Mrs. Malik's connections in Saudi Arabia, where her parents have been living for more than twenty years and her attendance of religious classes in Pakistan at Al-Huda—a network of Islamic schools for women—had contributed to radicalizing her. The Al-Huda management denied this, claiming that "The network has trained more than 20,000 women graduates in the last two decades and the authorities have never worried about or questioned them . . . We teach only the Koran and other subjects of Islam. Our message promotes peace."

After Marshal Zia's episode, various unsuccessful attempts ensued to reform the education sector. Benazir Bhutto (1988–1990) tried to prohibit the entry of Arab students and to regulate funding. Each province was required to report to the central government on the functioning of its madrassas. The government announced its decision to introduce their mandatory registration and audit. But Benazir fell before these measures were implemented.[121] Some provincial governments that tried to change the contents of the syllabus by removing references to Jihad faced a revolt by religious dignitaries, who promised a "bloody revolt" if the government sought to "mislead people by removing Koranic verses and Hadiths."[122] A provincial minister who had defended these changes hastened to add that "no Koranic verse or tradition of the Prophet Muhammad would be deleted."[123] In 2010, the government attempted an eighteenth reform of the madrassas, with no result. The nineteenth, announced by the current government, in particular after the attacks on high schools, schools and even a kindergarten (March 2016) faced the same opposition early on.

It should be noted that the real origins of anti-Shiite violence can be found in the sociology of the country and does not owe everything to Saudi influence. The use of death sentences for blasphemy is now widespread in countries such as Pakistan, where it was incorporated in the Criminal Code in 1986 by General Zia ul-Haq. At the time, the pretext was the need to modernize British colonial laws that punished outrages against different religions in order to preserve civil peace. Since that date, about 1,000 people have been involved in blasphemy charges in the country—half the cases were non-Muslims, Christians or Hindus. Salmaan Taseer, Governor of Punjab, had dared to criticize the regular use of the blasphemy law against Christians. He was assassinated by Malik Mumtaz Hussain Qadri, his bodyguard, on January 4, 2011. His murderer's execution triggered demonstrations glorifying his act throughout his funeral procession.

East Pakistan, traditionally a Muslim area, became Bangladesh in 1971 after an insurrection led by the Awami League (secular and socialist). The League established what was once a secular country there. This episode continues to be viewed as a failure of Islam. The efforts made by the Wahhabis since that time have borne fruit: since General Ziaur Rahman's coup d'état in 1977 (not to be confused with Zia ul-Haq), Islam once again became the official religion. Today, the Salafists persecute the 1 percent Buddhists, Shiites (4–5 percent of the population) and especially the laity (bloggers, editors, writers). "Those who write baseless accounts against the religion are also extremists," said the commissioner in charge of investigating the killings of these individuals.

Yemen—The Clash of Fundamentalisms

Yemen has been a thorn in Saudi Arabia's foot. Ibn Saud succeeded in robbing it of some of its northern provinces in 1934 and territorial disputes remain till this day. Over the past three decades, a mainly Wahhabi proselytism has gained popularity throughout Yemen, actively opposing both the main local schools—Zaydish and Shiite in the North, Shafi'i and Sufi in the South. Wahhabism was introduced in the province of Saada by local ulemas who had studied in Saudi Arabia or had been in Afghanistan. Upon their return, they set up Koranic teaching circles, religious institutes and Wahhabi mosques, then set themselves up in State schools and Islamic institutes, challenging the power of the "elders"—that is, Zaydism's elites—by advocating a direct relationship with God, without intermediaries, a literal interpretation of the Koran and social egalitarianism, all supported by a flood of free publications. Since September 2011, the Salafists of the Dammaj School, one of the main teaching centers supported by Saudi Arabia, started attracting students from around the world and conducted anti-Shiite activities. In the Zaydi bastions of northern Yemen, the surprising growth of Wahhabism may probably be explained by its capacity to mobilize a latent resentment against the elite and the key principles of Zaydism. The first conversions occurred in secondary schools and among some tribal chiefs, who were quite pleased to see the power of the Sayyids—the leaders of Zaydism—contested, as they were descendants of the Prophet on Ali's side. They had gone through the civil war years of the 1960s and the Wahhabis accused them of preventing the spread of the "true faith," of propagating superstitions, of refusing marriages with non-Sayyids, and so on. The latter responded by accusing the Wahhabis of broadcasting a non-Yemenite version of Islam. The quarrel took the form of prayers in the Zaydi mosques that the Wahhabis were breaking into ("arms extended" versus "crossed arms") and led to ceremonies peppered by violence in 1991 and 1992, which drove out the Zaydis. This clash of fundamentalisms continued until the present war, which began on June 18, 2004, against the Houthi rebels. The allied governments of Sana'a and Riyadh presented the latter as a group backed by Iran, accusing them of wanting to restore the Zaydi Imamate that had been abolished in 1962 after the civil war. In March 2015, Saudi Arabia launched an offensive against the Houthi rebels—not against Al-Qaeda in the

Arabian Peninsula (AQAP), which was considered the most dangerous of its subsidiaries by the CIA. The five Arab countries participating in the anti-Daesh coalition all withdrew their planes in order to go to war in Yemen. It is true that the monarchy had already mobilized seven times more combat aircraft against the Houthis in Yemen than in the Syrian–Iraqi theater. The Sunni coalition bombarded AQAP's positions in Mukalla only on April 23, 2016, presumably to look good in the eyes of the countries of the West, who had provided the coordinates for the targets. It was therefore the same posture as the one adopted for the fight against the Shiites, and one of non-aggression against Salafist jihadis, whether they were in Yemen, Syria or Iraq. So, as of now, the West is alone fighting Daesh. It may be added that the Dar Al-Hadith Salafist Center—which had been set up in Dammaj, Yemen, by Sheikh Muqbil Rahimullah, a graduate of the Islamic University of Madinah, expelled after the attack on the Great Mosque—is the center where the young American Talib, John Walker Lindh, also studied. The center was also particularly influential among Indonesian Salafists, due to Yemeni emigrant workers. It was also in Yemen that the Kouachi brothers—responsible for the attack on *Charlie Hebdo* in France—surrendered.

Egypt—The Great Arab Rival: "Soldiers Against Shiites"

The country had an estimated 5–6 million Salafists, marked by a deep opposition to Sufism. While many opposition activists joined the Muslim Brotherhood, a faction led by Mohammad Ismail Al-Muqaddim who was close to Saudi Arabia established the "Salafist Appeal" between 1972 and 1977, which gave rise to the Al-Nour Party after the Egyptian revolution. In the 2011 parliamentary elections, the Islamist bloc obtained 7.5 million votes out of a total of 27 million (27.8 percent), so it came in second place after the Muslim Brotherhood. As of January 2013, the party gradually moved away from Muhammad Morsi's government and joined the opposition during the July 2013 coup, which dismissed the president representing the Muslim Brotherhood.

But Saudi diplomacy seemed to be as concerned about Shiite activism as it was about domestic political ripples. In a telegram sent in July 2008, Faisal, the former Saudi Foreign Minister, said that the Kingdom's ambassador to Cairo was deeply concerned about "a new Iranian attempt to infiltrate Al-Azhar." An Iranian diplomat in Cairo had reportedly approached the university to open an Al-Azhar Institute in Iran, with graduates then joining the mother university as a "base to strengthen cultural and religious cooperation between Egypt and Iran." Imam Tantawy seemed to have liked the idea and agreed to admit Shiite students to Al-Azhar in 2007. The cable also expressed concern about the "number of writers who have announced their Shiite identity." Al-Azhar's denials followed closely on the publication by WikiLeaks of a 2011 Foreign Ministry document to King Abdullah. It stated that Al-Azhar's rector, Al-Tayyib, was seeking Riyadh's advice on a meeting proposed by Iran to discuss a rapprochement between Sunnis and Shiites. The letter was signed by the former Saudi Foreign Minister. The publication of the document forced the Al-Azhar authorities to deny having received any "guidance" from "any foreign entity or state." A spokesperson emphasized the independence of the religious institution by saying that its positions were based on religious principles rather than on the influence of outside actors. "However, [Al-Azhar] is coordinating with Islamic countries on Islam-related issues so as to avoid giving inappropriate opinions of the Islamic world in other countries."

A second "secret" cable, sent on May 30, 2012 by the same former minister to the Prime Minister on the activities of the Ambassador in Cairo, summarized what he called "resisting Shiite attempts to penetrate Egypt." He claimed that most religious institutions and personalities "reject holding Shiite gatherings in Egypt." Among them were the former Sheikh Al-Azhar, Muhammad Sayyid Tantawy, members of the Islamic Research Center, the Ansar Al-Sunna Al-Muhammadiya, Al-Gamiyah, Al-Sharia groups and others. Among these names, the Salafist preacher, Muhammad Hassan, was mentioned twice. In a conversation between the Saudi ambassador and the cleric, the latter said that he had spoken to Tantawy about the "danger of Iran's attempts to hold Shiite gatherings in Egypt" and he asked the Kingdom's Ambassador to play a more active role in the resistance. The cable quoted a press conference that the Salafist cleric had given under the patronage of Al-Azhar, "to resist the Shiite invasion, its books and periodicals of jurisprudence, and the organization of seminars and conferences in youth clubs and gatherings."

In another telegram the head of Saudi intelligence sent a document entitled "Shiite movements in Egypt" to various offices of the Kingdom: "The Shiite sect has found a vast area to expand in after the January 25 revolution. The confusion and instability and lack of security in the state helped it to do so [. . .] the Shiite movement has taken advantage of this opportunity and doubled its activities."

SAUDI ACTIVITIES IN THE MAGHREB COUNTRIES

Algeria

In June 2015, the Minister of Religious Affairs, Muhammad Aïssa, led a crusade against the increasingly aggressive emergence of Salafist fatwas. During a recent broadcast on the national channel, he dared to take the official discourse further. Asked about the devastation caused by Wahhabi ideology in society, Muhammad Aïssa did not beat about the bush in saying it as he saw it: "Wahhabism can be beneficial, but only in the society in which it was born. That is not the case with us, especially not in Algeria, where we have a religious referent." He confirmed at the beginning of January that the Saudi radical Salafist Imam, Muhammad Al-Arifi, a professor at King Saud University and a member of the MWL, would not be among the guests at a forthcoming symposium in Constantine: "The request as well as the visa have been refused, because we know that he is an actor in the subversion of the system called the Arab Spring and that he is also a promoter of propaganda for the benefit of the radical group, Jabhat Al Nusra (Al Nusra Front) of the Al-Qaeda in Syria."

It was Algeria that witnessed one of the worst religious wars during the "dark years" in the 1990s (about 150,000 dead). Its causes have been analyzed in depth by many, including the anthropologist, Abderrahmane Moussaoui, in an article entitled, "L'islam traditionnel mis à mal par les chouyoukh"[124] ("Traditional Islam Undermined by the Shuyukh" [religious scholars]). In his view, the establishment of the Islamic University of Madinah in 1960, a full-fledged academy and school for the management and marketing of the Wahhabi doctrine, was a major turning point and many Algerians from the newly independent country attended it to pursue a course in Islamic sciences, alongside the great Saudi masters. "They were made welcome, housed, and taught to gain a good command of the Arabic language and 'fiqh' [Islamic jurisprudence]. This was where the greatest theologians taught their precepts. The teaching of classical Arabic was the lure used to draw in followers. The Saudi university also granted scholarships to its students." Algerian students did internships in the great Saudi mosques, thereby enhancing their resumes, which did not fail to impress when they returned home. Many of the Algerian Salafists of the 1980s and 1990s benefited from these teachings under very comfortable conditions. In their biography, Algerian Islamists described this period as somewhat "magical," giving the impression that these encounters had been a moment of truth for them. They were the first to join the ranks of the Jihadi candidates when Russian troops entered Afghanistan. "In some respects, the Afghan epic could be considered the beginning of the restoration of the House of Islam. The first Arab martyr in Afghanistan was an Algerian, a former student of Madinah," concluded the anthropologist.

Boumédiène actually disregarded the initial terrorist acts at the Law Faculty in 1976, even though he knew full well that an Islamist political movement was gaining ground in the university, seeking to indoctrinate students and counter left-wing opposition. The process became even more challenging under the Chadli regime, which wanted to set the bearded men against the democrats demanding freedom of expression in 1980. Afterwards, he sought to share power with the Islamists, but the military viewed the advent of those who would have taken them to the gallows with disfavor . . . With the arrival on the scene of Salafist jihadism, a more radical current, Algeria was one of the first countries to be subjected to this nameless madness for ten years.

The newly established Salafist party, "Le Front de la Sahwa libre" (The Free Sahwa Front), tried to occupy the space left by the dissolved Islamic Salvation Front (FIS). Its founder, Abdelfattah Hamadache Zeraoui, reaffirmed in an interview for Algérie News: "Upon my return from Saudi Arabia, where I had spent three years gaining an education from the great ulemas, we began working in the mosques." It was during his studies that the idea of forming a Salafist party had been instilled, coupled with a commitment to provide him with the necessary support. According to him, there was nothing shocking about that: "If we start rejecting everything coming from the Gulf, we would also have to refuse everything that comes to us from the West." He said he was proud to be under the influence of the Saudi Arabian ulemas. The Front had recently published a document calling for the creation of an Islamic police in Algeria and going against the demonstration of anything that was "contrary to Islamic morality." In August 2013, he had already announced to Al Jazeera that if he were to become Algeria's president one day, he would establish an Islamic state with, of course, an Islamic police force. In an earlier video, as a good Salafist, he had attacked the Shiites in the country, where a movement for conversion seemed imminent.[125] He was present on July 5, 2015 during anti-fasters the protest against the "déjeûneurs" ("lunchers" or)—youth publicly opposing the constraints of Ramadan. He was also behind the initiative to form the "Hikmah Committees" ('Hikmah' meaning wisdom or putting things in their proper places or avoiding embarrassment) in order to monitor

Algiers' beaches and ban swimwear; finally, on July 11, he demonstrated at Belcourt against the Ministry of Religious Affairs' plan to reopen the synagogues. He was sentenced by the Algerian justice system to three months in prison for calling for the murder of the intellectual, Kamel Daoud, in March 2011.[126] However, his worries are far from over, given that about a hundred women participated recently in a public race along the streets of Algiers.[127]

Morocco: A Bulwark

In 2000, a confidential report,[128] entitled "Le wahhabisme, sa formation, ses menaces et son introduction au Maroc" ("Wahhabism, Its Formation, Threats and Introduction in Morocco"), affirmed that the country was facing a real "invasion" and expressed the great Tariqa Brotherhood's fears. In the 1970s, in the fight against the left and Nasserism, Saudi Arabia had provided support, opened madrassas, recruited young scholars, established new mosques, sent about twenty ulemas . . . so much so that that it started worrying King Hassan II who signed a decree recalling that Moroccan Islam followed the Maliki rite. To combat Wahhabi doctrine, Morocco used the crisis in the Sahel to assert its spiritual and diplomatic influence. In March 2015, it opened a training school for imams in Rabat. Five hundred students from Mali attended a two-year course, including training to counter calls for terrorism and jihad. The program also provided training on how to use the Internet and social media for the peaceful settlement of disputes. Morocco's efforts were both an attempt to challenge the influence of Algeria, its regional rival, but more broadly to contain organizations such as the Islamic State that was building its bases in Libya and Egypt, and more directly, to prevent deadly terrorist attacks such as those in Casablanca in 2003. On a different note, all the opposition did not lead to any hesitation by Riyadh as Ben Ali, the former Tunisian dictator and a sworn opponent of Salafists, had taken refuge in Saudi Arabia (along with his fortune).

SAUDI ACTIVITIES IN COUNTRIES WITH A MUSLIM MINORITY

Bosnia[129]

On February 2, 1996, the *Washington Post* revealed that since 1992, in cooperation with the United States, Saudi Arabia had been funding the Bosnian Armed Forces' armament plan worth $300 million. Washington denied the information, which would have constituted a violation of the embargo imposed by the international community on the warring parties, but Riyadh eventually refrained from going ahead with the plan.

It is important to recall the formation of the Seventh Muslim Mountain Brigade, which consisted of Salafists from different countries (including France). It was dismantled after the war, but some of the veterans stayed behind. The 1992–1995 civil war had appealed to the Wahhabis, such as the Mujahideen veterans, or "volunteers" from Islamic humanitarian agencies, such as the Benevolence International Foundation. Saudi Arabia reportedly raised over $373 million for the "Bosnian Jihad" in the 1990s. The Mujahideen, humanitarian workers and foreign-trained Bosnians were the vanguard of a local Wahhabi movement. Many of them stayed back in Bosnia, providing material support to the devastated Muslim community, but also influencing them ideologically. Shattered by the war, Bosnia could not afford to wait for help from its diaspora, which was in any case too poor. Furthermore, as Bosnian Islam's Sufi tradition—which had constituted a barrier against Wahhabism—had itself been dismantled during the Titoist regime, Saudi help was received with open arms.[130] The Wahhabi movement had taken root among a small section of the Bosnian Muslim population—about 3,000 of the 1.4 million Muslims. They lived mainly in isolated villages, which they governed according to strict Islamic law: men wore long beards and short pants, and women were entirely veiled. Two leaders guided the initial efforts: Jusuf Barcic and

Muhammad Porca, both former scholarship students in Saudi Arabia. In early 2007, Barcic and his supporters had (unsuccessfully) attempted to claim a certain number of mosques for their movement in Tuzla and Sarajevo. Proof of his notoriety came when more than 3,000 people attended his funeral after he lost his life in a car accident. Nedžad Balkan, a Wahhabi based in Vienna and known as the perpetrator of the attack on the Bugojno police station in June 2010, took over from him.

For years, analysts such as Stephen Schwartz, Esad Hećimović, Anes Alic and Vlado Azinovic had been raising alerts about the increasingly violent Wahhabization of Bosnian Islam: the assassination of a Croatian Catholic policeman in 1996; the Wahhabis arrested in 2008 and 2009 for planning to attack Christian sites and EU forces in July 2010, and so on. Nusret Imamovic, one of Barcic's disciples, introduced the Wahhabi code in Gornja Maoča as a model for similar communities, which he wished to extend to the whole of Bosnia. In early 2010, the Bosnian authorities took action, briefly detaining Imamovic and six other militants and seizing weapons, money and video files. The police again attacked the village after the Jašarević episode. In October 2011, a twenty-three-year-old Mevlid Jašarević shot at the US embassy in Sarajevo, wounding a police officer. Originally from the predominantly Muslim city of Novi Pazar in the Sanjak region, he had spent time among the Wahhabi communities in Vienna and Gornja Maoča. He was imprisoned for armed robbery in Vienna in 2005 and arrested in his hometown in 2010 when he brandished a knife during a meeting with the American ambassador. At the same time, the authorities arrested seventeen persons for their connections to Jašarević in Serbia's Sanjak region.

What's more, the organization, "Poziv u Raj" ("Invitation to Paradise"), put up placards and posters, distributed leaflets in Sarajevo, Bihac, Sanski Most, Maglaj, Zenica, Travnik and Tuzla, and organized public lectures in these cities, criticizing Bosnians who did not practice the "true Islam." In one lecture, one of the propagandists claimed that 60 percent of Bosnians did not pray, 70 percent of their women did not cover themselves and 90 percent drank alcohol. The campaign triggered protests by non-Muslims in the city of Maglaj (though a predominantly Muslim city) when leaflets urging conversion to Islam were posted on the Roman Catholic church. Members of the Wahhabi group also handed out similar leaflets to three Catholic nuns in Maglaj. Finally, Nedžad Balkan's supporters were to soon start advocating armed jihad.

Kosovo[131]

Radical Islam has gained prominence in Kosovo over the past five years. The country recorded 232 confirmed cases of fighters leaving for Iraq and Syria. According to journalistic sources, the estimated figure was of 300 out of a total population of 1.8 million inhabitants, which would make it one of the most affected countries.

In Kosovo, Wahhabism met with far more difficulties because of its Sufi traditions, which predominated in some areas (Gjakova, Prizren), and because patriotism was closely identified with Sufism. The most influential among the Sufi orders was that of the Bektashis, a highly anti-conformist sect with a long history in Anatolia and Central Asia. Bektashi practices, which accepted the consumption of alcohol, outraged the Wahhabis who had expelled them from Saudi Arabia in the past.

As early as in 1999, once the West's intervention had ended, Kosovo, like Bosnia and Herzegovina, had been flooded with propaganda and clerics trained in Saudi Arabia. How much money did the Saudis spend through the Saudi Joint Relief Committee for Kosovo (SJRCK)? Impossible to say. Humanitarian assistance to the most deprived—affected by unemployment and the lack of economic resources and often isolated from the political and economic center of Pristina, the capital—also funded the construction or renovation of mosques, schools and clinics. The aid seemed to be predicated on the adoption of a more rigorous lifestyle, such as wearing the veil for women and enrolling children in Koranic schools. By means of its religious diplomacy and by granting scholarships to theology students, Saudi Arabia therefore succeeded in establishing a conservative Muslim current, causing the first dissensions within Kosovo's Muslim community. According to Shpend Kursani,[132] radical and violent Islam was imported by the followers of the Takfiri movement, an extremist branch that developed mainly from 2005 onwards through the imams who had gone to the Middle East, Egypt in particular, to acquire their education. According to him, mosques were not the sole operating grounds of violent extremists, as few imams in Kosovo claimed to belong to the Takfiri current. On the other hand, he did not exclude the importance of the impact of discourses intolerant of other Islamic currents or the influence of radicalized individuals gravitating around mosques and spreading these beliefs in the private sphere, at meetings held in apartments or certain student dormitories, and through control over a number of video arcades and cafés. Finally, he emphasized the extensive the use of the Internet and social media. In fact, due to this digital strategy, it is not really possible to measure the real extent of the phenomenon.

According to the latest findings, most of the volunteers leaving for Syria are young (average age between twenty-three and twenty-eight), poorly educated (80 percent have not completed secondary school), often unemployed or in an insecure job, in search of a cause to serve and for the most part, with a criminal record. Radicalization also affects young people from secular families. The latter do not approve of the Islamization of their children, even going as far as to reject them, thus pushing them into the arms of the extremists. Conversely, in families with long religious traditions, young people seem to leave of their own volition, after a lengthy recruitment process that may last between six months to a year. While at the start of the phenomenon, the men left alone, some now take their families along, including their children.

Again according to Shpend Kursani, traditional Muslim leaders have been the priority targets of extremists. Capable of countering the latter with arguments based on Islam, they appear to be the main obstacle to radicalization. Considered non-believers or infidels, they have faced far more verbal or physical threats than those from liberals and atheists. The most recent physical aggression occurred in 2010.[133] Young people returning de-radicalized from Syria or Iraq and taking part in campaigns against extremist ideologies may also be the subject of reprisals.

In Pristina, on July 29, 2011, the final text of a lecture organized by the Muslim World League under the patronage of the King of Saudi Arabia called for the recognition of the country's independence, referring to the resolution adopted by the Organization of the Islamic Conference in this regard. Over 500 religious personalities had been invited, including ministers of religion, imams and Islamic community leaders from OIC member countries, as well as from countries with Islamic minorities across the world.

Mutual aid thus helped strengthen and bolster the rapid expansion of Wahhabism. For example, the Imam of the Great Mosque of Pristina, Shefqet Krasniqi, a former student of the University of Madinah, and Fadil Sogojeva, an imam who was a former student of the University of Riyadh, were arrested in the summer of 2014 and then released by the courts. The Imam of Pristina's Great Mosque was invited twice, in 2011 and 2013, by the Central Islamic Council of Switzerland (CCIS) for its annual conference. He also preached in Albanian mosques, where Mazllam Mazllami, the Imam of the Jeni Mahalles Mosque in Prizren, also preached. The latter had put several sermons online in which he called upon Muslim Kosovars, among others, not to allow their daughters to marry men of other religions. He also opposed the assimilation of Albanians into Switzerland (a classic policy followed by the MWL).

While the Saudi influence was firming up in this very unique territory, an episode called the "war of the mosques," which caused an upheaval among the Muslims of Bosnia and Kosovo, proved that the struggle was not easy. The Serbs destroyed almost half of the mosques, including several architectural treasures of the Ottoman era. At the end of July 2000, the Saudis, who had chosen to restore the Hadum Mosque in Gjakova, dating back to 1595, began to remove secular tombstones and destroyed the remains of the library . . . [134] The Kosovars reacted brutally. Gazmend Naka, an expert from the Institute for the Protection of Monuments, denounced the Saudi action: "The Serbs killed us physically, but these fanatics want to massacre our cultural heritage." The Saudis explained that NATO and the United Nations had given them carte blanche. The local authorities, backed by New York, stopped the mosque renovation work.

Bulgaria[135]

Bulgaria has one of the largest Muslim communities in Europe, with over 900,000 people (13 percent of the population), consisting of three groups: Turks (7 percent), a rather well-to-do homogeneous and well-knit community; the extremely poor and despised Roma, and 200,000 Pomaks (Islamized Bulgarians) who have commanded the attention of Islamist groups. According to an American agency report, the jihadists seek out Muslims of European appearance who are less easily detectable. The evidence being that Toni Radev, a Pomak, was part of the commando group that launched an attack in Madrid on March 11, 2004, causing 191 deaths.

On the other hand, there is also a strong community of 17,000 inhabitants, consisting of students who arrived in Bulgaria in the 1960s during the communist-era (Syrians, Lebanese and Palestinians, followed by Yemenis, Iraqis, Iranians and Afghans for the most part). A 2005 study estimated that immigrants adhering to the Wahhabi doctrine ranged between 2 and 8 percent (300 to 1,000 persons), with an active core group of 300 preachers working in the Roma ghettos.

Bulgaria's involvement in the coalition in Afghanistan and Iraq contributed to Salafist mobilization. But it would seem that the country was used rather as a transit and financing center, as well as a sanctuary, abetted by corruption in the security forces and links with organized crime. According to the Bulgarian and American agencies, groups such as Al-Qaeda, Ansar al-Islam, Hezbollah, the Chechen rebels, PKK and the Iranians worked in Pomak circles. Since there was no check on donations, religious schools, the construction of mosques or charities by the authorities, it appears that three Saudi NGOs were particularly active:

- The Taiba (Taibah) registered in 1995, to replace two NGOs (Dar al-Irshad and Al-Waqf al-Islamia) that had been shut down by the government in 1994 for radical propaganda and had directly financed the Grand Mufti. The founder, Abdurahman Takan, was expelled for "propaganda against the authorities." The searches proved that the NGO served as a front to fund Salafist groups in the Middle East and that the director, Hussein Odeh Hussein abu Qalbain, was planning attacks against the coalition forces in Iraq.

- The Neduwa (Neduba, Neoua, Nedlae), also funded by Saudi Arabia, was registered by a Syrian citizen in 1994. It provided services for pilgrimages, but also transferred funds for an illegal Pomak Islamic school in the city of Surnitsa.

- Al-Waqf al-Islamia, banned in 1994, was allowed to re-register in 2002 under the terms of the new Law on Religions. It was subsidized by a Dutch organization of the same name and linked to the Muslim Brotherhood and the former NGO, Irshad.

It is difficult to obtain information on the activities of unregistered NGOs. The most active, known as Igase (Igassa, al-Hayat al-Igathata), appear to be a branch of the International Islamic Relief Organization (IIRO). In 2005, it published two glossy publications: "Ikra," in the city of Madan, and "Miosiolmanska obshtestvenost" ("The Muslim

Community"), edited by The Union for Islamic Development and Culture in Smolyan, funded by Islamic NGOs.

The office of the Grand Mufti of Bulgaria, which oversees a system of regional muftis, sadly lacks in money and has no control over the activities of foreign foundations. A recent battle between two candidates for the Grand Mufti's post revealed the problem. The $62,500 received in public aid—insufficient to restore the 1,300 mosques and pay 1,050 imams—had forced the Grand Mufti to accept external aid. With the public system breaking down, an increasingly large number of Bulgarian Muslims moved to the educational system financed by foreign bodies. A mufti explained how he was obliged to use documents advocating "suicide" for his courses on religion, because of the lack of public supplies.

Add to that the hundreds of students trained in Saudi Arabia and other Arab countries who had begun to return and who seemed to be at the root of the friction with the elders concerning practices related to worship and the reading of the Koran. These preachers prefer to preach in private establishments and have apparently established two villages with new mosques in the Rhodope Mountains.

India[136]

India is the second largest Shiite country after Iran (50 million believers). To counter the Shiite influence, Saudi Arabia intends to propagate Wahhabism. One of the WikiLeaks telegrams listed the many Muslim organizations that have received the bulk of Saudi aid: nine institutions in Uttar Pradesh, West Bengal, Kerala and Maharashtra, to counter the growing influence of Iran among the Shiite community.

WHEN THE MWL GAINED A FOOTHOLD IN INDIA

According to documents translated by the daily, the *Indian Express*, the Saudi authorities planned to set up "The Custodian of the Two Holy Shrines' Indian Center of Salafist Studies." Similar institutions already exist in Pakistan and Afghanistan. India's intelligence services estimated that between 2011 and 2013, some 25,000 Saudi clerics paraded through the country, with more than $250 million to build mosques and universities, and to hold seminars. "We are talking about thousands and thousands of militant organizations and clerics who are part of Saudi Arabia's sphere of influence," said Osama Hasan, an Indian scholar in Islamic studies.[137] An amount of 4.5 million Saudi riyals (SAR) was traced to various institutions in Kerala, where Muslims account for 25 percent of the population. Similarly, in Uttar Pradesh (20 percent of Muslims), an amount of 75,000 Saudi riyals was promised to two different companies for a madrassa and a vocational training center for girls.

There is no doubt that Wahhabism is deepening its roots in the country, especially in Kerala, because of the radicalization of a large number of youth who had gone to Saudi Arabia seeking employment. Kerala was the only state where posters mourning the death of Osama bin Laden were put up and where a prayer meeting for Mohammed Ajmal Amir Kasab was held after he was hanged. Kasab was one of the Pakistani terrorists, members of the Lashkar-e-Taiba group, who were involved in the November 2008 attacks in Mumbai, killing 179 people. The sole assailant captured alive by the police, he was tried and sentenced to death on May 6, 2010.

French-Speaking Countries in Sub-Saharan Africa[138]

Sub-Saharan Africa is roughly divided into three parts: A Muslim north, a Christian south and an eastern region shared between the two. Christians are in the majority in southern Sahara (60 percent), but the proportions are changing, with the Muslim population being the largest, so much so that by 2050, Nigeria will be the third most Islamized country in the world.

Sub-Saharan Islam has several major characteristics. It is no longer confined to the Sahel alone, due to regional and internal migration. The boundaries between Christianity and Islam are now increasingly blurred. Muslim northerners have become the majority in many parts of the south, in Côte d'Ivoire, Cameroon and Nigeria, where ports provide employment. The conflict is therefore no longer head-on, with the exception of certain peripheries, such as central Nigeria, eastern Kenya or northern Central African Republic (CAR), where attempts were made by the followers of a Salafist interpretation of Islam to gain control of the Muslim population.

African Islam is also original in that it has witnessed different internal jihads, associated with different interpretations of the Koran. This has led to campaigns for the purification of Islam by abolishing pagan rites or by clamping down on messianic sects. These include the Almoravids in the eleventh century, the Fulani Jihad of the nineteenth century, or the Sudan in the second half of the nineteenth century. Two major movements have left a deep imprint on local Islam: The Mahdia, founded by Mohamed Ahmad ibn Abdallah (1844–1885) in the Sudan in the second half of the nineteenth century, and the teachings of Ousman dan Fodio (1754–1817) in Nigeria at the turn of the eighteenth and nineteenth centuries, which led to the foundation of the Sokoto Caliphate. Steeped in animist and syncretistic traditions, the local practice of Islam is considered deviant by Salafist–Wahhabis. In West Africa, Malikism, which predominates, is unique in that in addition to the Koran and all the official components of the religion (Hadiths, etc.), it uses the customs practiced by the ancient inhabitants of Medina as part of its jurisprudence. Transposed to Africa, Malikism also took pre-Islamic local customs into account, associated with esoteric practices in the case of confraternal Sufism, for instance. Fundamentalists consider sub-Saharan Islam as being perverted, because of the incorporation of paganism. Hence, the duty of true believers was to expurgate it. The destruction of the brotherhoods became an imperative because their masters were ignorant and responsible for all the impurities. Among the different kinds of "pollution" denounced by the fundamentalists were the consultation of marabouts, the sacralization of sultans and chiefs, the use of drums and dance, belief in amulets and spirits, festive and therapeutic Islam, and cults that believed in possession.

THE DISSIDENT BROTHERHOOD

The main brotherhood, the Tijaniyyah, was founded in the eighteenth century by Ahmed al-Tijani, who claimed to have descended from Hassan, son of Ali and grandson of the Prophet, who had appeared to him to announce that he had chosen him as a spiritual guide and taught him the religious ritual of the brotherhood to be founded. According to its followers, Tijanism is the ultimate revelation. In Fez, pilgrims turn toward Mecca to address Allah around his tomb, believing that Al-Tijani intercedes for them. The most visible forms of the practice are the rejection of long beards, praying to make requests and for intercession, possession cults, recitations of litanies invoking the spirit of the Prophet and Ahmed al-Tijani and death rituals with funerals. Not to mention the factorization of the five daily prayers. Tijaniyyah has several tens of millions of followers in West Africa—more than 50 percent of the population of Senegal and Cameroon, where the brotherhood is dominated by the Fulani and Hausa peoples.

The introduction of Wahhabism in sub-Saharan Africa began in the 1960s to circumvent Nasserism from the south. It gradually began to influence social norms by introducing new ones such as the wearing of the burqa, the separation of the sexes, funeral rites or the introduction of the night prayer—"Tahajjud," and the prohibition of marabouts and other saints. Wahhabism's success was largely due to its social role vis-à-vis minor ostracized elites, the vast majority being unemployed graduates who had also lost their Islamic values, undermined by a schooling system inherited from the former settlers. However, the madrassas proved to be totally unsuited, as while children learned Arabic and the Koran, attending them did not lead to greater access to employment, thereby doubling their frustration as only diplomas awarded by Western-type educational establishments were recognized. In Sub-Saharan Africa, radical Islam held the imitation of the West responsible for the country's backwardness. It challenged the economic and political order with its traditional values and chieftainship in order to promote adherence to the roots of Islam, the only harbinger of progress according to the advocates of radicalization. For a long time, black resistance opposed Arab Islam, accused of having been the vehicle for slavery. Today, radicalism is used by the heirs of those who were sold in order to take revenge on those who exploited them. What we have here is an adversarial Islamization, coupled with Arabianization. Radical Islam is breaking the structures of chieftainship and manufacturing a new Arabic-speaking African identity extraneous to traditional hierarchies. Cameroon and Somalia are an illustration of this reality. For all of them, the conversion to Wahhabi Islamism constitutes retaliation against the Fulani, who regarded them as second-class Muslims. Their revenge is all the more powerful as the new radicals speak Arabic and understand the Koran while the Fulani are content to merely recite it. They consider themselves closer to true Islam and its source, Saudi Arabia, while the Fulani believe in a local Islam, accused of being deviant. It is the fight of "Arabianness" against "Fulaniness."

Another characteristic continues to be a matter of concern for Riyadh's religious diplomacy, namely the importance of Shiite (Syrian and Lebanese) communities in some countries—Côte d'Ivoire, for instance. There are no accurate statistics, but probably over 60,000, or even 80,000 people are reported to be Shiites, the country being the primary home of the Lebanese diaspora in Africa and the fourth in the world after Brazil, Canada and Colombia. They are mostly from southern Lebanon, the region that fostered Hezbollah in 1982, and the community is suspected of maintaining alleged links with the Lebanese Party, deemed by several Western countries to be a terrorist organization. The Lebanese community in Côte d'Ivoire has a very strong hold on the country's economic sectors, controlling more than 50 percent, with nearly 4,000 companies employing 300,000 persons. The Shiite charitable association, Al-Ghadir, is purported to have received over 90 percent of its donations from members of Cote d'Ivoire's Lebanese community. The great mosque that it built in the Marcory district is the base for its activities. In fact, the difficulty lies in highlighting the channels used for providing Hezbollah financial support. A study on Salafism in Côte d'Ivoire, a country of particular importance for French interests, would prove useful.

Mali: A Textbook Case[140]

Mali, a secular state at birth as desired by Motibo Keïta, muzzled the Wahhabis. But the dictatorship of Moussa Traoré (1968–1991) put them back in the saddle. Hence, the country has long been a focus of the MWL's interest. Riyadh began to take action when tens of thousands of young Malians traveled to the Gulf countries. Harber Kounta, a Malian anthropologist, explained: "Many students had gone to study religion and then returned to build mosques and madrassas with Saudi money. That is how a number of animist villages made a direct transition to Wahhabism and they are now asking for the imposition of the Sharia, physical punishment or stoning." With the madrassas, they are taking control of associations and buying political influence. Along with mosques, water towers, clinics and Koranic schools, of course, the doctrines of Wahhabi Islam have sprung up. Two hundred mosques, 28 health centers and 4 universities have been built and 120 wells dug in 2015—the results are impressive. Since 2007, Malian students have had the right to take the baccalaureate exam in Arabic. Former President Alpha Oumar Konaré, in his "Education for All" program, announced more than a decade ago, granted madrassas the right to issue state diplomas. These schools, funded by Saudi Arabia and other Gulf charities, are required to teach French alongside Arabic and Koranic studies, but do not do so. The number of such institutions, approved but not regulated by the State, is growing constantly and many Sufi families are now sending their children to them. Not to mention the fact that the World Assembly of Muslim Youth has built a large Islamic education center in Bamako.

After high school, the poorest naturally go to universities funded by the Gulf countries, such as the one in the Sahel, supported by nine State-recognized Islamic NGOs. Its Director, Ibrahim Kantao, speaks Arabic and Bambara, but not French. The success achieved by these institutions can also be explained by the methods used by the Wahhabi imams, who may have a master's or double master's degree and preach in Bambara. Mahmoud Dicko, President of Mali's High Islamic Council (HIC), is a product of Saudi universities. Born in a Timbuktu family, he studied in Mauritania and then in Saudi Arabia. When he returned to his country in 1983, he was given charge of a Wahhabi mosque and began a meteoric rise that led him to the helm of the HIC in 2008, a position which made it possible for him to get forty-three articles modified in the new Family Code, which had given the same rights to girls as to boys.[141] He even managed to get a member of the HIC appointed to the National Electoral Commission. Although his term ended in 2013, he remains President of the High Islamic Council. The latter refused to condemn the Salafist attacks in the north of the country in

2012 and took a stand in favor of a dialogue with the Islamists, including Iyad Ag Ghali, the leader of Ansar Dine, the Salafist jihadi group in Mali. After the attack on the Radisson Blu Hotel on November 25, 2015, Mahmoud Dicko said, "The terrorists were sent by God to punish us for the promotion of homosexuality, imported from the West and prospering in our society." On December 12, 2015, at the Great Mosque, he concluded that jihadism was a "creation of Westerners" and of France, which sought to "recolonize Mali."

The lack of any response by the HIC to jihadi occupation in the north prompted a group of Sufi leaders to react. Cherif Ousmane Madani Haïdara founded the Malian Muslim Spiritual Leaders' Group (GLSM or GMSL) in May 2015 to highlight the nefarious nature of Wahhabism. "The HIC Wahhabis have shown their true face. As Muslims, we wanted to help the Malian army fight the Islamists, but the HIC refused to give us any funds. [. . .] The State should have control over what happens in the madrassas." Driven by an abundance of funds, mainly from Saudi Arabia and Qatar, Wahhabis and other conservative Islamist groups have built major infrastructure and gained support from local communities, frustrated by the lack of government support. He formally asked Qatar to block funding for groups in northern Mali. The GLSM/GMSL want the authorities to take a strong resolve to counter Wahhabi proselytism, but doubts the government's political will. The new Ministry of Religious Affairs, which has tried to thwart the Saudi influence, was established just three years ago, that is, after the occupation of northern Mali and the imposition of the Sharia by the Salafists. In fact, in Mali, the Wahhabis' diplomatic action preceded even that of the jihadists!

Riyadh's constant obsession with the Shiites takes a rather surprising shape in Mali. "Unlike Saudi Arabia, the Iranian strategy in Africa was not based on Islam,[142] but on a subtle opposition between the oppressed and the oppressor, with Shiism being presented as a third path."

This strategy has enabled it to gradually take root in certain African countries, such as Senegal and Nigeria, following the 1979 revolution. "Sunnis are still being converted to Shiism," underlined Bouba Nouhou, a professor and research scholar at the Bordeaux Montaigne University. But despite a certain attraction for Shiism, driven by a large Lebanese diaspora and by more or less clandestine Hezbollah cells, the Iranian influence is limited. Nevertheless, there are well-structured African Shiite breeding grounds, such as in northern Nigeria, in Zaria (Kaduna State), where the army carried out a major operation in December 2015 against the Islamic Movement in Nigeria, a pro-Iranian Shiite organization led by Imam Ibrahim El Zakzaky, who was arrested and detained. Since this attack, which claimed more than 300 lives, according to Human Rights Watch, thousands of the faithful regularly protest and defy the army in the country's mainly Sunni north and Tehran has been putting pressure on Abuja to free the Shiite leader. However, even this minor Shiite activism is enough to worry Saudi Arabia, which received the following cable from its embassy in Bamako in early 2009: "Despite efforts by the Embassy of Iran [in Mali], not many conversions have taken place, but there is always the possibility of their beliefs spreading widely in the future and Shiite activism could find a base here." The document went on to recommend funding for mosque, school, cultural and summer school projects in order to "strengthen the Kingdom's position" and promote Saudi Arabia's image as a "protector of the noble Islamic faith." It further added that this should be done "in a way that promotes peaceful coexistence between different ideologies and quashes the myths of Shiite propaganda because people in Mali love the Prophet's family." The Sufi Tijaniyyah order, which also honors the Prophet's family members as pure devotees, is therefore quite close to Shiism. There is a certain degree of porosity that has not gone unnoticed in Riyadh. "Not even 1 percent of Mali's population is Shiite, but there is a political presence, led by the Iranians," said Mahmoud Dicko, who, together with thirty other Malian clerics, signed an open letter addressed to Sheikh Yusuf al-Qaradawi in 2008 warning of the "dangers of the rising tide of Shiism," which sought to "transform Sunni African societies."

Niger: Signs Not as Weak as May Be Believed

A recent, excellent analysis by Jean-Pierre Olivier de Sardan, Emeritus Research Director at CNRS and Research Director at EHESS was published in the magazine, Marianne.[143] Some of his findings must be mentioned here, especially those concerning the work done by the Wahhabis since the fight against Nasserism. According to him, the riots that erupted in Zinder and Niamey on January 17, 2015, while President Issoufou was in Paris to participate in the demonstration for *Charlie Hebdo* in which ten people had lost their lives and a dozen or so churches had been burnt down, were notable signs. The riots were particularly violent, targeting churches and bars, apart from symbols of France and the ruling party. They clearly testified to well-planned organization and preparation.

This was the first time that the Christian religion had been attacked in Niger, testifying to the rise of an intolerant and violent Islam, the direct opposite of what Niger-based Islam had been for decades. For the article's author, the violence stemmed from the niche that the radical Salafist ideology had gradually made for itself since the 1970s, when the first batch of students that had gone to Saudi Arabia returned home. Niger's society is now increasingly driven by the new, rigorous Islam, which has also visibly insinuated itself in all public debates, with the rejection of the Family Code, the fact that judges swear their oath on the Koran, the upsurge in the number of veiled women or the presence of mosques within all public buildings. Every election is now a game of one-upmanship between candidates and to emerge as the "best, the most pious, the strictest Muslim," they make the maximum promises they can to the imams, marabouts and ulemas. These demonstrations have also highlighted the very dangerous game played by Niger's opposition

political parties, which have tried to exploit public reactions of indigna-
tion in the face of the issue of the Prophet's caricatures. As it were, even
before the Zinder and Niamey demonstrations, they had accused President Mahmadou Issoufou of going to Paris to "support *Charlie Hebdo*,"
thereby condoning the blasphemous caricatures. "Radical Salafism has
been able to prosper by making intolerance a cardinal value, multiplying
anti-Western and anti-Christian sermons, bolstering excesses and viewing jihadists as soldiers of Islam. The use of violence has therefore
become increasingly legitimized, through threats hurled at the African
Fashion Festival, or at young girls who are molested in markets for
wearing outfits that are too Western. "The demonstrations in Niamey
and Zinger are the first mass public outburst of such violence, out in the
open," said the journalist. Young people from the impoverished working
classes, especially the unemployed and largely unschooled informal
workers, or students from the Koranic schools, increasingly at odds with
the social and family norms of previous generations, have been particularly affected by the Salafist ideology. All the pillaging that has taken
place testifies to this situation. But the Salafist ideology has also permeated other categories: schoolchildren, students, junior and sometimes
even middle level executives (teachers, for example). In the context of the
Salafist ideology, jihadists can easily emerge as heroes. This does not
mean that jihadist movements are recruiting masses of people, but rather
that sympathies for the jihadists are increasing significantly. Even Boko
Haram, despite the attacks on Muslims in northern Nigeria, has had
some success among young adults. A fairly widespread conspiracy theory sees the hand of the West in the re-election of President Goodluck
Jonathan in Nigeria, thwarting a northern Muslim leader from being
elected in his place. On the other hand, Boko Haram's allure lies in its
overt radical rejection of the West and the modern democratic state. It
panders to anti-French sentiments, which have persisted, sliding into
much more general anti-West sentiments. Moreover, the jihadists from
northern Mali, like Boko Haram, also attack the Malian and Nigerian

states, respectively. These actions are well perceived in Niger, where there is massive and deep-seated rejection of the political class. Faith in the latter has been eroded by the growing corruption among the enlightened elite, the exasperating and sterile political games played by politicians, the public's powerlessness in the face of unemployment or the profound failure of the state school system. The same rejection extends to the moderate Muslim nomenklatura, official Islamic associations or brotherhoods, all accused simultaneously of collusion with the state and religious laxity. An organization like the Movement for Unity and Jihad in West Africa (MUJAO) has become the repository of all frustrations, preaching a radical change.

In a sense, Salafism and its jihadist extensions play the role of a revolutionary ideology in northern Nigeria, northern Cameroon and Niger. Followers of an Enlightened Islam, supporters of a tolerant Islam, moderate Muslims, Republicans defending secularism and democratic militants remain silent or grieve in silence, because laying into Salafism is likely to be perceived as an attack on Islam, so they risk being put in the Western camp, or even accused of being in the pay of the West. For instance, no demonstration was ever organized in Niamey in support of Boko Haram's victims in Niger or after the attack on the Kano Mosque. The icing on the cake was the statement by the Sheikh of the Grand Mosque of Niamey, Boureima Abdou Daouda, a former member of the Islamic University of Madinah, which is worth quoting: "As for these [anti-Christian attacks of 2015], I don't know anything. But Muslims did not do this [violent demonstrations], they were undoubtedly angry Christians; besides, bars had been plundered and the thieves had drunk the beer."

Indonesia: Laying the Groundwork and Rallying Support Based on Local Crises

The country is believed to have provided only between 700 and 2,500 fighters to the Islamic State. That may not be much, but this does not mean that Wahhabism has not made a mark in this Asian country. While speaking with the Australian Prime Minister, Malcolm Turnbull, President Barack Obama himself remarked that the Saudis and other Arabs from the Gulf had poured a lot of money into the Indonesian archipelago in the 1990s and sent a large number of imams and teachers to disseminate the fundamentalist version of Islam.[144] According to him, Islam in Indonesia was now much more Arab in its orientation. The Wahhabi ulemas' influence had begun to permeate university campuses from 1990 onwards and their followers define themselves as Salafists.[145] Funded by Riyadh, the Institute for Islamic and Arabic Studies (LIPIA) in Jakarta has acted as the spearhead in praising Saudi and Yemeni universities.

Ever since it was founded in 1945, Indonesia has upheld the principle of neutrality in religious matters, unlike its neighbor, Malaysia. And it is towards the revision of the Indonesian Constitution that a number of Salafist or Neo-Wahhabi groups—such as Laskar Jihad, the Hizbullah Front, the Islamic Defenders Front, the Hizb ut-Tahir group, KISDI, etcetera—have been working. The IIRO has sufficient monies to fund 575 new mosques for Indonesia alone. But the bulk of those funds are used for non-charitable purposes. A WikiLeaks cable mentioned various payments made to a series of publications for amounts ranging from $3,000 to $10,000 and a request for the Saudi Ministry of Culture and Information's participation through mass subscriptions to newspapers such as the *Kompas* and the *Jakarta Post*. In 2003, the "US News and World Report" noted, "Accompanying the money, there was invariably a blizzard of Wahhabist literature . . . Wahhabism's more extreme preaching teach mistrust of infidels, brand rival sects as apostates and lay emphasis on violent jihad."

After the attacks on the World Trade Center and especially after the American invasion of Afghanistan, these groups organized protests in front of the United States Embassy in Jakarta and marched through the streets of Java's major cities, riding the highly popular wave of anti-

American and anti-imperialist sentiments. Saudi money was poured into Wahhabi foundations that were very close to Laskar Jihad, such as Al-Irsyad. In fact, the ongoing sectarian conflict in the Moluccas, an archipelago divided between Christianity (essentially Protestant) and Islam, arose from a demographic imbalance and the adoption of a policy of preference for Muslims in the 1990s under pressure from the Muslim Committee, the "Ikatan Cendekiawan Muslim Indonesia" (ICMI), which rallied support for jihad. The Laskar Jihad, fairly quietist until then, also sided against the government's inability to protect Muslims and called for active solidarity.

The charismatic Jafar Umar Thalib was the prototype of an Indonesian Salafist. After studying in Saudi Arabia and Yemen, he went to Afghanistan to take part in the jihad. From 1994 to 1999, he confined himself to preaching, but the conflict in the Moluccas pushed him to violence. After September 11, he confessed that during his stay in Afghanistan he had met Bin Laden but did not consider him a pious Muslim. In order to make his attempt to distance himself more credible, he brought up a fatwa issued earlier by the Saudi Mufti, Ibn Baz, in which Bin Laden had been declared as being sectarian, led astray by his rebellion against the Saudi regime and was asked to repent. The Laskar Jihad, which he spearheaded, refrained from taking sides against the US aggression in Afghanistan, but later made very strong anti-American statements on his behalf. Like any good Salafist, he was completely anti-Shiite, labeling them "taghout" (i.e., traitors, infidels, "who do not open the doors to Paradise"). Suspected of influencing the October 2002 Bali attacks (202 dead), he was tried and acquitted. Another militant group, actually the first to get organized and make its mark on the streets of Jakarta, was the Islamic Defenders Front (Front Pembela Islam or FPI), perceived more as a heterogeneous group rather than a real movement. Its leader, Habib Rizieq Syihab, was a Sayyid (a Muslim claiming descent from Muhammad, especially through Husain, the prophet's younger grandson), born in Jakarta, who studied in Saudi Arabia.

The first signs of an anti-Arab reaction seemed to have emerged among indigenous Indonesian Muslims, who considered this kind of radicalism foreign to their culture. Former President Abdurrahman Wahid wrote in the *Wall Street Journal* that Wahhabism was making serious "incursions" into the tolerant Indonesian nation.[146] The two representative majority groupings in the archipelago—the Muhammadiyahs and the Nadlatul Ulema—fought against the Salafists. The first grouping consisted of 30 million members and the second over 35 million. However, as in other Muslim countries, some politicians did not hesitate to use the fundamentalist Islam card to oust adversaries, undermine rivals and come to power.[147]

Shiite Islam accounted for just 1.2 percent of the population, but seemed to be witnessing a certain growth, for example, with the 2 million Sunni converts. Two Saudi cables of March 14, 2012, written by Crown Prince Nayef ibn Abdulaziz in response to letters and reports received by the Minister of Foreign Affairs and Ambassador in Jakarta, focused on the activities of the Ahmadiyya Muslim community, a small Shiite sect of 400,000 members: "The Ahmadiyya issue was examined by the Preparatory Committee of the Supreme Council of Islamic Affairs in order to draw up a concrete plan with the help of the Ministry of Foreign Affairs, the Ministry of Islamic Affairs and the Supreme Islamic Council of Indonesia, to halt the spread of the Ahmadiyya sect. [. . .] The embassy in Jakarta is charged with explaining the danger the sect presents to the Indonesian government."[148] On April 23, 2012, a month after the letter, a mob of 80 Islamic extremists attacked an Ahmadiyya mosque in western Java, pelting it with stones and destroying objects of worship.

On May 15, 2012, in a second series of cables in response to those by Nayef ibn Abdulaziz, the following steps were recommended: first, advise international Islamic organizations to publish a statement specifying what the Ahmadiyya community was; and then, have the Islamic Affairs Ministry and the Muslim World League issue warnings against the community and its ideologies, while eschewing violence against its members. The Kingdom's Embassy was required to continue to support the Supreme Islamic Council of Indonesia in its efforts to propagate Islam against these beliefs. In August 2010, the Indonesian Minister of Religious Affairs, Suryadharma Ali, said that the Ahmadiyyas needed to be dismantled forthwith, otherwise the "problems will continue." In February 2011, three Ahmadi Muslims were beaten to death. Here, as in Algeria, Pakistan, or Afghanistan, the anti-blasphemy law is regularly used by Salafists against religious minorities.

SAUDI ACTIVITIES IN THE FORMER USSR

An overview of Saudi Arabia's activities in an area as vast and disparate as the former USSR is virtually impossible, firstly because Muslims there are dispersed and practice very different rituals, traditions and cultures. Secondly, because communism's religious policy varied greatly and the invasion of Afghanistan left its mark, which partly explains the present day radicalization. Indeed, according to experts of this region, re-Islamization may have begun in the 1980s, particularly during the Perestroika period. Finally, because the region is truly a "mission territory" for Muslims, often deprived of their roots, with Turkish, Iranian, Pakistani and Qatari religious diplomacy being especially competitive in the areas bordering Afghanistan. It is therefore difficult to determine what actual role Wahhabism plays in the current atmosphere of violent radicalization. It must be added that the undifferentiated use of the terms "Salafist" or "Wahhabi" or "preacher of a foreign Islam" to describe any perpetrators of attacks of any kind, any circumstances or targets, or even any opponents, further blurs the analysis.

The Central Asian countries have managed the transition with more or less flexible forms of dictatorship. Many radical activities have erupted around active trouble spots such as Chechnya or the Fergana Valley. However, inter-ethnic and intra-Muslim violence in some countries with borders inherited from the choices made by the Commissar of Nationalities, Joseph Stalin, is a source of crisis (for example, in 2010 the anti-Uzbek pogroms led by the Tajiks in Kyrgyzstan), which further complicates their study.

Russia[149]

Islam is the religion practiced by a number of minorities scattered across Russia. The largest of them live in the North Caucasus, the Urals and near the Volga. With nearly 20 million people, that is, 13–15 percent of the population, not including the 6 million Turkic-speaking Tatars, half of whom live in Tatarstan, Muslims are the largest minority and the second largest population group after Russians.

Wahhabism therefore spread across a dispersed Muslim population, supervised by religious authorities compromised by communism and lacking a real theological culture. It focused particularly on areas suffering open crises: the Caucasus and Tajikistan, to mention a few. The Wahhabi discourse—an exclusive adjective used in Russia to refer to radicals—developed in opposition to a traditional Islam, in particular to the official religions' imams and to confraternal Islam, widespread in the Caucasus and Central Asia. It was characterized by a strong rallying capacity vis-à-vis the youth, struck by economic recession and concerned about identity issues.

Under the Soviet regime, nearly 25,000 mosques were destroyed. In the Central Asian countries, out of the 12,000 pre-revolutionary mosques, fewer than 500, of which 27 were in Dagestan, remained in the 1980s. Islamic foundations were expropriated and Muslim clerics, trained exclusively by the State, were often discredited. The re-Islamization movement is purported to have taken off in the 1980s, facilitated by the Brezhnev regime, which had understood the utility of a more comprehensive and tolerant policy during the war in Afghanistan and then due to the slow decline of power during Perestroika. Today, Russia has about 7,000 mosques, including 5,000 in the North-Caucasus. Until 2005, the largest was in Makhachkala, Dagestan gave way to the future Kul-Sharif Mosque in Tatarstan, which was in turn "overtaken" in 2008 by the Akhmat-Kadyrov Mosque in Chechnya.

According to Mikhail Remizov,[150] President of the Institute for National Strategy, "Wahhabism and radical political Islamism as a broader concept have become the ideology of anti-Russian protests that has the greatest appeal in the Muslim areas of traditional Islam. The risk of long-term propagation is growing due to mass migration in Russia." He echoed the same concern about the State's disengagement that has been felt in major western suburbs: "If the Russians were to leave, the State would leave a strategic vacuum, perhaps not at one go, but gradually." Ever since 2000, a kind of "Salafist holding" has taken shape in Russia, which includes imams, civil servants and businessmen. Roman Silantyev, Director of the Human Rights Center, quoted his counterpart in the Russian Federation's Federal Security Service (FSB): "The terrorists' geography has expanded to include Siberia, the Middle East and the Urals, and the first conflicts have erupted in the autonomous district of Yamalo-Nenets and in Tatarstan."

Afghanistan's invasion was the first blow (the mostly Muslim troops sent in December 1979 were quickly relieved); today, the intervention in Syria alongside the Alawite (Shiite) minority of Bashar al-Assad conveys the impression of a desire to fight against the Sunnis and, finally, the strong-arm tactics used in the dispute with Erdoğan's Turkey has made the situation of some Russian Muslims even more complicated. Indeed, the Syrian adventure is perceived diversely by them. There are an estimated 3,000–7,000 Russian-speakers in the ranks of the Islamic State (according to Putin), therefore constituting the third-largest foreign nationality. About 1,700 came from the North Caucasus and around 200 from the Volga region. The rest came mainly from the Urals, Moscow, St. Petersburg and Siberia. Approximately between 600 and 5,000 are considered to have left Dagestan. They began leaving at the start of the Syrian crisis and the outflow then gathered momentum with the proclamation of the Caliphate. The call for a jihad against Russia, launched a few months ago by some forty Saudi imams, has muddied the waters in the minds of many—something that could be exploited by extremists, worries Alexei Malachenko, a Caucasus specialist in Moscow's Carnegie Center.[151] He stated, "Nearly 100,000 Russian Muslims consider the Islamic State an honorable organization defending the rights of Muslims. Between 2,500 and 4,000 Russian Muslims are already fighting in Syria against Assad's forces. Their possible return to Russia is a major security risk." Ample evidence has been provided by the Caucasian branch of the IS, comprising twenty-six heads of groups, which was formed in 2015. A Federal Security Service (FSB) officer, whom the author met during one of his visits to Central Asia, confessed that Russia's bombing strategy in Syria specifically targeted Russian-speakers (1,000 are purported to have already been eliminated) in order to preclude their return.

Tatarstan

Facing stiff competition from Turkish diplomatic action and its great religious brotherhoods, Wahhabism in Tatarstan is still in a "crypto-phase." A WikiLeaks telegram mentioned the case of a dozen people from the Trans-Kama region who had gone to study in Saudi Arabia. The imam of the main mosque of Kazan Kul Sharif had also studied there from 1992 to 1997. Valiulla Yakupov, head of the Education Department of the DUM (Muslim Religious Administration) in the Republic of Tatarstan explained, "Changing the size of one's beard and the extent of the arm movements during prayers is the easiest thing in the world. [. . .] The problem is that, having accepted the 'Salaf akidah' (the faith), a Muslim also accepts the idea of violent actions. One might believe that such a person will at the least help the jihadists materially. It must also be said that the 'taqiyya'—the art of dissimulation for the greater good of Islam—leads one to conceal one's true religious convictions if necessary; this is an important element of the Wahhabi ideology."[152] In the opinion of experts, this area is extensively permeated by radical Islamism. The four churches that were set on fire within a period of two weeks in the Autonomous Republic of Tatarstan in December 2015 may be construed as an illustration. And on July 19, 2012, Tatarstan's Mufti, Ildus Faizov, appointed in January 2011 after the ouster of his predecessor, Osman Iskhakov, deemed too complacent vis-à-vis radical Islam, was seriously injured when his car exploded. Faizov had, among other things, banned books from Saudi Arabia. His deputy, Valiulla Yakupov, was shot dead on the same day in Kazan. "The explosions and gunfire that have just rung out are only the beginning," said Mufti Farid Salman, Director of the Holy Koran and Sunnah Research Center at the BBC.[153] According to him, there were already over 3,000 radical Islamists in Tatarstan, but many had likely taken a peaceful stand. However, several radical Internet forums had already called for the assassination of people who frequently and openly criticized the spread of "Wahhabism" in Russia. Radicalized Tatars were arrested from the ranks of insurgents in Chechnya and even among the Taliban in Afghanistan. "The authorities claim that there is peace and quiet in the region," said Rais Suleimanov, head of the Volga regional branch of the Russian Strategy Research Institute. "In fact, the situation has degenerated and now, peace and tranquility are merely an illusion." After the publication of his research on the development of Islamic fundamentalism in Tatarstan in 2010, he was dismissed from his post at Kazan University and, shortly afterwards, the center itself was closed down. Mufti Farid Salman believed that the July 2012 attacks were "a proclamation, a provocation . . . we had already reached a point of no return. A generation of committed Wahhabis had reached maturity in Tatarstan." After the assassination attempt on Ildus Faizov, the local Interior Minister, Artyom Khokhorin, suddenly realized that an undeclared war was being waged in the region for the past thirteen years. The State tried to respond by initiating a dialogue with official Islam and by building mosques and an Islamic academy for training religious representatives.

Central Asia

Historically, the region was divided into countries with arbitrary borders and voluntarily heterogeneous populations only at the end of the civil war, in 1920. The sudden independence, following the dissolution of the Soviet Union after seventy years of the communist regime, left societies traumatized by the abrupt cessation of enterprises, the nonpayment of pensions and wages, the interruption of economic flows and political uncertainty. . . .

As early as in 1991, Riyadh had donated $1.5 billion to Russia for cultural and religious activities, mainly for the Central Asian countries, and had offered far greater access to the Hajj. Just under a year after independence, by June 1992, 130,000 people had gone on the pilgrimage.[154] The Saudi religious authorities recruited and mobilized members of the Uzbek refugee community in the peninsula in the 1930s to be sent as missionaries to preach and encourage people to go on the pilgrimage to Mecca. Within the first two years of independence, 25,000 Uzbeks had gone for the Hajj.[155] In Uzbekistan, where confraternal Islam was born and is still widely practiced, the Wahhabi discourse was shaped in opposition to traditional Islam, in particular to the imams of the official religions. The Islamist party, Hizb ut-Tahrir, close to the Taliban, has been making inroads in Uzbekistan, just as it has in Tajikistan and Kyrgyzstan, with the mushrooming of small cells.[156] It preaches peaceful change through a mass popular movement that would eventually rise up against the current rulers.

The Uzbek government has been waging a fierce battle against "extremists" since the assassination of police officers in the Namangan region in late 1997,[157] attributed to "Wahhabi militants." The authorities have carried out hundreds of arrests and the repression intensified after the attack in Tashkent in February 1999, which resulted in the death of sixteen people. The battle against the Islamists also served as a pretext for fighting against the political opposition, which had already been considerably suppressed since 1993. At the recent trial of the leading members of the Islamic Movement of Uzbekistan (IMU), Mohammed Salih, the leader of the Erk Democratic Party, in exile since 1993, was accused of working with the Islamists and was sentenced to fifteen years in prison. The demands by the IMU, classified as a terrorist group in some western countries, have gradually evolved, first calling for a theocratic regime, not just in Uzbekistan but throughout Central Asia, through a new organization: the Islamic Movement of Central Asia, which seeks to restore the former Khanate of Bukhara and which announced in 2015 that it was going to join the Islamic State. The repression by Emomali Rahmon, the dictator in power for twenty-three years, has created the most volatile situation among the region's countries. Tajikistan, the poorest state in Central Asia, is under both internal and external pressure. The reign of the incumbent president is characterized by violence, a lack of responsibility, corruption and mass migration. The transfer of funds and drug trafficking are now the main sources of income. With the economic crisis and the West's embargo against Moscow, 300,000 to 400,000 migrants returned to the country in 2015, with little hope of finding a job. Control over religion and political opposition, including the banning of the Islamic Renaissance Party of Tajikistan (IRPT), has only turned the country into a hotbed for rebellion. Finally, the 1,400-kilometer-long border with Afghanistan and the growing instability in the north, where Central Asian militants have allied themselves with the Taliban, has heightened the element of vulnerability. The IRPT, accused of preparing a coup d'état, was declared illegal by the country's Supreme Court. Its leader, Muhiddin Kabiri, was charged with allegedly organizing attacks against the security forces, such as the attack led by Abduhalim Nazardo around the seat of power in early September 2015. The attack occurred a few months after Colonel Gulmurod Khalimov, Commander of the Ministry of the Interior's special forces, deserted and announced that he was joining the Islamic State, further demonstrating the fragility of the power structure. On December 2, 2015, in a joint initiative, the

country's ulemas issued a fatwa declaring war on the Salafists and calling on all the country's Muslims to fight against them, and obviously
the Islamic State. The initial measures were more symbolic than effective, with the police announcing that they had shaved the beards of
some 13,000 Tajiks and closed more than 160 shops selling traditional
Muslim clothing.[158] According to Serghei Massaulov, a Kyrgyz specialist in Central Asia who was interviewed, the jihadist guerrillas of Central Asian origin present in the Syrian–Iraqi theater of operations,
estimated to be over 3,000, likely consist of:

- 1,200–1,300 fighters belonging to the Islamic Movement of
  Uzbekistan (IMU), which includes an undetermined number of Caucasians (Chechens, Dagestanese, etc.), 800 Turcomans and Turkmens, including Turkmens from Afghanistan,
  but also Turcomans of other origins

- About 600–700 Tajiks from Tajikistan, but who are trying
  to recruit Tajiks from North Afghanistan and have a considerable breeding ground in Iraq and Syria. According to
  the Tajik Minister of the Interior, 692 fighters in Iraq and
  Syria are wanted and 154 Tajik families have left for the
  war zones

- 200–300 Kazakhs

- Around 100 Kyrgyz, supplemented by 200 Uzbeks from
  South-Kyrghystan

Like the IMU, most of these groups are beefed up by external elements,
especially Caucasians.

It is not easy to determine the limitations of Wahhabi influence in the
Central Asian countries: local Islam, by its specificities, traditions and

languages, is considerably original in nature and the authorities have been emphatic about curbing foreign influences. Turkey, which is linguistically closer, has given stiff competition to Saudi Arabia. Wahhabism and its discourse on Muslim identity therefore seem to be struggling and in a sort of "crypto-Salafist" phase. By way of illustration, the pogroms that tore Kyrgyzstan asunder in 1992 and 2001 targeted the Uzbeks while avoiding the Russian citizens living there. On the other hand, in each of the countries, the local authorities organized the representation of cults around a Grand Mufti and instituted curbs to control madrassas and funds from abroad. Some multicultural countries proclaimed themselves secular (e.g. Kyrgyzstan, with its new 2015 religious freedom law). Although Saudi money had been used to build nearly 5,000 mosques in Central Asia,[159] Wahhabism's impact cannot be measured by these figures.

On the other hand, doubts persist about the Afghan Taliban's strategic ambitions with regard to the Central Asian countries. According to Serghei Massaulov, they are believed to have remained fundamentally driven by the idea of a Pashtunistan straddling Pakistan rather than by a hypothetical Khanate of Bukhara. The hypothesis of a possible spin-off effect of the Afghan crisis therefore lacks credibility.

Caucasus

The biographical journey of Doku Umarov, the Chechen insurgent leader, demonstrates the volatile and changeable nature of data. Of Uzbek origin, radicalized after his time with the Red Army in Afghanistan, he was responsible for a number of anti-Russian terrorist acts since 2009, such as the Moscow metro explosion in 2010 or the one at Domodedovo International Airport in 2011. He called himself both a denouncer of the "Wahhabis" and, after becoming a champion of Chechen nationalism, also proclaimed the Emirate of the Caucasus, which he wished to expand to the Volga region, in order to build the Greater Emirate of the Caucasus. Would this be the reason for his opposition to Chechens leaving to join the Islamic State?

"The presence of Islamic humanitarian organizations close to Salaf-ism, such as the 'Social Reform Society' (Kuwait), the 'International Charity Society' (Qatar) and the 'International Islamic Salvation Congress' (Saudi Arabia) on Chechen soil is well-established. Over 80–90 percent of Chechnya's fighters are local, while those from the Middle East (1,000) are mostly Mohajirs—Caucasians exiled in the 19th century at the time of the Russian conquest,"[160] according to Eva Kochan. In addition to these fighters, the Chechen jihad received foreign funds, often from the same sources as Al-Qaeda. The Saudi Arabian foundation, Al-Haramain, whose assets have been frozen since 2004 in the United States, is believed to have sent it $50 million. The Benevolence International Foundation, based in Chicago, is deemed to have funded it in the same way before the US authorities closed its offices in December 2001. According to a 2002 Russian security services estimate, the Gulf countries, including Saudi Arabia, have reportedly paid $1.3–2.5 million per month since the mid-1990s to fund "terrorist activities" in Russia. The same services proclaim that telephone calls to and from the Gulf countries that they intercepted around the time of the deadly attack on the Moscow theater on October 23, 2002, stand proof of this fact.

Furthermore, the *Guardian* published startling unconfirmed information: the Saudi intelligence chief, Prince Bandar bin Sultan, was reported to have given Russian President Vladimir Putin "guarantees to protect the Winter Olympic Games" in Sochi during a visit to Moscow in August 2013.[161]

Adeeb Khalid, a specialist on Central Asia, observed that the local situation has essentially shown that Islam is a complex phenomenon that cannot be easily categorized into "good" and "bad," or "moderate" and "extremist." Here too, Islam has a specific form. "It is essential for observers to have a historical perspective, to clearly discern the political stakes, the ethnic differences involved . . . and to separate the disinformation provided by the regimes from the actual conduct of Muslims."[162] In conclusion, the reasons—both for conflicts and radicalization—are so varied in the Central Asian and Caucasus countries that it is difficult to determine Saudi diplomacy's direct responsibility.

For Ramzan Kadyrov, Chechnya's pro-Russia President, it was an extremely simple matter, "All Wahhabis are not only enemies of Islam but all humanity," and he saw no other solution than their complete physical elimination. He was supported by Sultan Mirzaev, the Grand Mufti, who views Wahhabism as an emanation from hell.

SAUDI RELIGIOUS ACTIVITIES IN EUROPEAN COUNTRIES

An article by Al-Azab Abdul Khalil, published in "Al-Alam al-Islami" ("The Islamic World") on the MWL's website in December 2004, entitled, "Saudi Arabia's Decisive Role in the Dissemination of the Divine Message of Islam in the West," summarizes the research conducted by Dr. Sheikh Rafat Gunaimi, Director of the Egyptian Research Institute at Zagazig University. Europe is seen as a promising "territory" for Islamization. In another article on the same site entitled, "Muslims in Switzerland Are Seeking Ways of Training Their Own Imams," the author, Ali Salekh, based in Paris, explained in detail how Wahhabi imams could be introduced into European mosques without alarming European authorities: "An Imam must familiarize himself with all aspects of life in the concerned country in order to be able to issue fatwas that are in line with the Sharia on the one hand and, on the other, take the actual living conditions in that country into account."

Salafism had virtually no presence in Europe in the 1980s. In the mid-2000s, it burgeoned, leading to some thirty terrorist attacks in European territory from 2001 to 2010 in its jihadist version, amidst a wave of departures to Syria. The April 2015 UN report on the 25,000 foreign fighters who went to join the jihad,[163] provides startling results about the proportion of departures to the overall population: Belgium was in the lead, with 500 to 800 departures, that is, 39.4 departures per

million inhabitants, ahead of Denmark (26.7), Sweden (18.8) followed
by France (18.3) and Austria (17), followed by Great Britain (9.5) and,
finally, Germany (7.5).[164] Thirty to fifty Irish citizens were also suspected to have gone to Syria and at least three of them were killed there.
Compared with its miniscule Muslim population (50,000 persons), Ire-
land was deemed to have the highest participation rate of Muslims in the
Syrian conflict among all European countries. The same report noted a
70 percent increase in arrivals of foreign combatants since March 2014,
the date when the Western military engagement in Iraq and Syria started.

Yet, Europe remains a sanctuary even today. Al-Qaradawi and
other Islamic clerics have consolidated their authority by setting up a
number of jurisprudential boards that issue fatwas on matters ranging
from the participation of Muslims in political life to financial activities
through the Dublin-based European Council for Fatwas and Research
and the International Union of Muslim Scholars (IUMS). Various local
councils are scattered across Europe, particularly in Great Britain,
where the issue of the Sharia in the British legal system has been a subject of intense debate in recent years. Their influence on the daily lives
of most Muslims living on the continent is not known. But given the
ethnic and national divisions within Muslim communities in Europe,
no single council has a monopoly. For instance, Al-Qaradawi's European Council appears to exert influence over certain sections of the
Arab community. On the other hand, South Asian Muslims are more
likely to turn to other networks. African Muslims remain attached to
their own preachers who stayed back in their countries. According to a
study by the Pew Research Center's Global Attitudes Project, a majority
of British Muslims seem more inclined to seek advice from local imams.
But the fact remains that as of now, no modernist Islamic European
center can claim to hold complete sway over all Muslims.

Belgium: Sumptuous Expenditure, Communitarianism, Radical Associations and Ghetto Sanctuaries[165]

Belgium, a major exporter of fighters, appears to be an important Salaf-ist center (in terms of financing, logistics and departures). The story of the country's relationship with Saudi Arabia reads like a shoddy piece of writing, first with the establishment of a Muslim identity based on bilateral diplomatic relations, followed by the burgeoning of a number of local associations and field actions in the ghettos.

In 1969, King Baudouin thanked Saudi Arabia for helping the vic-tims of the fire at the department store, L'Innovation, and agreed to the establishment of the Islamic and Cultural Center of Belgium (ICCB) under the MWL's control in the eastern pavilion of Brussels' Parc du Cinquantenaire. Later, the ICCB became the Muslim World League's European headquarters.

The ICCB's Board of Directors consists of all the ambassadors of Muslim countries, but the Saudi ambassador is its ex-officio President. The Belgian government recognized Islam in 1974 and, in May 1978, by means of the "Schools Pact," King Khaled managed to obtain grants to pay six hundred religious teachers in primary and secondary schools. A training institute for imams, whose director is empowered by the Belgian Ministry of National Education to designate teachers for classes on Islam and Arabic in public schools, was inaugurated in 1989. There are reportedly seventy-seven mosques at present in Brussels alone. And the first beneficiary of Saudi donations in Belgium was the Jardin des Jeunes (Garden for Youth), set up to impart courses in Arabic and reli-gion in Brussels in 1997. Several Islamic booksellers depend on it. The Al-Imam al-Bokhari Center, established in 1998, coordinates pro-Saudi movements in Belgium. Led by Wahhabis of Turkish origin, the Youth Education and Culture Center set up in Saint-Josset-en-Noode in 1998, better known as Al-Maarifa, has its own printing house, Dar al-Hadith. The Faculty of Islamic Sciences of Brussels, which provides courses in Arabic and offers a five-year theological course, though not recognized by the French-speaking community, is also located at the same address. The ICCB played a central role in spreading Salafism in Belgium throughout the 1980s, and even conducted activities that are now considered counterproductive for the integration of Muslim immigrants, to the extent that in 1990, it was divested of its status as the official interlocutor and of its role in the selection of Islamic religious teachers by the Belgian authorities.

Beyond the official Saudi presence, a swarm of semi-official organizations mushroomed, drawing on clerics of the Wahhabi dissent movement, such as Abu Chayma, who was convicted in 2012 for torture in an exorcism trial in Brussels and who, having served his sentence, continues to give courses on religion. Mustapha Kastit, a Moroccan who spent eight years studying in Saudi universities and was the founder of the Al-Bokhari Center is the very embodiment of Salafism. In 1998, his services were engaged by the MWL. But following an article calling for a boycott of Israeli products in order to fight the Occupation of the Territories, he was denounced by the MWL's top leadership and a Saudi sheikh, Ubaid al-Jabiri, branded him as someone who was "misguided and adrift" [sic!].

The newest member of the Belgian Islamic galaxy is the "Collectif réflexions musulmanes" (CRM or Muslim Reflections' Group), founded in Brussels at the end of 2012, with a view to "propagating an authentic Islamic discourse," part of which consists of denouncing "Islamophobia" and disrupting public debates.

The most paroxysmal case of forbearance by European countries vis-à-vis hate militants is that of Sharia4Belgium, founded in 2010. Very active on the streets and on the net, the group and its leaders heaped together all that could be considered as racism and called for murder and the legitimization of violence before finally being banned in 2012. The trial of forty-six of its members, suspected of being the biggest suppliers of jihadists for the Syrian front, took place in September 2014. Of the number of Belgians who left to wage the holy war, 10 percent were affiliated with it or had gravitated to it. Fouad Belkacem, its spokesperson and main facilitator, in pre-trial detention since April 2013, was facing up to twenty years in jail along with fifteen other members. He only got twelve.

MOLENBEEK: A DANGEROUS EXAMPLE OF A GHETTOIZED DISTRICT

Testimony of a French Specialist on the Arab World

I go regularly to Molenbeek at the invitation of the commune's Secular Moral Circle to give lectures on the issues facing the Arab and Islamic world. That is how, on October 18, 2011, I met with Ms. Firouzeh Nahavandi, a professor at the Université Libre de Bruxelles, to give a lecture entitled "Different perspectives about the Arab Spring uprisings." Mr. Philippe Moureau, the Socialist Party Mayor of the commune, seated in the first row of spectators, had arrived flanked by two athletic bodyguards in djellabas, with dark jackets, caps on their heads and long beards, who stood giving a fierce look on either side of the front door. As the average age of Molenbeek's Secular Moral Circle members was around sixty-five, the risks of anyone disturbing public order appeared limited to me and did not justify a show of force of such magnitude and with so many connotations. It goes without saying that the tone of the lecture was neither political nor partisan—although both of us were worried about the Salafist grip on the Arab revolutions—and was merely limited to considerations validated by information sources as neutral and academic as possible. However, this did not prevent Mr. Moureau from indirectly casting doubts on Ms. Nahavandi's intellectual honesty, because, being of Iranian origin, she undoubtedly supported a "Shiite interpretation" of events, and espe-cially mine—because, since my country had tortured Muslims in the 1960s, I was not qualified to speak about the Arab world. Then, visibly satisfied with his outing, he left with his bodyguards.

Somewhat surprised by the violence of the charges, I asked the journalists present what they thought. They laughingly replied that it was all part of local folklore. Philippe Brewaeys, in particular, a jour-nalist with *Marianne Belgique* and a Molenbeek resident, explained to me that Philippe Moureau, who had been the mayor for over ten years (from 1992 to 2002), had built his entire career on votes by Moroccan immigrants in his commune (who by then accounted for 60 percent of the population), that he won over their votes by granting them different benefits and municipal employee posts (several members of the Abde-slam family were actually municipal employees), by building a number of places of worship financed by Saudi Arabian NGOs and by seeking to limit—with the support of certain Socialist Party federal ministers—any "interference" of Belgium's State security agencies within his commune. Several people assured me that this kind of thing was not unusual and that similar issues could be found in a slightly less carica-tural manner in municipalities like Schaerbeeck, Anderlecht, Vilvoorde, Forest, etc.

Things seem to have changed somewhat with Moureau's departure and his replacement by a less "spectacular" bourgmestre (mayor).

The name of Molenbeek, one of the nineteen districts in Brussels, comes up in a startlingly large number of terrorist cases: it was the sup-port base of the AIG network responsible for the Paris attacks. It was also the place where Abdessatar Dahmane lived—he was one of the two who murdered Commander Massoud on September 9, 2001; Has-san al-Haski, one of the backers of the 2004 Madrid attack also lived there; Mehdi Nemmouche, the perpetrator of the massacre at the Jewish museum in Brussels, had lived there for over six weeks before committing the crime (May 2014); as did Abdelhamid Abaaoud, the brain behind the Verviers cell, who was readying himself to assassinate police officers in Belgium (January 2015) and was the alleged sponsor of the four perpetrators of the Paris bombings. Amedy Coulibaly, one of the perpetrators of the *Charlie Hebdo* attack, had gone there to procure weapons; Ayub El-Khazzani, the terrorist behind the August 2015 Thalys attack lived there and, finally, it was the ultimate hideout of Salah Abdeslam and his accomplices in the Brussels attacks. Molenbeek, with a population of 90,000, has nineteen mosques. According to Imam Abdel Hassani, not all of them deliver a message as "clear" as his. "Some imams will point out that French diplomacy is bad. You have to know the society in which you live to talk to its members," he emphasized. "I have been here for forty years, and for thirty-four years I have worked in the Delhaize supermarkets." This is one of the peculiarities of Belgian Islam, taken to extremes in Molenbeek. Many imams have been trained in Saudi Arabia, many more are being sent there by the countries of origin of the immigrant population groups living there. In a way, it is the key to understand the Belgian community model in which extreme communitarianism predominates: Walloons–Flemish; Moroccan–Turkish–Pakistani and Somali mosques.[166]

At the beginning of the last decade, the Belgian federal police had learned of the existence of an arms depot in an apartment in the Brussels commune. The local authorities opposed a search that could potentially disrupt the local climate, "managed by the Muslim elite, who had given assurances about keeping a check on the few hotheads." It finally took place the day after the Paris bombings.

The fact remains that while half of the Belgians who left for Syria came from Brussels, which is actually one of the three main regions of Belgium, the other half came from the Flemish part, notably Vilvoorde and Antwerp, where "Sharia4Belgium" held sway.[167]

Great Britain: Koranic Schools and "Sharia Zones"

Britain is home to 2.8 million Muslims, accounting for 5 percent of the population. On an average, 5,000 people convert to Islam in the UK each year, 60 percent of whom are women. The entire fabric of British society is changing. There are already 100 mosques in Waltham Forest, Newham and Tower Hamlets in Greater London, along with 24 Islamic primary and secondary schools, which, in addition to the national educational program, may devote time to Koranic studies. Hundreds of post-school classes where boys and girls wear robes, skull caps or hijabs and learn to recite the Koran by heart thrive in the mosques of British cities.

The Saudi government's reluctance to carry out national textbook reforms emerged in the midst of a debate initiated by the BBC,[168] which broadcast a report on the forty part-time Islamic schools in the United Kingdom in 2010. Despite the Saudi ambassador's denials, journalists found that in fact the embassy's religious office held authority over the network of schools that taught the Saudi curriculum, imparting courses on how to kill apostates, polytheists and homosexuals, as well as teaching a violent anti-Semitism. In 2014, a report by the Office for Standards in Education (OFSTED)—equivalent to the National Education Inspectorate in France, covering six schools in Birmingham, the second largest city in the UK and 22 percent Muslim, sparked a lively debate. In the schools concerned, the headmasters had imposed full-fledged religious rules: separation between boys and girls, calls for prayer over the loudspeaker, pilgrimages to Mecca presented as school trips; images of Christ banished from the nativity play performed at Christmas. The plan was also to ban art and music classes. Moreover, private detectives were recruited to monitor the relations between school children of both sexes and to inform parents of conduct considered to be indecent. In particular, the headmasters appear to have kept tabs on the teachers' emails. Since then, these schools have been placed under the OFSTED's control.

The "Sharia Law Zones"[169] are localities marked by signs at the entrance as spaces governed by Sharia rules. The example of Waltham

Forest, a London suburb, served as a model for a new kind of zone instituted in recent years. There are twenty-five such zones currently in Great Britain, in predominantly Muslim localities such as Bradford, Dewsbury, Leicester and Luton. According to Abu Izzadeen, a self-styled "Muslim Director" of one of these zones, "We want to transform all neighborhoods into united Islamic zones, away from the excesses of Western civilization: with a ban on alcohol, gambling, drugs, music, smoking, homosexuality, and co-education." The campaign in favor of Sharia Zones is spearheaded by a new organization whose name is sufficiently explicit: "Muslims against Crusades" (MAC). According to the Association of Police Chiefs, every year, 17,000 Muslim women in the United Kingdom fall victim to forced marriages, are raped by their husbands or subjected to genital mutilation—practices tolerated by the most radical of Islamists. There is also the issue of the civil jurisdiction of Islamic courts and the Islamization of public services (hospitals, transport, etc.), also mentioned earlier.

Hungary

A WikiLeaks telegram mentioned a request from the Saudi embassy in Budapest. Saudi Arabia considers its religious work, supported by donations, as a means of improving its reputation. The Saudi ambassador in Budapest asked for $54,000 a year for an Islamic association and for permission to found a religious center. This grant would help fight extremism and "play a positive role in promoting the kingdom's image as a moderate power."

Germany: Refugees and Saudi Concern[170]

The landscape in the country is quite similar to that of other major European states: it includes a quietist Salafism and a jihadist minority. Germany has committed itself to hosting nearly one million refugees from the Middle East. Faced with the difficulties of its generous refugee policy, Berlin was offered Saudi assistance for the construction of 200 mosques. According to the Lebanese newspaper, *Al-Diyar*, the kingdom apparently made the decision after being requested to do so by a committee of the country's Sheikhs. It also committed to pay the country at least $200 million. But perceived as Saudi provocation, the announcement did not go down well. On December 7, 2015, Vice-Chancellor Sigmar Gabriel called for a halt to funding from Saudi Arabia,[171] accusing it of encouraging radicalism, in the newspaper, *Bild am Sonntag* —an extremely rare stand taken by a Western political leader. "We can no longer close our eyes. Saudi Arabia funds Wahhabi mosques worldwide. Such communities are a breeding ground for potential terrorists in Germany," he said. "The radical fundamentalism of the Salafist mosques is no less dangerous than right-wing extremism," he declared. Anton Hofreiter, the leader of the Greens in the Bundestag, also appealed to "Westerners [who] needed to seriously consider economic sanctions." The public denunciation is considered to have come after a report submitted by the German intelligence service to the Chancellery, demonstrating the noxious nature of Saudi diplomacy in the Arab world.

France: The Country That Prefers Principles to Facts

For France, Saudi Arabia is the country offering the prospect of "$10 billion worth of contracts." The writer of these lines, who has had dealings with this lucrative customer, heard this figure mentioned for the first time in . . . 1992. "Slippery prospects" indeed! It is therefore understandable that at the highest level of the State, there is no desire to mix Salafism and Wahhabism.

But while it is true that the MWL did face a few problems in France, it was not because of the policy of police control over Salafist preaching posts, but because it discovered the variegated and conflictual nature of the Muslim community with its "shikayats" (complaints) and interference from the Maghreb countries. The financing of some mosques sometimes led to major public works–related litigation, as we have seen.

However, the network of former students of Wahhabi religious universities continues to function and some of the imams from the Paris region continue to be in Riyadh's pay (the figure of 5,000 euros per month has been mentioned). In October 2002, the MWL tried to bring these different components together under the umbrella of a French Council of Muslim Worship (CFCM—"Conseil français du culte musulman"), hoping to sit on its board. Although they met in the beautiful Hilton Suffren Hotel, Abdallah bin Abdulmohsen al-Turki, a former Saudi minister of religious affairs, a prince of the blood and secretary-general of the League, failed to achieve either. Politely turned away from the body that later became the CFCM by the Minister of the Interior, Charles Pasqua, the League nonetheless participated indirectly in debates in the person of Salah Djemaï, its legal adviser for the territory and board member of the Mantes-la-Jolie–based Ibn Abd al-Aziz Mosque. And so, France was protected from the MWL by its own Muslims.

However, this did not preclude the disturbing presence of Salafists. In the 1990s, Abdelkader Bouziane and Abdel Hadi Doudi, the imam of the mosque on the National Boulevard in Marseille, introduced Salafism in France. Both Algerian, they arrived in France in the 1980s and studied for a while at the Islamic University of Madinah. The latter, the brother-in-law of Mustapha Bouyali, founder of the first armed Islamist organization in Algeria, was a fellow traveler of Ali Belhadj, one of the founders of the Algerian FIS (Islamic Salvation Front). Imprisoned in Algeria, Doudi was released in 1986 and, of course, immigrated to France, the cradle of human rights . . . In September 2001, the National Security Directorate (DST—"Direction de la sûreté nationale") was already alarmed by the "presence of ulemas from Saudi Arabia who had come to conduct seminars in the La Rose des Vents Mosque in Aulnay-sous-Bois, the Al-Ihsan Mosque in Argenteuil, or the Tariq-Ibn-Zyad Mosque in the Mureaux," as became evident from an internal note.

In July 2001, Abdullah al-Bukhari, Sali al-Zubaydi and Muhammad Bazmoul gathered over a thousand young people at the Aulnay-sous-Bois Mosque to recruit followers for theological studies in Saudi Arabia. Abdelali Mamoun, the moderate imam of Yvelines, attended the meetings held in 1999 and 2000 at the Mantes-la-Jolie Mosque in the presence of officials from the University of Madinah. "More than eighty boys applied for a scholarship," he said. Highly aggravating proselytizing, given that on their return, "these young Muslims turn into referents—they coordinate the local Salafist community, organize video-conferencing with Saudi Arabia, Jordan or Algeria, co-opt new converts . . . ," underlined an Île-de-France intelligence official. According to police estimates, 100 Muslim communities out of 2,500 are Salafist, that is, the numbers doubled in five years. French Salafists continue to consult extensively with Saudi ulemas. Of the list of the twelve clerics most frequently mentioned on French Salafist sites, nine are based in Saudi Arabia or trained in Saudi universities. The rest are Yemenis.[172]

The documents published by WikiLeaks also show that the Saudi authorities, in their fight against the regime of the mullahs, finance a certain number of Iranian opponents living in the Paris region. A note drafted by the Saudi Embassy in Tehran rationalized this generous aid by evoking the "frustration of Iranian citizens and their strong desire for a regime change." According to another document, "Members of the Iranian opposition abroad must be brought together and encouraged to organize exhibitions featuring images of the acts of torture committed by the Iranian regime." It is up to the readers to identify the fortunate beneficiaries of this generosity, who organize an extravagant demonstration each year in June in Villepinte, bearing no relation whatsoever to their own financial capacities!

A final French characteristic is its secularism, which has proved to be both quite an effective and at the same time paralyzing defense. Any repressive or restrictive action is immediately denounced as "destructive of freedom" or "islamophobic." It has thwarted any movement demanding Koranic schools or Islamic courts. It has now been found, however, that Koranic schools are being conducted in apartments, leading to the dropping out of 5,000 young people, despite compulsory education. But academic inspectorates, deprived of any means of sanction, can only record these facts. The Ciotti law that allowed for the suspension of family allowances in case of school absenteeism was repealed by the left in 2012 and replaced by a "structure whereby social services and educational staff are together able to analyze what is wrong and what can be done to remedy it." So, officially, there are no Koranic schools, but unauthorized classes continue to be held . . . without fear of retribution!

The same can be said about deportation orders, for example, as regards incitement to hatred or violence. In April 2004, in an interview with the monthly magazine, *Lyon Mag*, Abdelkader Bouziane was found justifying the stoning of unfaithful women in the land of Islam in the name of the Koran and admitting that in France, a husband could beat his wife in "specific cases," such as adultery. He should not hit her on the face, but aim lower, at the legs or stomach, hit hard to scare her into not doing it again. Two months earlier, in February 2004, he was issued a first deportation order, but it was never enforced, although it cited absolute urgency and the "imperative need for it, for State and public security." This procedure makes it possible to override certain rules established to protect foreigners. Brought before it for an urgent interim order, the Administrative Court of Lyon suspended the second deportation order issued on April 20 by the then Minister of the Interior, from April 23, 2004, probably considering that depriving the imam of the right to strike his wife would cause him damages that could not easily be repaired. Permitted to return to France, the expelled imam was back on May 22. In October 2004, the State quashed the suspension. The next day, the imam was again arrested and taken to the airport to board a flight to Algiers. The following year, the criminal component was instituted. Abdelkader Bouziane was acquitted at the first instance by the Lyon Criminal Court on June 21, of charges of "direct incitement, not followed up in practice, to commit the offense of willful assault on the integrity of a person" for his remarks published in *Lyon Mag*. In October 2005, the decision was revoked by the Lyon Court of Appeal, which sentenced Abdelkader Bouziane to six months' suspended imprisonment and a fine of 2,000 euros. His appeal to the Supreme Court was dismissed on February 6, 2004. As of 2006, the imam's presence in Belgium became a problem as he was reported to the police in the Schengen Area. He should have been arrested and deported, but that did not happen, although numerous police and judicial sources confirmed that they were aware of his presence. All these twists and turns clearly demonstrate both the difficulty in repressing violent or hate speech as well as the security gaps in the Schengen area.

The same applies to the expulsion of former terrorists sentenced. Saïd Arif, an Algerian terrorist who was convicted by the French courts in 2007 for acts perpetrated on French soil in 2002, including the abortive attack on the Christmas market in Strasbourg, was released from prison in December 2011 with the obligation to leave the country—a decision that was never enforced. The European Human Rights Court of Appeal opposed his extradition to Algeria because of the threat of torture hanging over him. Saïd Arif was then placed under house arrest in Millau, which he violated by escaping. Found in Sweden and extradited again to France, he was then sentenced to six months in prison, but was in fact placed under house arrest once again in Langeac, and later in Brioude in October 2012. In April 2013, he was back in the limelight, extolling terrorism in the columns of an Haute-Loire weekly newspaper. He escaped again in the summer of 2013 (by stealing a hotel car) and after being on the run for a long time, he was declared dead in Syria in May 2015.

The debate on terrorists forfeiting their nationality, eventually withdrawn by the Government, could also be used as an example. For instance, none of the forty people making up the Franco–Belgian network responsible for the Paris and Brussels attacks (161 dead and 622 wounded) will be stripped of their nationality, neither the bomb-maker nor the person who made the suicide-bomber jacket, nor the various other participants in the network. The entire debate is focused on the acquisition of a nationality based on jus soli or the right of soil principle, presented as a republican principle. For the record, the right of soil was introduced in the Civil Code by Napoleon in 1804 to com-pensate for the lack of troops. It is still unclear whether Napoleon was a "leftist" or from the "right." France is a country in which human rights are protected far better than the people themselves! And the debate on French diplomacy with regard to Saudi Arabia has yet to take place.

SAUDI RELIGIOUS ACTIVITIES IN NORTH AMERICA AND AUSTRALIA

Australia: A "Mission Territory"

WikiLeaks has made it possible to analyze Saudi Arabian activities in Australia in the media, religious groups and the control of scholarship students there. Saudi Arabia has been heavily involved in funding local Islamic institutions, with estimates of up to $100 million, which has created tensions between Muslim organizations and concerns within the Australian community in general. Diplomatic messages and email exchanges show the direct relationship between the Saudi Foreign Min-istry and the Embassy, seeking to influence the Arab and Muslim com-munities' political and religious opinions. Checks totaling $10–40,000 from the Ministries of Culture and Information have been disbursed to Arab media and mainstream organizations. Students are also moni-tored by the Embassy and the reports are sent directly to Mabahith, the Interior Ministry's General Directorate of Investigation, which is also responsible for selecting mosques and communities to be funded. One of the recurring concerns remains the surveillance of the Shiites, mainly refugees from the Middle East, so as to be able to counter their role in the Australian Federation of Islamic Councils.[173]

The current Grand Mufti, Ibrahim Abu Muhammad,[174] a former student of Al-Azhar, made a shocking remark following the 2015 Paris bombings: "It is [. . .] imperative that all causal factors such as racism, Islamophobia, infringement of freedom through securitization, duplicitous foreign policies and military intervention are dealt with in depth." Ameer Ali, the former President of the Australian Federation of Islamic Councils, immediately responded with an excuse, "The problem with the mufti is that he cannot communicate in English. This means that he must rely on the people around him." Anthony Albanese, the Deputy Prime Minister, labeled the grand mufti's statement as "totally unacceptable" and, together with other senior political leaders, urged moderate Islamic leaders to speak against extremism with one voice.[175]

Canada[176]

The Saudis have funded mosques in Ottawa, Calgary and an Islamic Center in Quebec, according to Riyadh's official statements. None of the imams of these three centers and mosques is able to say how much money was paid. Gamal Solaiman, of the Ottawa Mosque, allegedly questioned the Board of Directors about the investigations underway but received no reply. Hussein Paiman, of the Calgary Mosque, whose imam was a professor at King Saud University in Saudi Arabia, did not know much more than that about his own institution. And this is quite apart from the fact that the Islamic Center in Quebec is managed by Sheikh Syed Bukhari, who is also a graduate of the University of Madinah. The three institutions are mentioned on the Kingdom's website.[177] A 2002 Saudi report noted that "King Fahd had donated $5 million for the founding of the Islamic Center in Toronto and $1.5 million annually for its functioning."

The Saudi government has also made donations to help finance private Islamic schools in Canada. WikiLeaks documents, including cables between diplomats in Ottawa and government officials in Riyadh, mention payments of $211,000 to a school in Ottawa and $134,000 to Mississauga between 2012 and 2013. The latter "needed support and assistance for the school's second phase of development and construction." The institutions' administrators denied any Saudi influence and claimed that they accepted donations with no strings attached: "This is not the way we operate. We are exclusively Canadian and we have our own way of doing things," claimed Sharaf Sharafeldin, Executive Director of the Muslim Association of Canada (MAC), which manages several mosques and private Islamic schools.

United States of America

Long a haven and refuge of jihadists at a time when they were fighting the USSR, fostering recruitment sites for candidates for Afghanistan, hosting Salafist student association websites on university blogs, refusing the extradition of Bin Laden proposed by the Sudanese authorities in order to eschew all risks (before September 11), negotiating with the Taliban regime to find a way for transporting oil from Central Asia— again before September 11—the United States' ambivalent and at times even spineless attitude towards Wahhabism-Salafism has always suggested that they were "the" religious sanctuary as opposed to secular European countries.[178] Moreover, former CIA officials readily recall that they were forbidden from gathering intelligence on the great Saudi ally.

Hence, the retaliation following the World Trade Center attack was limited to a few expulsions and other paltry measures. In February 2004, the State Department ordered twenty-four Saudis with diplomatic visas to return home and the Saudi government closed the Department of Religious Affairs at its Washington embassy.

However, a report by "Freedom House"[179] described in detail how the Saudi government had widely disseminated "hate propaganda" in the country's Koranic schools, inciting Muslims, among others, to hate

Christians and Jews and conduct themselves in America as if they were on a mission behind enemy lines.

The few geographic examples cited here are merely a small sample of the phenomenon. A systematic study of the WikiLeaks documents would probably reveal the global nature of Riyadh's religious action further, solely concerned with ghettoizing Muslim population groups wherever possible, around the Wahhabi-Salafist conception of Islam, while attempting to counter a hypothetical Shiite influence. For an exhaustive study, the religious activities of other major actors, such as Erdoğan's Turkey, Qatar, with its immense resources and its anti-Saudi action, Islamabad and its innumerable activists and, finally, Tehran, which has never renounced its ambitions, will have to be weighed against each other. And there are an ever-growing number of arenas for these rivalries to play out. Countries in an open religious war such as Syria, Iraq, Yemen, Bahrain, Lebanon, Afghanistan and Pakistan and now Nigeria are joined by the former Soviet Central Asian countries, a region in total disarray after the collapse of communism, permeated by violent ethnic rivalry, cross-border population movements and the cancerous spread of the Afghan crisis. It is therefore surely the premise of internal wars within Islam that is being laid by these rival religious diplomacies, the most serious probably being the multiple Saudi–Iranian battlefields.[180]

Where does Saudi foreign policy stand today? Is the system continuing to develop or has it witnessed failures? The initial difficulties that emerged over thirty years ago have only grown, combining various internal and external developments. Moreover, Riyadh has begun to count its increasingly scarce pennies more carefully, with oil at just $30 a barrel.

CHAPTER 5

WHEN SUBMUNITIONS EXPLODE

THE 1990–1991 CRISIS: WHEN "OPERATION DESERT STORM" SWEPT AWAY THE "GHUTRAHS" (ARAB HEADDRESS)

Saudi Arabia is the only regime in the world that is challenged neither by the left, which is non-existent, nor by the right, but from the sky. There is no liberal political organization, contrary to what the West would hope for. The real opposition is religious and, each time, the monarchy's response to any crisis or criticism has been with "more religion"! Any liberal reform would be seen as a concession to non-believers. It is therefore a country of continuous religious reforms, as described in previous chapters.

Granting women the right to drive is a rather Kafkaesque example. In 1990, during the Gulf War, forty-seven women defied the ban. Some were arrested and imprisoned, while most were simply given a ticket. And the husbands were accused of not abiding by the Koran and not "restraining their wives." A second movement called "women2drive"[181] came into being thirty years later, led by Manal al-Sharif, a thirty-seven-year-old IT specialist, with no arrests reported during the first few weeks. But pressures ultimately weakened the movement. While the head of the powerful religious police, Abdel Latif Al Sheikh and the Minister of Justice, Mohammad al-Issa, now assert that no religious text disallows women from driving—recalling that the Prophet's consorts used camels—a conservative cleric, Saleh Al-Luhaydan, averred that women who drove risked having abnormal children "because of the pressure on their ovaries," without, however, quoting the Koranic sources for his medical diagnosis. Prince Salman's recent decision to authorize women to drive till June 2018, is symbolic of the blind and shortsighted vision westerners have of this country, considering that reform is symbolic of change—just thirty years to change so little: what a race!

In the 1980–1990 decade, the wealthy Saudi monarchy seemed to rejoice in the glory of the anti-Soviet jihad's victory in Afghanistan, the fact that the Iranian revolution was running out of steam and the persistent decline faced by Iraq, worn out by eight years of war. Its entire religious diplomacy seemed to be paying off. But when Iraq invaded Kuwait in the summer of 1990, the blackout lasted three days in the local media. King Fahd, in disarray, wanted to call for the assistance of the West's armed forces. However, the country's princes and top religious leadership failed to see eye to eye and the king urged Sheikh Abdulaziz Ibn Baz to formulate a positive fatwa. Convinced by the satellite imagery provided by the Americans, but not without calling for a conference of 350 colleagues, the old sheikh theologically justified that it was possible for a Muslim state to ask for the help of non-Muslims in a situation of extreme urgency when "Islam was under threat."[182] Shortly thereafter, he went further by calling the war against Iraq a jihad. He was rewarded by being named Grand Mufti in 1993, although he was not from the Al-Shaikh tribe.

The 550,000 GIs (including 60,000 Jewish American soldiers, according to unverifiable local rumors) landed within a few weeks near the Islamic Holy Shrines and were perceived by a large section of the population as an army sent to invade a sanctuary that the Wahhabi dynasty was duty-bound to guard and protect. The appeal to infidels was denounced as a sign of collusion by the "Custodian of the Holy Shrines" with the oppressors of Muslims and protectors of Israel. Many Islamic groups, including the Muslim Brotherhood, disapproved of the alliance and broke away from the monarchy. As was his wont, the king gave in on at least the issue of form—the troops were to respect Saudi laws and leave the country as soon as the threat was removed. The Committee for the Promotion of Virtue and the Prevention of Vice was given greater powers, but ran up against American practices like women soldiers at the wheel, among others—unprecedented occurrences in the Kingdom's history. The GIs settled down and then stayed on. Anger against the American presence then stirred up attacks. The first attack broke out in 1991 (during the war, two American soldiers and one Saudi man were wounded by a bullet in a bus), the second in 1995 (car bomb explosion in front of a National Guard building), the third in 1996 (a truck full of explosives pulverized the entrance to the US base in Khobar). Others followed.

Then, in 1991, four hundred ulemas petitioned the king to ensure greater respect for their religion (i.e. for their own power), for the eradication of corruption and nepotism and for lessening dependence on America. They considered Sheikh Ibn Baz as one of their own, and the latter certainly concurred with their main demands. But, to his great embarrassment, the petition was made public. In December 1992, seven out of the four hundred ulema signatories also demanded political reforms, some of them inspired by the Iranian system of a "Guide" or "Guardian Council," but also the "Islamization" of foreign policy and the creation of an armed force of 500,000 men to protect the Holy Shrines. They were dismissed from office by the King. Ibn Baz, the "great legitimator," apologized, as did other signatories, claiming that the document was supposed to remain private. But the harshest of sermons denouncing the ruling family were copied and broadcast across the country on tapes. Once again, the old sheikh was obliged to intervene, branding the recordings as "toxic allegations . . . against the will of God." With his help, the House of Saud seemed to have managed to weather the storm. Later, he went on to issue a fatwa approving the peace process in the Middle East. From his Sudanese exile, Osama bin Laden called for the Sheikh's resignation, detractors of the Saud family urging him to express his true convictions before his death and to endorse the Islamic opposition. Although he had spoken in private, Sheikh Ibn Baz refused to change his stand, convinced—not without reason—that Wahhabism and the Saud family had no option but to sink or swim together.

In 1999, the "great legitimator" died. The Kingdom was saved, but not spared the dissent that the king had feared. Criticism erupted from persons such as the Syrian Sheikh Muhammad Surur, exiled in Great Britain. The Islamization of the world was temporarily put on hold to focus on safeguarding the regime against protesting Islamists, including the Muslim Brotherhood, who had taken up the cudgels for Saddam Hussein, proclaiming him "the hero of the Arab world." To counter both religious and western criticism, a more consensual target emerged—the war against Iran, a Shiite, anti-imperialist power. Riyadh began reorienting the Muslim World League's activities, with the organization being transformed into a legitimization structure for the Saud dynasty,[183] and focusing its activities against Shiites. Its leaders (mostly diplomats), were proficient in doublespeak: the Saudi regime was the guarantor of the fight against Salafism and the drift towards terrorism by former students from its own universities, while ensuring the representation of Muslims among Western authorities on the basis of conservative ideas and of being totally opposed to republican values.

On January 1, 2005, the regime dismissed 44 clerics, 160 imams, and 149 muezzins: a total of nearly 1,350 religious leaders. Those who had issued murderous fatwas, such as Nasser al-Fahd, Ali al-Khudair and Ahmed al-Khalidi, retracted their words. Despite reassuring official statements, the education sector remained untouched (see the 2006 "Freedom House" report). Apart from repression and face-lifting reforms, it was Islamic one-upmanship that allowed the regime to bail itself out. To this end, several arguments were put forward: the disqualification of the opposition as being "contrary to real Islam," by Prince Bandar, ambassador to Washington, and as being contrary to the

Sharia according to Prince Nayef; the refusal to use the term "funda-mentalist" and solely using the term "extremists"; the growing rigor against women; the endorsement of repressive measures against the sig-natories by the Senior Council of Ulemas, etcetera. The most symbolic protesters, if they agreed to make amends, were restored to favor, proof that the regime did not want to go too far in repressing religious dissidents.

Three examples of "Sahwa" ("Islamic Awakening") dissenters illus-trate this point: first, Ali al-Duwayhi, who had been heading the Al-Ahsa faculty of theology since 2001, although he had signed several political petitions defending the Saudi school curriculum and declared himself in favor of holding municipal elections. As for Abdul-Muhsin al-Ubaykan, who had openly called on the government to undertake reforms between 1992 and 1994, he was marginalized and dismissed from his many functions, including from his post as a judge in the Riyadh court and as imam of a mosque. Restored to favor in 1999–2000, he nevertheless continued to criticize certain decisions, especially those relating to jurisprudence and the judicial system, gainsaying those of the Senior Council of Ulemas. To put things right, he issued fatwas on the lawfulness of the salute to the national flag, the condemnation of Sahwist opponents or the ban on joining the jihad in Iraq for Saudis. Even when he was restored to favor, the ulemas vetoed his entry into the council. He was initially appointed to the Ministry of Justice and as a member of the Advisory Board before becoming one of the King's advisers in 2009. Finally, Abdullah Ibn-Jibreen, a high-ranking cleric and a potential candidate for the Senior Council of Ulemas, was one of the sponsors of the Islamist protests of the early 1990s, a veritable critic of the regime and of the major ulemas, who publicly disowned him. He was dismissed from his official duties, but subsequently restored to favor. Although he was an excellent theologian, he was never able to claim the post of a senior "alim" or ulema because of this "blunder." His atonement and recent support to the government did not suffice.

On the other hand, the Shiite, Ayatollah al-Nimr, also a non-violent critic of the regime, was arrested, imprisoned, sentenced to death and finally executed. A case of sheer double standards!

In this Muslim version of Stevenson's novel, Dr. Saud cloaked Mr. Jihad in a shroud of secrecy, only allowing the latter to reveal its hideous face in its ulemas' sermons.

SALAFISTS FLEE THEIR MASTER

On May 12, 2003, Saudi Arabia itself was the subject of a triple suicide bombing: thirty-five victims, including nine Americans. While until then, it had denied the presence of Al-Qaeda on its territory, the government uncovered cells of the organization in Riyadh, Mecca, Medina and Jeddah, as well as in the Jouf area, in the North. The Saudis, who had laid the ideological and financial foundations for the development of Al-Qaeda and its sister organizations, including Hamas, discovered that the fire they had lit could also devour their own country. Bin Laden, who had denounced the call to the West's armed forces while he was in Sudan, issued a "declaration of war" aimed at driving Americans out of the peninsula. After the attacks in the 1990s and, especially since 2000, individual acts of aggression and the attack on the World Trade Center aroused enthusiasm in the country. In February 2003, the authorities in Riyadh announced that about 100 citizens and some 20 others had been arrested for their Al-Qaeda ties, but on May 12, a series of attacks took place in a compound in Riyadh, inhabited by foreigners; and, earlier in April, a car exploded outside the security forces' headquarters in Riyadh. Attacks multiplied until hostages were taken in the Al-Khobar oil site in May 2004, claimed by Al-Qaeda in the Arabian Peninsula (AQAP). That year, some twenty attacks on Saudi territory killed 274 people. There was now an internal jihadist opposition to the Saudi system.

In recent years, the Muslim World League and the World Assembly of Muslim Youth have been losing credibility and are increasingly competing with the organizations they had once sought as partners. Many Muslims prefer local organizations, such as Young Muslims UK, which had emerged from the Jama'at-Islami movement, or the European Council for Fatwa and Research, affiliated with the Muslim Brotherhood. Samir Amghar distinguished between transnational preachers, extremely concerned about respecting those in power and the princes (Saudi as well as Yemeni or Qatari), from local clerics, leading a small group of cohorts, far more critical of the systems in the Gulf countries—in a way, like the "mad dogs" of Salafism seeking causes to defend and new jihad territories.[184] New technologies have made it easier for preachers to reach out to wider audiences. Discussions on issues relevant to Muslims are increasingly present on the web via blogs and social networks. Those who lead the discussions, such as Tariq Ramadan, teaching at Cambridge, Abdullah Ibn Jibreen Murad or Mustafa Cerić, Bosnia's Grand Mufti, have gained the legitimacy that affiliation to a transnational organization such as the League or the Assembly no longer confers. When European Muslims seek information about Saudi Arabia, they can visit the websites of Saudi ulemas such as Salman al-Ouda, who runs the popular www.islamtoday.com, or that of Nasiruddin al-Albani. The Internet provides an ever-increasing space for decentralized and direct debates with individual preachers rather than with heavyweight international structures such as the MWL.

Added to this is the fact that the most virulent forms of Salafist action in Europe are now being propagated by leaders who no longer have a Wahhabi background, such as Choudary in Great Britain, Fouad Belkacem with "Sharia4Belgium," or Muhammad Achamlane of the "Forsane Alizza" in France. Finally, the last stratum—fighters returning from jihad areas, such as Afghanistan—are asserting their authority, of whom Abu Qatada is perhaps the only Londonistan leader to have received religious training (in Pakistan). Others, such as Abu Hamza al-Masri or Abu Musab al-Suri, are fighters or combat theorists. The latter has no traditional religious education. He writes about jihad without being a theologian, simply adapting the theories of "leftist" guerrillas to an Islamist framework.[185] Worse still, characters such as Abu Musab al-Zarkawi, a former thug, radicalized in prison, or Abdelmalek Droukdel, the head of the Al-Qaeda in the Islamic Maghreb (AQIM) in Algeria, an engineer by training who had fought in Afghanistan, or Abu Bakr Naji, the author of the book *The Management of Savagery*,[186] are cropping up in battle zones. A few other no less disturbing preachers escaped to Saudi Arabia. Zakir Naik, based in Mumbai, is the founder of the satellite TV channel, "Peace TV." He is a doctor rather than a conventionally trained cleric, influencing young South Asian people in Britain because of his ability to answer contemporary questions through a combination of common sense and an encyclopedic knowledge of the Koran. He is a polemicist, dotting his speech with frequent comparisons between Islam and other religious traditions (he is also at ease quoting the Bible), always stressing that Islam is superior to them. Naik had expressed support for Osama bin Laden, called America the "biggest terrorist," and said that the Taliban's limitations of women's rights could have positive aspects.

In June 2010, the British Home Office denied him access to the country, citing "a number of unacceptable comments" uttered on a widely relayed YouTube video. The Canadian government also denied him a visit to the country for a major Islamic conference in Toronto.

THE MUSLIM BROTHERHOOD, EXPELLED, TRIUMPHS IN THE ARAB SPRING

The Sahwa movement was an outcome of reflections that emerged in the late 1950s, based on the Muslim Brotherhood's doctrine, which had managed to take root in the Kingdom's political and religious fabric. As early as in 1954, the Brotherhood persecuted by Nasser, and which had taken refuge in the Gulf countries and Saudi Arabia, became increasingly associated with anti-Nasserism, to the point of becoming its core as of 1962,[187] as explained earlier. A second wave of "brotherhood-related" emigration in the early 1970s was less the result of Egypt's authoritarian policies than the attraction of the Gulf countries following the oil boom and the extraordinary professional prospects that ensued, although divergent, relations between the two entities were very long-standing. Stéphane Lacroix emphasized this, recalling the remarks made by King Abdulaziz, when Hassan al-Banna, the Egyptian teacher who founded the Muslim Brotherhood, had asked him for the right to open a branch of his organization in Saudi Arabia: "What's the point? Here, we are all brothers, and we are all Muslims." The request was in any case counter to the prohibition of political parties on the territory.

The Brotherhood tradition was a political tradition that was primarily founded in opposition to the imperialist West and, secondarily, against the "impious regimes" of the Arab world.[188] The Wahhabi tradition, on the other hand, was more strictly religious and specific to the Kingdom—its main enemy was not the West, nor Arab regimes, but religious innovations, all of which were considered perverted as compared to the original creed ("aqidah"). Obviously, the ultimate perversion was Shiism. The gradual politicization of the Wahhabis occurred under the Brotherhood's influence, which proposed a religious, but also social and political interpretation of Islam. Their doctrine has therefore been fundamentally hostile to the strict separation of politics and religion as established by the Saudi dynasty and the Wahhabi muftis. The two traditions converged in the educational system dominated by the Brotherhood's methods and thoughts, while continuing to preserve the Wahhabis' power over the dogma's foundations. At King Abdelaziz University in Jeddah, founded in 1967, as well as at its annex in Mecca, the Brotherhood was virtually in the majority in the educational apparatus, with the Syrian Brothers, Muhammad al-Mubarak and Ali al-Tantawi, as well as the Egyptian, Mohammed Qutb, the brother of Sayyid Qutb, who played a key role in bringing the two theological schools closer together. He purged the Brotherhood doctrine of some "left-wing" or even socializing influence of texts such as "Social Justice in Islam" ("Al-adalah al-ijtima'iyyah fil-islam"), a theory that was completely inadmissible to the Kingdom. Allied with the Saudi authorities in the 1970s, the Sahwis gradually moved towards dissent in the 1980s—indirectly, to begin with, and then through gradual mediation. During these difficult years, social discontent was attributed by the Sahwists to the "secularists" and "modernists," and sometimes the Wahhabi ulemas. Their criticism had not yet been directed against the authorities.

The Sahwa movement was a purely Saudi cross-breed that then spearheaded internal dissent. The types of actions used—petitions, sermons, demonstrations, addresses to the royal family—gave it time to sensitize many young Saudis. But the massive presence of American troops on Saudi soil was the catalyst for all the mute crises faced by this frustrated generation, struck by the economic recession. This was the only truly destabilizing movement for the Saudi authorities. The Sahwist discourse was now directed against the State itself. The movement collapsed in 1994, both because of the repression by the Saudi regime and because of its own structural weaknesses, such as the lack of organization or a recognized leader.

Expelled for supporting Saddam Hussein against the arrival of Western troops, the Brotherhood gradually organized opposition to the regime, encouraged by the Arab uprisings. Both of them preached a "Sunni Islam," but their politico–religious interests were adversarial in nature. The Wahhabi establishment, in particular, considered the Muslim Brotherhood as a threat to its religious interests. Its ideological authority was called into question by the Brotherhood, which believed it necessary to go beyond the juridical schools, viewed as being divisive for the Muslim community. Saudi Arabia always favored religious movements, but provided they did not interfere with its domestic politics. However, after Kuwait's invasion by Saddam Hussein and the Gulf War, the Muslim Brotherhood began demanding reforms that Riyadh rejected outright.

In the 1960s, the Saudi regime's sense of encirclement came from the triumph of pan-Arab movements influenced by Nasserism. Bad memories resurfaced during the Arab Spring uprisings, which had a domino effect in Egypt, Syria, Tunisia and Yemen. The issue was far from new, but it had been underestimated before the 2011 events. And yet, from that date onwards, the clerics began to reinvest in political dissent. Fresh petitions were signed by the movement's leading representatives. Pro-Muslim Brotherhood stands multiplied. At the same time, repression against the Brotherhood also grew in the peninsula; indeed, a total purge was carried out in all the Gulf countries. The overthrowing of the Egyptian President, Hosni Mubarak, and the assumption of power by the Muslim Brotherhood, with the tacit assent of the Americans, was a shock to Riyadh, which considered the early departure of someone who had eventually become its ultimate regional ally in its fight against Iran inconceivable. A system of close, quasi-clientelistic personal relations existed between the two regimes, combined with massive legal and illegal Egyptian immigration in Saudi Arabia. When a Muslim Brotherhood member, Muhammad Morsi, came to power in 2012, Saudi Arabia threatened to send all the immigrants back to Egypt. The authorities in Riyadh recovered a sense of serenity only after he was overthrown by the army in 2013, with the active support of the Salafists, closely linked to the Kingdom. The Brotherhood was then branded a "terrorist organization" by Riyadh in 2014.

Since 2011, dissent had begun to gain traction within Saudi Arabia itself. Three major petitions signed by local political leaders were sent to King Abdullah.[189] The first, called "Demands of Saudi Youth for the

Future of the Nation," called for the release of political prisoners and the establishment of a constitutional monarchy. The second, "Toward a State of Rights and Institutions," repeated the same grievances and added a demand for the separation of the king and prime minister's functions. The third, "National Declaration for Reform," advocated the recognition of fundamental rights by the regime. All these demands were based on theological foundations. The Saudi Arabian Association of Civil and Political Rights (ACPRA), based in London, was founded in 2009 and was quick to take center stage. But it soon lost eleven of its cadres, who were arrested by the Saudi regime for "breaking allegiance and disobedience to the sovereign" or "manipulation of public opinion against the authorities."

Saudi Arabia's youth was quite receptive to leading preachers who were close to the Brotherhood. Aware of this problem, the government implemented a purge policy from 2012 onwards, which intensified in 2014. In October 2015, the cleric, Muhammad al-Arifi, with a Twitter following of more than eight million people, was excluded from the Riyadh-based King Saud University, probably because of his criticism of the government's policy on Egypt.

Public education, largely under the Brotherhood's influence, was the quintessential arena for the ideological purge. The measures taken included a Saudi Arabian Director of Education's Circular No. 37300769 of November 22, 2015, which drew up a list of books to be withdrawn from school and training center libraries within two weeks, which was aimed primarily at Muslim Brotherhood authors, including:

- Yusuf al-Qaradawi, a theologian, a refugee in Qatar, a member of the fraternal Brotherhood with significant global influence, known for having called for jihad in Syria or taking up arms against General Gaddafi. He was President of the European Council for Fatwa and Research and was also sought after by Interpol at the request of Egypt, his country of origin. An ulema, who had been taken in by the rival, Qatar, he was all the more dangerous.

- Sayyid Qutb, one of the leading theorists of the thinking about the "general excommunication of Muslims," called "mass 'takfir'," and one of the primary references for Islamists and terrorists.

- Muhammad Qutb, Sayyid Qutb's brother, who largely contributed to spreading his elder brother's work and the Muslim Brotherhood's ideology in Saudi Arabia.

- Abul A'la Maududi, the main instigator of "political Islam" in Asia in the last century. Founder of the Pakistani party, Jemaah Islamiyyah ("Islamic Party"), similar to Egypt's Muslim Brotherhood, he remains one of the primary references for Islamists.

- Hassan al-Banna, founder of the Brotherhood, who had made the struggle for power a key element for the establishment of an Islamic state.

There seemed to be a tilt in Saudi Arabia's position with the advent of the new King Salman, who now placed Daesh before the Muslim Brotherhood in the official hierarchy of threats. A Palestinian Hamas delegation was received in Riyadh, as well as delegations from Ennahda (Tunisia) and Al-Islah (Yemen). The Kingdom, benumbed by the threat that Iran represented in its eyes, tried to set up a Sunni front, while remaining extremely cautious, as the slightest movement always represented a danger on the domestic scene.

It was once again in the religious sphere that the Saudi regime sought to neutralize political dissent. All the measures taken to modernize the State in this area have indeed been very ambiguous. Hence, as of 2010, the right to issue fatwas without State authorization was restricted to just a few leading ulemas. Presented as a way of restricting Islamist fundamentalism in the country, the measure made it possible, above all, to reserve monopoly over religious speech solely to an inner circle of the regime. At the same time, the issue of putting Saudi civil and criminal laws down in writing was regularly brought up (but never decided) by the government. The purpose was not to discuss Western legal norms, but to reduce room for maneuver for local religious leaders, as they still retained the monopoly on interpreting the Sharia. Their decision-making power would be diminished if laws were written down. Once again, still more religion!

For its part, the Brotherhood, which had emerged victorious in almost all electoral processes, was soon swept away by the exhilaration of power and went too far in Tunisia and Egypt. Disavowed, it was either forced to accept compromises or was forcibly evicted by the military (the scenario in Algeria one day, Egypt the next). It was tempted to resort to violence, without, however, using the jihadist discourse. On May 28, 2015, on the Brotherhood's official website, www.ikhwanonline.com, 159 ulemas called for an armed struggle against the Egyptian military regime, but once again targeted journalists, politicians, "and whosoever may be responsible, even solely through incitement, for having violated the honor of women" [sic]. The Deputy Supreme Guide, Mahmoud Ezzat, a refugee in Turkey, tried to regain control by closing down the site, but in eleven of Egypt's twenty-seven governorates, the Brotherhood spoke out in favor of an armed struggle.

DAESH: DR. JEKYLL VERSUS MR. HYDE

On March 1, 2016, the Saudi Sheikh al-Qarni was the target of an assassination attempt at the Western Mindanao University's auditorium in Zamboanga City, Philippines. He was speaking at a conference on extremism funded by George Washington University (what a strange mix of genres!). The attack was claimed by the Islamic State, which had been formally condemned by Sheikh al-Qarni. The former, in turn, had listed him as a target in the group's magazine, *Dabiq*. The Sheikh headed one of the world's 100 largest Twitter accounts, having twelve million followers. Some of the highest dignitaries of Islam, Sheikhs al-Qaradawi and al-Arifi, expressed sympathy. This was, yet again, a demonstration of the fight that Daesh had decided to engage in against the Sunni religious supremacy claimed by the Saud dynasty. In 2015 alone, it opened an internal front by perpetrating six attacks in the country. Three were evidently aimed at Shiite regions (noblesse oblige!). Yet, the Sauds had carefully avoided engaging in the "Inherent Resolve" Operation against the Islamic State. Of the 20 participating countries, 11 were part of NATO (plus Australia), and only seven were Arab countries, including five from the Gulf. Saudi Arabia had sent in fifteen combat aircraft, as many as Denmark and the Netherlands combined, before withdrawing all of them for the benefit of the conflict in Yemen, leaving the West alone to fight Daesh.

Daesh now projected itself primarily as the true defender of oppressed Sunnis in Syria and Iraq. It achieved its first goal by marginalizing Al-Qaeda and its local branch in Syria, Al-Nosra. The recent call by Al-Zawahiri, Bin Laden's successor, enjoining the caliph, Al-Baghdadi, to place himself under his authority, was the fourth pathetic and desperate attempt to regain control of the situation. Daesh's rallying of jihadist groups in thirteen countries is proof of the new dynamic that it was able to create, but which eluded Al-Qaeda.

The Islamic State can now rely on "foreign fighters" coming from around a hundred countries, while the coalition led by Riyadh in Yemen has only about ten Arab supporters, often close affiliates. The Muslim coalition against terrorism, hastily formed by Riyadh with thirty-four Sunni countries (some of which, like Pakistan or Egypt, have mentioned that they had not been consulted), was a declaratory act, with limited military impact.

The Islamic State's final stage was therefore to establish the religious legitimacy of the Caliph, who dubbed himself the Commander of the Believers. Competition became theological between these two Sunni powers who claimed to lead the Ummah across the entire Arab–Muslim world and represent Islam.

There was nothing ambiguous about Riyadh's military counter-strategy. Riyadh, like the other Gulf Cooperation Council (GCC) capitals, could not consider Daesh as the main threat, for fear of being challenged by its own civil society. Despite recent announcements, there was no question of Riyadh putting boots on the ground against the Islamic State, especially to defend the Shiite regimes of Baghdad or Damascus. Most of its 150,000 men were deployed along the Yemeni border. And the Saudi military intervention in Bahrain came to the monarchy's rescue in 2010 against the popular Shiite revolution (70 percent of the people), which had challenged the Sunni Al-Khalifa family. More recently, in Yemen, Operation Decisive Storm, launched in March 2015, sought to reinstate President Mansur Hadi, overthrown by the Shiite Houthi revolt, and not fight the "Al-Qaeda in the Arabian Peninsula" (AQAP), considered by the former CIA Director, David Petraeus, as "one of the most dangerous regional nodes in the global jihad." The fact that Yemeni Shiism is closer to Saudi Sunnism than Iranian Shiism from an ideological point of view, and that former President Saleh, himself a Zaidi, had waged six wars against the Houthis, was of course of no consequence. It matters not, for they were the only Shiites within his reach! In the coalition led by Riyadh, there were about ten Sunni Arab countries, with 170 aircraft from the GCC countries, of which 35 were sent against Daesh. Just to bear a simple scale of measurement in mind, it is important to know that Yemen, a country that is more densely populated than Syria, cannot evacuate its nationals to its bordering countries, as they are all members of the coalition. The war, going on since 2004, has caused more than 340,000 displaced persons, 15 percent of whom have been living in camps, according to the UN Office for the Coordination of Humanitarian Affairs. In addition, the country has taken in 246,000 Somali refugees.

Daesh had become a deadly threat for Saudi Arabia. The latter had to once again keep its hold over its population by tightening religious rules, for instance, by decapitating forty-five Sunni radicals at the same time as a high Shiite dignitary and by acquiring the help of the West with the utmost of discretion. Thus, USA provided the coordinates for targets in Yemen that Saudi airplanes would miss in a spirit of unending enthusiasm. A demonstration—if one were required—that collateral damage (Shiite) was not a constraint for the Wahhabi strategy.

SAUDI ARABIA VERSUS IRAN: SEEING SHIITES EVERYWHERE!

The Khomeinist revolution was a turning point for the Shiites; it changed the agenda of the world's Muslims and, to some extent, blurred all the lines.

Imam Khomeini was the first to unsheathe the weapon that was destined to be highly successful in all its avatars: the death sentence for blasphemy. In his treatise on jurisprudence, written during his exile in Turkey in the 1970s, the Ayatollah wrote, "Anyone can kill a person who insults the Prophet within his hearing—as long as he does not fear for his life, his honor or those of a believer [. . .]—without the need for any permission from an imam or his replacement." The fatwa against the writer, Salman Rushdie, was first issued from India, as he was of Indian origin, but it became globalized only when it was taken forward by Ayatollah Khomeini's condemnation. Violent demonstrations erupted, for instance, in the Indian subcontinent and even on the streets of Paris in 1988 and 1989, forcing the Organization of Islamic Co-operation to speak out. On the other hand, the eight-year war against Iraq, supported by all the great powers, enhanced the rising popularity of the new anti-imperialist Iran. For eight years, President Mahmoud Ahmadinejad had been the face of the same anti-West steadfastness.

Finally, on "Arab streets," the Lebanese Hezbollah became the hero of the fight against Israel in the summer of 2006, inflicting its first defeat on the Israeli army.

But in religious terms, would these different events translate into conversions to Shiism? Leastways, that was what the Saudi authorities believed. According to Israel Elad-Altman, "Fantasy or reality, it is difficult to know the magnitude of the phenomenon—many 'converts' likely kept the secret, which is permitted by Shiism." In Syria, a close ally of the Islamic Republic, engaged in a sustained missionary effort to change the country's religious landscape, turned upside down by the presence of tens of thousands of Iraqi Shiite refugees, the conversion rate was deemed to be high among the Sunni majority. The country was home to several Shiite shrines, such as the Sayyida Zaynab, which attracted thousands of Iranian pilgrims and Shiites each year from the Gulf's Emirates. A number of madrassas too were established here and there by Iran in Syria. Indeed, Tehran was even accused of buying conversions. The sentiment (real or supposed) of a wave of conversions in Egypt and Jordan, and further in Morocco and Algeria or Sudan became a ritual element of speeches by the authorities, who called for Saudi Arabia's help. Although limited in scope, the movement was seen as an unacceptable risk in Riyadh, which could be infiltrated in this way by agents in Iran's service."[190]

The leading Sunni dignitaries were quick to speak up. Sheikh Yusuf al-Qaradawi accused Tehran of proselytizing in Egypt. If the movement of conversions were to intensify, he warned, " . . . there would be an Iraqi-style civil war in the country in twenty years' time." He directly attacked the Lebanese Hezbollah leader, Hassan Nasrallah, whom he called a "fanatic." In October 2005, one of the leading figures of the Saudi clergy, Sheikh Salman ibn Fahd al-Awdah, accused Shiite missionaries of being a "threat to Islam" and blamed Iranian leaders for failing to get the measure of the risks this posed for the Muslim world. Yet, in 2006, the two men, the Egyptian and the Saudi, enthusiastically defended Hezbollah in its fight against Israel. The Egyptian, Muhammad Mahdi Akif, the highest authority among the Brotherhood, also supported Hezbollah. The same was true for the Brotherhood in Jordan, close to the Palestinian Hamas. On the other hand, the Syrian branch of the Muslim Brotherhood, which was opposed to the Assad regime, strongly criticized Iranian proselytism in the country, accusing the Damascus regime of turning Syria into a "province of the Islamic Republic," cutting it off from its Arab "profundity" and changing its religious identity. That is why Sunni leaders in Saudi Arabia, Jordan and Egypt were concerned in the face of the emergence of a triptych with combative pretentions: the Islamic Republic of Iran, the new regime in Iraq and, finally, the Lebanese Hezbollah.

That was why Riyadh failed to fathom the reasons behind the US decision to invade Saddam's Iraq. In a congressional hearing, Prince Saud al-Faisal declared: "It seemed impossible that such a thing could occur. We thought that this war would prevent Iran from occupying Iraq, after saving Kuwait's independence. Now it is the entire country that is under Iran's control." In the Saudi and Daesh press, the Iranians were now referred to as "Safavids"—the seventeenth and eighteenth century dynasty behind the adoption of Shiism in Iran. The reciprocal dramatization gave the crisis an increasingly politico-religious and belliferous dimension.

Saudi diplomacy indicated an intense fear of the Shiites as evidenced by telegrams from China,[191] the Philippines, Uganda (a predominantly Catholic country) and Mali expressing concern about their growing presence. Every diplomatic post had to draw up a detailed report and an action plan to obtain financial support. A telegram from the embassy in Sri Lanka reported meetings between the Iranian ambassador and a group of clerics. Another telegram mentioned that Wakil Ahmad Mutawakil, founder of the Afghan Foundation in Kabul, had fruitlessly asked for help, while the Hazara Shiites managed to get assistance from Tehran. A cable from the Tehran embassy called for the adoption of a plan to support Salafist religious television channels in order to extend their coverage, arguing about Iran's interference in Arab countries such as Bahrain. The plan was to be entitled, "Unmasking the Iranian media." The telegram further stated that this was only part of the plan, because although the Al-Wisal channel had been shut down, there were many other channels that the Iranians could use. According to the telegram, the signal strength needed to be reduced, at least so that it did not reach Bahrain or Saudi Arabia. Between 2010 and 2013, the Arabsat satellite blocked the channel granted to the Al-Alam (a Persian and Arab channel) on royal orders. The Iranian channel then started broadcasting through European satellites. Diplomats were also asked to estimate how many Eritrean students were studying in Iran (40) or the number of Shiite Muslims in Mauritania (50,000). They had to send an alert when a public debate took place between Shia and Sunni Muslims, for example near Al-Dahab, the mosque in Manila. Although Shiites accounted for less than 1 percent of the Muslim population in the Philippines, a memorandum dated February 4, 2010 warned that the religious message of minorities "had managed to breach its limited circle and reach out to the public."

A Saudi Foreign Ministry document showed the categorization of newspapers and journalists in Bahrain, occupied by the Saudi forces, because the country's identity cards did not specify religious affiliation. A cable dated October 1, 2011, a few months after local demonstrations started, revealed that the Riyadh intelligence agency had asked for precise information on Shiite activities, including the "methods used to infiltrate and take control of the situation." Saudi diplomats went far beyond merely gathering information by blackmailing the Bahraini authorities and linking Saudi aid to information on the different religious movements. A Saudi Intelligence Directorate document recalled an earlier request that sought "to exclude all Shiites from the Kingdom's projects." The cable specifically mentioned the Persian Arab University and King Abdallah Medical City, calculating the number of Shiite employees working there. Another cable stated that Saudi Arabia would only award scholarships to Bahraini students if they were Sunnis. The ambassador then explained in his reply that the student selected for one of the scholarships granted by Saudi universities had been "born in a well-known Sunni family." Even humanitarian aid was sectarian. In 2011, the Saudi Foreign Minister provided aid to flood victims in Thailand, noting that "this would have a positive impact on the country's Muslims and would limit the Iranian government's impact in extending the Shiite influence."

Another example concerns Pakistan. When the Islamabad-based International Islamic University President, Mumtaz Ahmad, invited the Iranian ambassador to a cultural week on campus, the Saudi Arabian ambassador called him to express "his great surprise" and suggested that he invite the ambassador's wife instead. As the Rector refused to obey, the Saudi diplomat suggested that Suliman Aba al-Khail, a Saudi theologian, who was a member of the university council, should summon the Board of Directors in order to "select a university president who was true to our orientations." Mumtaz Ahmad, a professor of political science with a doctorate from the University of Chicago, confronted the conservative faculty members in order to try and lessen the Saudi influence on the campus, but to no avail. He had to resign from his post as president in 2012, after the Saudi ambassador finally worked directly with the then Pakistan President, Asif Ali Zardari, to ensure that a Saudi subject became the university's president. "At the end of the day, they won," said a faculty member, speaking on the condition of anonymity.

Hassan, the son of Sheikh Suhaib Hasan, an Indian Muslim theologian and a former student in Saudi Arabia, who had been employed for four decades in Kenya and Britain, was well placed to testify to the authorities' obsessive nature. Hasan was a penitent and currently an associate of the Quilliam Foundation, which studies the phenomena of radicalization. According to a WikiLeaks cable, he described the policy of fighting the Shiite influence systematically,[192] coordinated by the Supreme Council of Islamic Affairs and the King's Office.

WHAT ABOUT RELATIONS WITH WASHINGTON?

The chaos in the Middle East would dissuade any country from getting involved. The major regional balances (or imbalances) can no longer be managed without Iran. Riyadh has due cause to be concerned about the difficult, yet "stop and go" normalization of relations between Washington and Tehran after the signing of the nuclear agreement. Indeed, the agreement recognizes the Islamic Republic as a "threshold State," that is to say a State with nuclear technology, but which has foresworn its development. On the other hand, the new bill, adopted unanimously by the Senate on May 17, enabling US citizens to sue countries for terrorist attacks on the United States, baptized the "Justice Against Sponsors of Terrorism Act," (JASTA) should not really keep the King awake. The House of Representatives, however, did not necessarily present the same convergence of views and former president Barack Obama pointed out that "if we open up the possibility that individuals and the United States can routinely start suing other governments, then we are also opening up the United States to being continually sued by individuals in other countries."[193] The vote, more symbolic than effective, reflected the real aversion the Kingdom arouses in public opinion across the Atlantic. Would Donald Trump, the US President, be able to convince the public of the need to send GIs to defend the obscurantist monarchy? The declassification of the twenty-eight "Defense Secret" pages of the US Congress report on the 9/11 attacks has opened up new perspectives and the US justice system, which has never forborne from indicting foreign powers, should be able to make the most of them.

The times, they are a-changin'!

CONCLUSION

In conclusion, it must be said that Saudi religious diplomacy is almost global in nature. As such, it should be a subject of international relations' studies, which is not the case at the present time. Indeed, the Saudi soft power incites respect: with a mix of the American system with its multiplicity of public and private actors heading in the same direction and a Soviet-style propagandist capacity with its inflexible ideology and its policy of training political commissars of Salafism, it has succeeded in remaining below the academic radar. And yet, the resources at its disposal, notably financial (US $6–7 billion a year), make it a much better-endowed actor than Soviet propaganda was in its heyday (US $2 billion a year) and should logically be a factor in the debate on the financing of jihadism.

While this study may seem incomplete, it merely demonstrates the need for much more ambitious and systematic work. The current debate on the funding of the Islamic State is futile until the ideological matrix that gave rise to Salafist Jihadism is taken into account. "Political Islam" may be dead, but Saudi religious diplomacy is not and neither is Salafism. Others have attempted to compete with Riyadh, but with fewer resources, such as the tiny Qatar or Turkey, within their geographical area and certainly not with the intention of propagating ideas of tolerance, but without the gigantic resources of Wahhabism.

Saudi religious diplomacy is not a foreign policy that has been totally coordinated and thought-out at the highest level. It was initially a policy pursued by the Muslim Brotherhood, the only cadres that the

country had at its inception, and it only gradually became Saudi, before
assuming the offensive against the confraternal congregation. But
although there may be a multiplicity of processes and actors, certain
indicators, by their sheer constancy and repetition, reflect a rare conti-
nuity and an abundance of resources that explain the dispersal and the
(sometimes uncontrollable) nature of the various activities conducted in
different parts of the world. There also remains a global capacity for
intervention—and that is the most important. Whereas Salafism is not
the only religious radicalism today, it is the only religious radicalism to
have been bolstered, encouraged and propagated by a State with
resources as vast as those of the enormous Saudi "Small and Medium
Enterprise."

The degree of danger Wahhabism presents seems to be better perceived in Arab–Muslim countries, from where the strongest reactions
have come (Morocco, Algeria, Indonesia, Uzbekistan, Tajikistan, Pakistan, Tunisia, etc.), rather than in the countries of the West, which react
to individual attacks rather than being able to anticipate the threat
posed by this ideology. An expert analysis of the areas where Saudi
religious diplomacy has been applied in different places across the
planet is the only way of predicting forthcoming crises, such as those
that surprised us so much in Mali and the Central African Republic.

The extraordinary level of empathy generated by the subject of jihad
among young Saudis as a key episode of the National Gesture taught in
the Kingdom's schools probably inspires the same calling from similar
programs taught in Koranic schools in the world's great democracies.
Reason enough to act! It is perhaps the only school system capable of
training "democrats" with racism, sectarianism, misogyny, homophobia and a hatred for others, formalized in textbooks. The theory put
forward by certain analysts who present the Salafists (or Quietists) as
"agents of democratization" therefore remains disputable.[194] Had that
been the case, the same descriptor would also have to be applied to the
ideology of the Khmer Rouge, or the racist theorists of Nazism. The

trauma of 9/11 pushed the Saudi ulemas, who found themselves in the eye of the storm, to preach a "quietist" Salafism and to denounce terrorism, especially when it was turned against the monarchy.

How can one explain that Salafism has replaced Third-Worldism and that it is as rallying an ideology in a certain number of countries of the Global South? It should be recalled that during the entire Cold War, the Near and Middle East region witnessed the greatest number of clandestine operations by Western intelligence agencies, giving rise to the so-called conspiracy theory so popular on "Arab Streets," fully aware of the various coups d'état attempts in Jordan, Syria (1949), Iran (1953), Iraq (1959) and Egypt. In the aftermath of the destruction on 9/11, the American neo-conservatives, overcome by a warlike hubris, sent armies to invade the Taliban's Afghanistan, the benchmark Emirate for all Salafists, followed by Iraq, Libya and then the allied intervention in the Syria-Iraq stage and, finally, Mali and the Sahelian zone. At the same time, a second Intifada, with two air strikes against Gaza and a land-and-air operation against Lebanon left them speechless. The "duty to protect," a newly coined phrase, was used to defend the Libyan people being massacred by Colonel Gaddafi, but never in the case of the Palestinians. Western capitals have sought to refer President Bashar al-Assad to the International Criminal Court, whereas Arab opinion believes George W. Bush to be the main culprit for the misfortunes of the Middle East, though the only punishment meted out was in the form of the shoes thrown at him in 2008 by Muntadhar al-Zaidi, an Iraqi journalist (unfortunately, not a good marksman!). Applying the most outrageous of double standards, the West has led to the worst case scenario—the exacerbation of a feeling of injustice—to the absolute delight of all the world's Salafists. It is this mountain of lies that has become the breeding ground within which Salafist Jihadism flourishes.

And it has flourished so well that even Riyadh feels threatened by the monster: should it fight to defend the progenitor? Shiite radicalism against Sunni radicalism—the plague against cholera! Should a stand be taken in the civil wars that the two radicalisms have set off in Iraq, Syria, Bahrain, Afghanistan, Pakistan, Yemen, Lebanon and Nigeria? Should the accusation of Islamophobia be allowed to stand, whereas 90 percent of the victims of terrorism are Muslims killed by Muslims? And when the minimum religious rights of Muslim minorities are not guaranteed in Saudi Arabia, Iran, Turkey, Kuwait and Malaysia, among others? The Arab–Muslim world has embarked upon a religious war wherein the West has no legitimacy to intervene. Will we be able to protect ourselves from it? Should the fight be against Daesh rather than Riyadh?

Saudi Arabia has just forged an "alliance against terrorism" with thirty-four Sunni countries—in other words, a way of promising troops to fight the IS. Undoubtedly, this is one of those initiatives in which no further action will ever be taken and which all diplomats are trained to proclaim when their power is on the wane. Destroying the Islamic State militarily will not solve the problem—on the contrary, it may even exacerbate it by mobilizing an even greater number of terrorist candidates in the West, presenting propagandists with the ideal arguments and dispersing trained fighters across the continents.

The monarchy only regained control of the system when it sparked a backlash that had the potential to destabilize royalty—and not when the West, no matter how powerful, demanded it. It would be futile to expect the regime to change its religious diplomacy, so deeply ingrained is it in its DNA. Listening to Wahhabi ulemas or the Saudi regime describe their "Islam" as a "religion of peace and love" is an oxymoron. No cause has done more harm to the image of Islam in the world than Wahhabism. It may, like other ideologies, decide on periods of "peaceful coexistence," but it cannot change its genetic fingerprints.

No one appears to have enough diplomatic clout today to change Riyadh's religious diplomacy. The Americans do not want to, none of the European countries has the means to do it alone—that too, unless they want to run the risk of being economically penalized by Riyadh, to the cynical satisfaction of other member countries. Perhaps "European" diplomacy needs to make its voice heard on this subject of collective interest. A check on the foreign funding of mosques and imams, legislation governing the freedom of speech and calls for hatred and the verification of the curricula of Koranic schools, for example, would go a long way in preventing the continent from becoming a "mission territory," or even a sanctuary for Salafists. But is there any European diplomacy capable of taking a coherent stand in the face of such a danger?

ANNEX 1

An overview of Saudi Arabian religious diplomatic activities, with or without a moderate royal contribution (2002).[195]

A QUICK OVERVIEW OF SAUDI ARABIA'S RELIGIOUS DIPLOMACY, WITH OR WITHOUT A MODERATE ROYAL CONTRIBUTION, AS ON MARCH 27, 2002

USA

Dar Al-Salam Institute; the Fresno Mosque in California; Islamic Center in Colombia, Missouri; Islamic Center in East Lansing, Michigan; Islamic Center in Los Angeles, California; Islamic Center in New Brunswick, New Jersey; Islamic Center in New York; Islamic Center in Tida, Maryland; Islamic Center in Toledo, Ohio; Islamic Center of Virginia; Islamic Center in Washington; Islamic Cultural Center in Chicago; the King Fahd Mosque in Los Angeles; the Mosque of the Albanian Community in Chicago; the South-West Big mosque, Chicago; and the Omar Ibn Al- Khattab mosque, Los Angeles.

Canada

Calgary mosque; Islamic Center in Quebec; Islamic Center in Toronto (US $5 million out of King Fahd's pocket, in addition to US $1.5 million given annually for operating expenses) and the Ottawa mosque.

Europe

The Brussels cultural center, which received a contribution of Saudi riyals (SAR) 19 million ($5 million in the 1960s); Geneva's Islamic Center, which received a grant of SAR 19 million for the construction of a mosque, a cultural center, a school and a reading room; Madrid's Islamic Center, one of the largest in Europe (SAR 27 million or $7 million), including a clinic; London's Islamic Center (contribution of SAR 25 million); Edinburgh's Islamic Center, located in the city center, with a seating capacity of 1,000 (SAR 15 million); Rome's Islamic Center ($50 million from King Fahd's coffers, amounting to 70 percent of the total construction cost) plus $1.5 million annually for operating costs; Gibraltar's Custodian of the Two Holy Mosques (more than SAR 30 million); and in Malaga, one of the largest projects, the Islamic King Fahd Center, with an area of 3,848 sq. m.

The Construction of Mosques

The Kingdom is believed to have directly financed over 1,359 mosques, for an overall grant of SAR 820 million, that is, $220 million, in Zagreb, Lisbon, Vienna, New York, Washington, Chicago, Maryland, Ohio, Virginia, plus 12 other cities in Latin America, where the Saudi contribution was only partial. The Great Mosque of Lyon received SAR 11 million.

University Chairs

The King Abdulaziz Chair in Islamic Studies at the University of Santa Barbara, California, was established by the Saudi Royal Family in 1984. The King Fahd Chair in Sharia Islamic Studies was established in 1993 at the Law Faculty of Harvard University, with a donation of $5 million from the King himself; the King Fahd Chair in Islamic Studies at the School of Oriental and African Studies (SOAS) of the University of London was established in 1995 with a £ 1 million grant from King Fahd. The "Custodian of the Two Holy Mosques" chair in the Gulf University was set up to provide a resident professor at the Moscow Faculty of Medicine and Science.

Koranic Schools

The commitment to teach Islam and create Koranic schools has been a constant focus since King Fahd bin Abdulaziz's reign. Schools are designed to strengthen the attachment of Muslim children abroad to their culture, religion and the Arabic language:

- The Islamic Center of Washington, established in 1984, teaches Arabic and Islamic studies. There are 1,200 male and female students, 549 of whom are Saudis, the remainder representing 29 nationalities. For a space of ten years, from 1984 to 1994, the center's operating cost was over SAR 100 million.

- The King Fahd Academy in London has 1,000 students, including children of Arab diplomats as well as other Arab and Muslim children living in the capital and belonging to 40 different nationalities.

- The King Fahd Academy in Moscow is not only a quality educational institution but also a "pedagogical attempt to counter the communist regime's lies and persecution with regard to Islam." It is a step in the cultural reaffirmation of Islamic values.

- The King Fahd Academy in Bonn, opened in 1995, includes a school for 500 pupils and a mosque for 700 worshipers. It teaches Arabic and Islam in order to build bridges with German society. The total cost was DM 30 million (equivalent to SAR 76.5 million).

- The Islamic Academy of Bihac (Bosnia) cost SAR 5 million as part of a comprehensive program of assistance to the Republic of Bosnia and Herzegovina.

Funding Islamic Research Institutions

Outside the Arab–Muslim world, many Islamic research institutes are supported by the Kingdom. Among them are the American University of Colorado, the American University of Washington, the 'Institut du monde arabe' in Paris, Duke University in North Carolina, Howard University in Washington, the Institute of Arab History and Islamic Sciences of Frankfurt; John Hopkins University in Maryland, the Middle East Institute in Washington, Shaw University in North Carolina and Syracuse University in New York.

ANNEX 2

SOME FAMOUS ALUMNI OF THE ISLAMIC UNIVERSITY OF MADINAH

Abdul Aziz Al-Harbi, member of the academic board of Umm al-Qura University. Famed for having asserted that Harut and Marut, mentioned in the second Surah of the Koran, were human beings and not angels.

Bilal Philips, a teacher in Canada who condemned the Boko Haram group during a visit to Nigeria. Philips also said that there was no rape in marriage because a woman had to give herself to her husband. He was barred from staying in Australia, the United Kingdom, Germany and Kenya. He was described by the US government as an "unindicted co-conspirator" of the 1993 terrorist attack on the World Trade Center.

Abu Usamah, Imam in Birmingham. According to a report published by the Center for Social Cohesion, Usamah advocated "the legitimacy of the holy war in an Islamic state; preached hatred against non-Muslims; declared that apostasy and homosexuality are punishable by death; and that women are inferior to men," in an undercover recording, which featured in a Channel 4 episode on "radical Islam at British universities." In the documentary, Usamah also expressed his support for Osama bin Laden and defended his right to freedom of expression, saying, "If I were to call homosexuals perverted, dirty, filthy dogs who should be murdered, that would be my freedom of speech, wouldn't it?" Usamah also stated that "He [Osama bin Laden] is better than a million George Bushes, he's better than a thousand Tony Blairs."

Abu Ammaar Yasir Qadhi, an American Muslim scholar and writer of Pakistani descent, he served as Dean of Academic Affairs at the Al Maghrib Institute and at the Islamic Educational Institution. In January 2010, the *Daily Telegraph* reported that in 2001, Qadhi had described the Holocaust as a "hoax" and had claimed that "Hitler never wanted the mass destruction of the Jews [. . .] he actually wanted to expel them to neighboring territories." Qadhi later denied having said this but acknowledged that for a while, he had held erroneous views with regard to the Holocaust.

Muhammad Al-Shareef, founder of the ISIS Institute for Managers, called for Yasir Qadhi, an American professor at Rhodes College and Dean of Academic Affairs at the Al Maghrib Institute, to be assassinated because his colleague had condemned the attacks on *Charlie Hebdo*. An investigation was conducted by the institute. It must be noted that the works of Anwar al-Awlaki, an American imam and active member of Al-Qaeda, were still on sale at Al Maghrib events, even after they were banned by the institute in 2009. Among the famous students at the center were: Umar Farouk Adulmutallab, who attempted to blow up Northwest Airlines Flight No. 253 from Amsterdam to Detroit in December 2009; Al-Awlaki, killed by an American drone in Yemen; Daniel Maldonado, a convert, convicted in 2007 for having formed a group linked to Al-Qaeda in Somalia; Tarek Mehanna, a pharmacist arrested for conspiring to attack Americans. The Al Maghrib Institute has been accused of being "liberal" and "apolitical" by some American Salafist groups. As a result of this polemic, the institute decided to dispense with the "Salafist" label.

Ehsan Elahi Zaheer, a Pakistani teacher and theologian, was the leader of the Ahl-e-Hadith movement. He died in an attack in 1987.

Rabee al-Madkhali, a former lecturer in the Faculty of Hadiths and Head of the Department of Sunnah in the Department of Advanced Studies of the Islamic University of Madinah. He also founded the Madkhalism movement. He is considered one of Salafism's most radical thinkers. Gilles Kepel has described him as being the perfect example of a "court scholar," as opposed to more radical trends within the Salafist movement. Despite his early opposition to the Saudi government, Al-Madkhali is now one of the Saudi royal family's staunchest defenders. While politically quietist within his own country, he has supported violent conflict elsewhere, such as when he called on Muslims both inside and outside Indonesia to participate in the Maluku sectarian conflict.

Shefqet Krasniqi, Imam of the Grand Mosque of Pristina (Kosovo), was arrested for his radical preaching and then released by the Kosovar justice system.

Muqbil bin Hadi al-Wadi'i, a religious scholar and founder of Dar al-Hadith al-Khayriyyah in Dammaj, Yemen. One of his books accuses bin Laden of "sectarianism," "partisanship," "fitna" (rebellion) and "religious ignorance." He never compromised by siding with the Sahwa movement.

Attique Ahmed Khan, a moderate politician from Jammu and Kashmir.

Saeed Abubakr Zakaria, a Ghanaian preacher, who served in Canada from 1997 to 2007 and then returned to Ghana to lead an Islamic institute.

Safiur Rahman Mubarakpuri, a preacher and writer from Uttar Pradesh.

Ismail ibn Musa Menk, Grand Mufti of Zimbabwe, an openly homophobic Islamic preacher. In 2013, his planned tour to six UK universities—Oxford, Leeds, Leicester, Liverpool, Cardiff and Glasgow—was canceled after opposition from student unions and university officials.

Pierre Vogel, a convert, an active preacher in Germany who believes that polygamy is justified because Germany has more women than men. In January 2016, Vogel shared a video criticizing a woman raped by a Middle Eastern man in Cologne, accusing her of Islamophobia.

Muhamed Ciftci, director of an Islamic school in Germany. He was accused in 2010 of having links with the Sauerland Group, which was planning a bombing in 2007, and with Arid Uka, who wanted to bomb Frankfurt airport.

Hussain Yee, a Malay politician of Chinese origin. He denied the role of Muslims in the September 11 attacks, as according to him, the accusation was based on unproven suspicions. He further argued that "Jews were behind the September 11 attacks."

Abdul Hadi Awang, a Malaysian MP.

Muzammil Siddiqi, imam at the Islamic Society of Orange County in Garden Grove, California. He is the current President of the Academy of Judaic, Christian and Islamic Studies at UCLA and is very active in interreligious dialogue.

Ahmed Omar Abu Ali, a US citizen accused of supporting Al-Qaeda and conspiring to assassinate President G. W. Bush.

Mohyeldeen Muhammad, a Norwegian of Iraqi origin, a political activist associated with the Profetens Ummah group, one of whose members wanted to "protect Jews with an AK-47 and a hunting license." A controversial figure in Norway after stating that the country was at war with Muslims and threatening Norwegians with a September 11–like incident. Following a series of statements concerning Norway, homosexuality and Islamism, he was deported from the country in 2011.

Abdel Salam al-Bourjis, a disciple of the former mufti of Saudi Arabia, frequently visited France to give lectures.

Muhammad Bazmoul, an Egyptian national, a lecturer at the University of Mecca, who condemned the Paris attacks.

Muhammad Al-Maghraoui, a Moroccan Salafist theologian, is a refugee in Saudi Arabia. His fatwa allows girls to marry at the age of nine, citing the example of the Prophet.

Ali Ferkous, a professor at the Faculty of Islamic Sciences at the University of Algiers, justifies the use of ruqya, an exorcism operation that has already claimed victims, for it is devoid of any polytheistic signs.

Sheikh Ja'afar Adam, a Nigerian, was the director of one of the grand mosques in Kano, Nigeria for many years. One of his favorite students was Mohammed Yusuf, who later founded Boko Haram. After many trips to Saudi Arabia, Yusuf turned radical, seeking to destroy rather than change the regimes of African states and rejected all Western influence. In 2007, Ja'afar Adam publicly condemned his former disciple, who, in exchange, ordered his assassination.

Ahmad Musa Jibril, a Salafist preacher who incites people to go to Syria but "not to join armed groups." A study by the International Center for the Study of Radicalization showed that 60 percent of the youth who had left for Syria were Jibril's followers.

Hamid bin Abdallah al-Ali, identified by the United States as an Al-Qaeda fundraiser and facilitator.

Zahran Alloush, a Syrian Salafist, who was active during the civil war. He was the commander of Jaish al-Islam, a major component of the Islamic Front. He issued a call to "clean" Damascus of all Alawites and Shiites.

Umar Sulaiman al-Ashkar, a professor at the Islamic Law Faculty in Amman, Jordan, he was close to the Muslim Brotherhood. He called on all Muslims to support the second Intifada.

Sheikh Khalid Hafiz, an Indian, was an imam in New Zealand from 1982 to 1999.

Ahmad Kutty, born in Kerala, India, is a well-known preacher in North America. Currently, he is a senior resident scholar at the Islamic Institute in Toronto.

Sabir Mahfouz Lahmar, a Bosnian citizen, who won his lawsuit in the United States for having been illegally detained for eight years in Guantanamo.

Abdur Rahman Madani, a citizen of Bangladesh, has been serving the Khatib of the Darul Ummah Mosque since April 2002. He is also Chairman of the Global Aid Trust and an executive member of the preaching committee.

Tomasz Miśkiewicz, a Polish mufti.

Feiz Muhammad, an Australian preacher of Lebanese origin, who disputes the idea of marital rape. In 2007, a box set of 16 DVDs of his sermons, called *The Death Series*, drew the attention of the Attorney General because some of them called for the killing of infidels and non-believers.

Othman Al Omeir, a British businessman, journalist and editor, who was born in Saudi Arabia.

Muhammad Omran is supposed to have founded Salafism in Australia. He expressed his appreciation of the path taken by bin Laden in different ways. Despite his denials of his personal ties with Abdul Nacer Benbrika, convicted of attempted terrorist attacks, the Australian government suspects him of encouraging terrorism.

Nizar Rayan, the head of Hamas, in charge of the ties between the political branch and the military branch.

Abdullah Saeed, currently a professor at the University of Melbourne, the Sultan of Oman's Chair in Arabic and religious studies.

Omar Shahin, born in Jordan, lives in the United States. He expressed doubts that any "sincere" Muslim was in any way responsible for the 9/11 attacks. He was one of the six imams taken off a domestic flight in 2006.

Salem Sheikhi, a Libyan citizen, is currently the "Khatib" (person who delivers the sermon during the Friday prayer and Eid prayers) at the Didsbury Mosque in Britain.

Abu Anas al-Shami, a Palestinian professor, writer and jihadist, born in Kuwait but originally from the West Bank town of Yabroud, Palestine. In the mid-1990s, he went to Bosnia and Herzegovina to teach Islam in cities and refugee camps. He later returned to Jordan. In the late 1990s, the Jordanian authorities shut down an Islamic center that Al-Shami had established in Amman on the grounds that it was promoting a fanatical interpretation of Islam. In 2003, al-Shami joined Abu Musab al-Zarqawi in the north-east of Iraq.

Ali al-Tamimi, a former resident of Fairfax County, a biologist and professor, convicted of inciting terrorism as part of the Virginia Network and sentenced to life imprisonment.

Muhammad Sayyid Tantawy, the Grand Mufti of Egypt, author of a fatwa legalizing abortion in case of rape. This sparked a controversy with the Mufti Ali Gomaa, who believes that life exists after 120 days of pregnancy. Tantawy also opposed female circumcision and revealed that his daughter had not been circumcised.

Faris Al-Zahrani, one of the twenty-six longest-sought terrorists by the USA. He is one of the forty-six executed on January 2, 2016 in Saudi Arabia.

Larbi Becheri, member of the new theological committee set up by the French Council of the Muslim Faith (CFCM), a PhD in Islamology from the University of Aix-en-Provence, a graduate in the field of the Sharia from the University of Madinah, a graduate of Sorbonne University, a member of CEFR and UISM, a professor of Muslim theology and in charge of the IESH in Château-Chinon (European institute for human sciences).

Ounis Guergah, a graduate in the Sharia from the University of Madinah, a graduate in philosophy from Sorbonne University, a member of the CEFR and the UISM, a professor of Muslim theology and an academic advisor at IESH in Paris. He is a member of the theological committee of the CFM and has proposed adaptations of the late and morning prayers for the Ramadan period.

Shukri Aliu was born in Kosovo, but lived in Macedonia. He studied in Syria for a few years and was subsequently allegedly thrown out and expelled from Saudi Arabia because of his Takfirist ideas. A refugee in Egypt, he studied his ideology of excommunication in depth before going to Macedonia, where he practiced in Skopje in the 2000s. He was a member of the Macedonian Islamic Community (MIC), in which he appears to have participated in debates, holding weapons in his hands. Prosecuted, he took refuge in Kosovo, where he remained nearly seven years without being bothered by the justice system, but was eventually expelled to Macedonia in 2012.

Genci Balla, an imam, who had recruited the Albanian, Mariglen Dervisllari, killed in Syria in the ranks of Daesh while he was studying in Madinah in 2010–2011.

Juhayman al-Otaybi, leader of the attack against Mecca's Grand Mosque in 1979.

Sheikh Boureima Abdou Daouda, a former student of the Faculty of Medicine at the National University of Niamey and a graduate of Islamic University of Madinah. He collaborated with several international Islamic centers and organizations in Madinah, including: the preaching center, the World Assembly of Islamic Youth, the King Fahd Complex for the Printing of the Holy Koran and the Ministry of Islamic Affairs in Riyadh, among others. Apart from being a preacher, he was also a trainer, an Islamic lecturer, the founding president of the Islamic

Translations Bureau, the founder of the School of Life and president of the International Good Life Organization.

Rexhep Memishi, a Macedonian, was expelled from Medinah in the 2000s because of his Takfirist diligence, under pressure from an Imam of Albanian origin from Kumanovo. He settled in Egypt between 2004 and 2006, where he also had disagreements with imams from Kosovo and Albania, listed as Salafists. On his YouTube account, Udhëzimi Islam, whose profile features a portrait of Osama bin Laden, posted a large number of videos.

Abdelkader Bouziane and Abdel Hadi Doudi, both Algerians, arrived in France in the 1980s to introduce Salafism. Abdel Hadi Doudi was the brother-in-law of Mustapha Bouyali, leader of the first armed Islamist organization in Algeria, a fellow traveler of Ali Belhadj, one of the founders of the Algerian FIS. Imprisoned in Algeria, he was released in 1986, and immigrated to France. In September 2001, an internal memorandum showed that the Directorate of National Security (DST) was already alarmed about "the presence of Saudi Arabian Ulemas, who had come to conduct seminars in the mosques of La Rose-des-Vents in Aulnay-sous-Bois, Al-Ihsan in Argenteuil and Tariq-Ibn-Zyad in Les Mureaux." In July 2001, Abdullah al-Bukhri, Sali al-Zubaydi and Muhammad Bazmul gathered more than a thousand young people at the mosque in Aulnay-sous-Bois to recruit the young faithful so that they could be sent for theological studies to Saudi Arabia. In April 2004, Abdelkader Bouziane justified the stoning of unfaithful women in the land of Islam in an interview given to the monthly magazine, *Lyon Mag,* and declared that in France, a husband could beat his wife in "some specific cases," such as adultery. In February 2004, a first deportation order was issued, but never enforced. Brought before it for an urgent interim order, the Administrative Court of Lyon suspended the deportation order on April 23, 2004. Allowed to return to France, the expelled Imam was back on May 22, 2004. In October 2005, he was sentenced by the Lyon Court of Appeal to six months' suspended imprisonment and a fine of Euros 2,000 for "direct incitement, not followed up in practice, to commit the offense of willful assault on the integrity of a person." As early as in 2006, the confirmed presence of the imam in Belgium posed a problem, whereas he should have been arrested and deported.

Syed Fida Bukhari, born in Pakistan, had learnt the Koran by heart at the age of nine. He received a MWL scholarship for studying at the Islamic University of Madinah. After his studies, he was sent to Quebec where he sat on the Sharia Council, also called the Islamic Jurisprudence Council, which rules on "civil and matrimonial" disputes.

Nedzad Balkan, born in Vienna, is the son of a Bosnian Muslim dignitary. In his thirties, after a dissolute life, he took charge of the Sahaba Mosque in Vienna and was believed to be the one who funded the Wahhabis who went to fight in Bosnia. Like many Bosnian leaders, he had studied at the University of Madinah in the early 1990s. Apparently disappointed at the lack of Islamism in the Saudi regime, he left before graduating. Back in Vienna, he preached at the Al-Tawhid Mosque, which he also left, after a dispute with another radical, Muhamed Porca.

SELECTED BIBLIOGRAPHY

We shall limit the references given here to books that relate most directly to the subject of Saudi Arabia, in alphabetical order. We would like to express our sincere apologies in advance to all those who may have been overlooked. Moreover, most of the regional sources that helped analyze the thrust areas of Saudi religious diplomacy used can be found on the WikiLeaks website: https://wikileaks.org/saudi-cables/db/. The conclusions I have drawn have been compared with those inferred by specialists on the regions concerned and it is not possible to name all of them here. Finally, interviews were conducted with various persons who, with a few exceptions, all wished to remain anonymous: French diplomats, French and foreign theologians, armed forces personnel, intelligence specialists, journalists, specialists of Islam from France, politicians, MWL officials and Lebanese political figures, among others. We regret our inability, therefore, to express our gratitude individually to each of them.

WORKS
Anouar Abdallah, *Les Oulémas et le Trône*, Al-Rafed, 1995.
Khaled M. Abou El Fadl, *The Great Theft: Wresting Islam from the Extremists*, HarperOne, 2005.
Charles Allen, *God's Terrorists: The Wahhabi Cult and the Hidden Roots of Modern Jihad*, Da Capo Press, 2007.
Samir Amghar, *Le Salafisme aujourd'hui*, Michalon, 2008.

Scott Atran, *L'État islamique est une révolution*, Éditions Les Liens qui Libèrent, 2016.

Antoine Basbous, *L'Arabie saoudite en question*, Perrin, 2002.

François Burgat, *L'Islamisme en face*, La Découverte, 2005.

François Burgat, *L'Islamisme à l'heure d'al-Qaeda*, La Découverte coll. Poche/Essai, 2010.

Jason Burke, *Al-Qaeda, la véritable histoire de l'islam radical*, La Découverte, coll. "Cahiers libres," 2005.

Olivier Corancez (de), *Histoire des wahabi: depuis leur origine jusqu'à la fin de 1809*, Les Cahiers de l'Orient, 2008.

Olivier Da Lage, *Géopolitique de l'Arabie saoudite*, Éditions Complexe, 2006.

Fatiha Dazi-Héni, *Monarchies et sociétés d'Arabie. Le temps des confrontations*, Presses de Sciences Po, 2006.

Michael R. Dillon, *Wahhabism: Is It a Factor in the Spread of Global Terrorism?*, thesis, Naval Post-Graduate School Monterey, 2009.

Anoushiravan Ehteshami, *From the Gulf to Central Asia: Players in the New Great Game*, University of Exeter Press, 1994.

Jean-Pierre Filiu, *L'Apocalypse dans l'islam*, Fayard, 2008.

Bernard Godard, Sylvie Taussig, *Les Musulmans en France. Courants, institutions, communautés: un état des lieux*, Robert Laffont, 2007.

Andrew Hammond, *Popular Culture in The Arab World*, The American University in Cairo Press, 2007.

Hazem Kandil, *Inside the Brotherhood*, Polity, 2014.

Adeeb Khalid, *Islam after Communism: Religion and Politics in Central Asia*, University of California Press, 2007.

Gilles Kepel, *Jihad: The Trail of Political Islam*, Harvard University Press, 2002; French translation: Jihad.

Gilles Kepel, *Expansion et déclin de l'islamisme*, Gallimard, 2000, coll. "Folio actuel," 2003.

Gilles Kepel, *Fitna. Guerre au cœur de l'islam*, Gallimard, 2004.

Gilles Kepel, *Terreur dans l'Hexagone*, Gallimard, 2015.

Farhad Khosrokhavar, David Bénichou, Philippe Migaux, *Le Jihad-isme, le comprendre pour mieux le combattre*, Plon, 2015.

Robert Lacey, *Inside the Kingdom: Kings, Clerics, Modernists, Terrorists, and the Struggle for Saudi Arabia*, Penguin Press, 2010.

Stéphane Lacroix, *Les Islamistes saoudiens. Une insurrection manquée*, PUF, 2010.

Brynjar Lia, *Architect of Global Jihad: The Life of Al- Qaeda Strategist Abu Mus'ab al-Suri*, Columbia University Press, 2008.

Pierre-Jean Luizard, *Le Piège Daech. L'État islamique ou le retour de l'histoire*, La Découverte, 2015.

Pascal Ménoret, *L'Énigme saoudienne. Les Saoudiens et le monde, 1744–2003*, La Découverte, 2003 (blog: http://pascal-menoret.over-blog.com).

Fabrice Monti, *La Coke saoudienne au cœur d'une affaire d'État*, Flammarion, 2004.

Nabil Mouline, *Les Clercs de l'islam*, PUF, coll. "Proche-Orient," 2011.

Thierry Mudry, *Guerre de religions dans les Balkans*, Ellipses, 2005.

Madawi al-Rasheed, *A History of Saudi Arabia*, Cambridge University Press, 2nd ed., 2010.

Philippe Raggi, *Indonésie, la nouvelle donne*, L'Harmattan, 2000.

Hamadi Redissi, *Le Pacte du Nadjd ou comment l'islam sectaire est devenu l'islam*, Seuil, coll. "La Couleur des idées," 2007.

Bernard Rougier (dir.), *Qu'est-ce que le salafisme?*, PUF, coll. "Proche-Orient," 2008.

Olivier Roy, *L'Échec de l'islam politique*, Seuil, 1991.

Olivier Roy, *L'islam mondialisé*, Seuil, coll. "La Couleur des idées," 2002.

Olivier Roy, *La Peur de l'islam*, Éditions de l'Aube, 2015.

Ben Salama, *Au nom de l'islam. Enquête sur une région instrumentalisée*, Éditions de l'Atelier, 2009.

Reinhard Schulze, *Islamischer Internationalismus im 20. Jahrhundert: Untersuchungen zur Geschichte der islamischen Weltliga* (Islamic

Internationalism in the 20th Century: Studies in the History of the Muslim World League), Brill, 1990.

Antoine Sfeir, *La Démocratie en danger, l'enseignement islamiste saoudien*, Center for Monitoring the Impact of Peace (CMIP), Berg International, 2004.

Antoine Sfeir, *L'Islam contre l'islam. L'interminable guerre des sunnites et des chiites*, Grasset, 2013.

REVIEWS AND REPORTS

Samir Amghar, "La Ligue islamique mondiale en Europe: un instrument de défense des intérêts stratégiques saoudiens," *Critique internationale*, Presses de Sciences Po, no. 51, 2011.

Iyad el-Baghdadi, "Salafis, Jihadis, Takfiris: Demystifying Militant Islamism in Syria," el-baghadi.com, January 15, 2013.

Samar Batrawi, "The Dutch Foreign Fighter Contingent in Syria," *Combating Terrorism Center*, October 2013.

James Dorsey, "Creating Frankenstein: the Saudi Export of Wahhabism," lecture at the Institute of South Asian Studies, March 2016.

Steven Emerson, Testimony of Emerson Steven before the House Committee on Financial Services Subcommittee on Oversight and Investigations, "Terrorism Financing & U.S. Financial Institutions," March 2003

Per Gudmundson, "The Swedish Foreign Fighter Contingent in Syria," *Combating Terrorism Center*, September 2013.

Jonathan D. Halevi, "Al-Qaeda's Intellectual Legacy: New Radical Islamic Thinking Justifying the Genocide of Infidels," *Jerusalem Viewpoints*, no. 508, December 1, 2003.

Daniel H. Heinke and Jan Raudszus, "German Foreign Fighters in Syria and Iraq," January 2015

Timothy Holman, "Foreign Fighters from the Western Balkans in Syria," *Combating Terrorism Center*, June 2014.

Seth G. Jones, "A Persistent Threat: The Evolution of al Qa'ida and Other Salafi Jihadists," *Rand Corporation*, consulted on May 28, 2015.

Evan Kohlmann and Laith Alkhouri, "Profiles of Foreign Fighters in Syria and Iraq," *Combating Terrorism Center*, September 2014.

Martin Kramer,"Coming to Terms: Fundamentalists or Islamists?," *Middle East Quarterly*, 2003.

Shpend Kursani, "Report Inquiring into the Causes and Consequences of Kosovo's Citizens' involvement as Foreign Fighters in Syria and Iraq," *Kosovo Center for Security Studies*, 2015.

Stéphane Lacroix, "Les nouveaux intellectuels religieux saoudiens, le wahhabisme en question," *Revue des Deux Mondes*, no. 123, July 2008.

Stéphane Lacroix, "Saudi Islamists and the Arab Spring," London School of Economics Kuwait Program, May 2014.

Bruce Livesey, "The Salafist Movement," *PBS Frontline*, consulted on October 24, 2014.

John J. Mearsheimer, "America Unhinged," *National Interest*, 9-30, consulted on May 30, 2015.

Patrick Mennucci, Report on the surveillance of jihadi networks and individuals, Assemblée nationale (National Assembly) no. 2828, October 4, 2015.

Nabil Mouline, "Les Oulémas du Palais. Parcours des membres du comité des grands oulémas," *Archives des sciences sociales des religions*, no. 149, 2010.

Ahmad Moussalli, "Wahhabism, Salafism and Islamism: Who Is the Enemy?," A Conflicts Forum Monograph, 2009.

Raffaello Pantucci, "The British Foreign Fighter Contingent in Syria," *Combating Terrorism Center*, May 2014.

Fernando Reinares and Carola García-Calvo, "The Spanish Foreign Fighter Contingent in Syria," *Combating Terrorism Center*, January 2014.

William A. Rugh, "Education in Saudi Arabia: Choices and Constraints," *Middle East Policy*, vol. 9, no. 2, 2002.

Aaron Y. Zelin, "Up to 11,000 Foreign Fighters in Syria. Steep Rise Among Western Europeans," *International Center for the Study of Radicalization and Political Violence*, King's College London, December 2013.

Aaron Y. Zelin,"The Saudi Foreign Fighter Presence in Syria," *Combating Terrorism Center*, April 2014.

ICSR Report, *Victims, Perpetrators, Assets: The Narratives of Islamic State Defectors*, January 2015.

International Crisis Group (ICG) Report, Asia, 2002.

Report on the mission to the Republic of Kosovo from June 10 to 20, 2015, by the *Office français de protection des réfugiés et apatrides* (OFP) with the participation of the *Cour nationale du droit d'asile* (CNDA) and the *Bundesamt für Migration und Flüchtlinge* (BAMF).

Report on "Saudi Publications on Hate Ideology Invade American Mosques," Freedom House, 2005.

Report on "The State of Education 2002–2003," Social Policy Development Center (SPDC), 2003.

Report on "La Salafisation des Tatars: Questions de préservation de la langue, de la religion, de la prédication, de la culture nationale et ethnique" (The Salafization of the Tatars: Issues regarding the preservation of the language, religion, preaching and national and ethnic culture), Symposium on International Studies by Islamic Experts in Contemporary Russia and the CIS countries: Achievements, Problems and Prospects," March 15–16, 2011, University of Kazan.

Soufan Group Report:"Foreign Fighters: An Updated Assessment of the Flow of Foreign Fighters into Syria and Iraq," December 2015.

"The Global Salafi Jihad," The National Commission on Terrorist Attacks upon the United States, July 9, 2003, consulted on June 1, 2015.

ENDNOTES

1. www.pbs.org/wgbh/pages/frontline/shows/saudi/interviews /holbrooke.html
2. For the record, a book on the religious history of the US was also recently published: *Histoire religieuse des États-Unis*, by Lauric Henneton, Flammarion, 2012.
3. Hamadi Redissi, *Le Pacte de Nadjd ou comment l'islam sectaire est devenu l'islam*, Le Seuil, coll. "La Couleur des idées," 2007.
4. bigbrowser.blog.lemonde.fr/2015/11/21/letat-islamique-a -unpere-larabie-saoudite-et-son-industrie-ideologique/
5. Lumumba University is the other name for the People's Friendship University of Russia that used to train cadres for the Communist Party.
6. Dominique Chevallier, "wahhabisme," Encyclopædia Universalis [online], www.universalis.fr/encyclopedie/wahhabisme, consulted on October 24, 2015.
7. Henri Laoust, *La Profession de foi d'Ibn Batta*, Ifpo, 1958.
8. Hamadi Redissi, *Le Pacte de Najd ou comment l'islam sectaire est devenu l'islam*, op. cit, p. 30.
9. Nabil Mouline, *Les Clercs de l'islam*, PUF, coll. "Proche-Orient," 2011.
10. Ibid.
11. Quoted by Madawi al-Rasheed, *A History of Saudi Arabia*, Cambridge University Press, 2nd ed., 2010, p. 17.
12. Hamadi Redissi, *Le Pacte de Najd ou comment l'islam sectaire est devenu l'islam*, op. cit., p. 74.

13. Georges Jawdat Dwailibi, *La rivalité entre le clergé religieux et la famille royale au royaume d'Arabie Saoudite*, Publibook, 2006, p. 9.

14. Fatiha Dazi-Héni, *Monarchies et Sociétés d'Arabie. Le temps des confrontations*, Presses de Sciences Po, 2006.

15. Hamadi Redissi, *Le Pacte du najd ou comment l'islam sectaire est devenu l'islam*.

16. Stéphane Lacroix, "Islam, droit et radicalisme," *Moyen-Orient*, no. 29, 2016, op. cit.

17. Article by Henri Laurens, http://orientxxi.info/magazine /la-legende-du-pacte-du-quincy, 1213.

18. Quoted by Ben Salama, *Au nom de l'islam. Enquête sur une région instrumentalisée*, Éditions de l'Atelier, 2009, p. 42.

19. Michel Foucault, "Il mitico capo della rivolta dell'Iran" ("The Mythical Leader of the Iranian Revolt"), *Corriere della sera*, vol. 103, no. 279, November 26, 1978, pp. 1–2.

20. Antoine Basbous, *L'Arabie saoudite en question*, Perrin, 2002, p. 84 et sq.

21. Contrary to what Thomas Lippman, an American expert, stated in *Le Point* on January 21, 2016, young Saudis, who account for 70 percent of the population, do get influenced by the jihadist mythology taught in schools. See Gilles Kepel, *Fitna: Guerre au cœur de l'islam*, Gallimard, 2004.

22. Jason Burke, *Al- Qaeda, la véritable histoire de l'islam radical*, La Découverte, coll. "Cahiers libres," 2005.

23. Op. cit.

24. A very pious Muslim school of thought, highly prevalent in the Indian sub-continent, which emerged in the British Isles in 1867 as a reaction to colonization; it advocates the return to a "just Islam and respect for Islamic principles".

25. www.who.int/substance_abuse/publications/en/saudi_arabia.pdf

26. "Behind the façade of Wahhabi conservatism in the streets, the underground night life of Jeddah's elite youth is thriving and throbbing [. . .]. The full range of worldly temptations and vices are available–alcohol, drugs, sex–but strictly behind closed doors . . . The freedom to indulge in carnal pursuits is possible simply because the religious police keep its distance when parties include the presence or patronage of a Saudi royal and his circle of loyal attendants," according to a memo by the US consulate in Jeddah, quoted by WikiLeaks.

27. Murphy Caryle, "For Conservative Muslims, Goal of Isolation a Challenge," *The Washington Post*, September 5, 2006.

28. Mark Durie, "Salafis and the Muslim Brotherhood: What is the difference?," *Middle East Forum*, June 6, 2013.

29. Khaled M. Abou El Fadl, *The Great Theft: Wrestling Islam from the Extremists*, HarperOne, 2005, p. 75.

30. Michael R. Dillon, *Wahhabism: Is it a Factor in the Spread of Global Terrorism?*, thesis, Naval Post Graduate School, Monterey, 2009.

31. Ahmad Moussalli, "Wahhabism, Salafism and Islamism: Who Is The Enemy?," A Conflicts Forum Monograph, 2009, p. 3.

32. Introduction by Gilles Kepel, *Jihad: The Trail of Political Islam*, Harvard University Press, 2002, pp. 219 222.

33. Hamadi Redissi, *op. cit.*, p. 31.

34. James Dorsey, "Creating Frankenstein: the Saudi Export of Wahhabism," lecture, Institute of South Asian Studies, March 2016.

35. Olivier Roy, *L'islam mondialisé*, Seuil, coll. "La Couleur des idées," 2002, p. 133 et seq.

36. Samir Amghar, *Le Salafisme aujourd'hui*, Michalon, 2011.

37. See Yussuf al Qaradawi, *Le Licite et l'Illicite en Islam*, Al Qalam, 2005.

38. Quoted by Antoine Basbous, *L'Arabie saoudite en question*, *op. cit.*, p. 71.

39. See an anthology of the Sheikh's thoughts at www.pbs.org
     /wgbh/pages/frontline/shows/saud/interviews/alomar.html

40. Olivier Da Lage, *Géopolitique de l'Arabie saoudite*, Éditions
     Complexe, 2006, p. 39.

41. http://www.madamasr.com/sections/politics/wikileaks
     /saudiarabia-and-azhar-shia-encroachment-egypt

42. http://www.lemonde.fr/attaques a paris/article/2015/11/18
     /fabien-clain-la voix-du-massacre-de-paris-avait-deja-menace
     -le-bataclan-en-2009_4812298_4809495.html

43. Quoted by Olivier Dalage, op. cit., p. 34.

44. www.cia.gov/library/publications/the world factbook/geos
     /sa.html

45. https://reprieve.org.uk/saudi-arabia-stop-the-crucifixtion
     -of-ali-al-nimr/

46. http://news.bbc.co.uk/2/hi/middle_east/1874471.stm

47. Ziauddin Sardar, *Une histoire de La Mecque, De la naissance
     d'Abraham au xxie siècle*, Payot, coll. "Payot histoire," 2015.

48. www.independent.co.uk/news/world/middle east/the destruction
     of mecca saudi hardliners are wiping out their own heritage
     501647.html

49. See Gilles Kepel, "Jihadist Salafism" in *Jihad: The Trail of
     Political Islam, op. cit.*; Bruce Livesey, "The Salafist movement,"
     PBS Frontline, 2005, updated on October 24, 2014; Martin
     Kramer, "Coming to Terms: Fundamentalists or Islamists?,"
     Middle East Quarterly, 2003, pp. 65 77; Iyad El Baghdadi,
     "Salafis, Jihadis, Takfiris: Demystifying Militant Islamism in
     Syria," el baghdadi.com, January 15, 2013, updated on March
     10, 2013; "The Global Salafi Jihad," The National Commission
     on Terrorist Attacks Upon the United States, July 9, 2003,
     updated on June 1, 2015; Mearsheimer, John J., "America
     Unhinged," *National Interest*, 9 30, updated on May 30, 2015;
     Seth G. Jones, "A Persistent Threat: The Evolution of al Qa'ida

and Other Salafi Jihadists," *Rand Corporation*, pp. ix x iii, updated on May 28, 2015.

50. For this debate, see Nabil Mouline, *op. cit.*, p. 320 et *seq.*

51. Gilles Kepel, *op. cit.*, p. 225.

52. www.cairn.info/zen.php?ID_ARTICLE=OUTE_014_0255 #re5no5

53. John R. Bradley, "Kingdom of Peace Transformed into al Qa'eda's Latest War Zone," *The Telegraph*, August 1, 2015.

54. Jonathan D. Halevi, "Al Qaeda's Intellectual Legacy: New Radical Islamic Thinking Justifying the Genocide of Infidels," *Jerusalem Viewpoints*, no. 508, December 1, 2003.

55. oumma.com/11522/ un-religieux-saoudien-decrete-une-fatwa-rendant-licite

56. geopolis.francetvinfo.fr/des religieux-saoudiens-appellent-au -djihad-contre-la-russie-en-syrie.83051

57. Ibrahim bin Mohamed al Malek, *King Abdullah's Counter Terrorism: Strategy and Philosophy*, Ministry of Education, undated official publication.

58. *Arab News*, November 25, 2015.

59. www.amnesty.fr/Presse/Communiques-de-presse/La-lamentable -reponse-du-monde-la-crise-des-refugies-syriens.13536

60. Olivier Roy, *op. cit.*, p. 7.

61. Ahmed Rashid, *op. cit.*

62. www.courrierinternational.com/article/2008/07/03/la -schizophrenie-du-touriste-saoudie

63. Former retired police officer, Fabrice Monti, *La Coke saoudienne au cœur d'une affaire d'État*, Flammarion, 2004.

64. Daniel Yergin and Joseph Stanislaw, *La Grande Bataille, les marchés à l'assaut du pouvoir*, Odile Jacob, 1998, pp. 383–384.

65. http://english.alarabiya.net/en/News/middle-east/2015/12/28 /Saudi-Grand-Mufti-Islamic-alliance-will-defeat-ISIS-.html

66. Pascal Ménoret, *L'Énigme saoudienne. Les Saoudiens et le monde, 1744–2003*, La Découverte, 2003. See also his blog: http://pascal-menoret.over-blog.com

67. The magazine, *Moyen-Orient*, no. 29, 2016, p. 31.

68. Op. cit., p. 88.

69. Nabil Mouline, "Les Oulémas du Palais. Parcours des membres du comité des grands oulémas," *Archives des sciences sociales des religions*, no. 149, 2010 and https://assr.revues.org/21954

70. *Arab News*, Tuesday, March 22, 2005.

71. Broadcast on the website: islamonline.net

72. Ignace Leverrier, "L'Arabie saoudite, le pèlerinage et l'Iran," *Cahiers d'Études sur la Méditerranée Orientale et le monde turco-iranien*, no. 22, 1996, uploaded on March 4, 2005; http://cemoti.revues.org/137#bodyftn64

73. www.theguardian.com/world/us-embassy-cables-documents/220186

74. www.ibe.unesco.org/National_Reports/ICE_2008/saudiarabia_NR08_fr.pdf

75. William A. Rugh, "Education in Saudi Arabia: Choices and Constraints," *Middle East Policy*, vol. 9, no. 2, 2002, pp. 40 55.

76. http://www.axl.cefan.ulaval.ca/asie/arabie saoudite.htm

77. Antoine Sfeir, *La Démocratie en danger, l'enseignement islamiste saoudien*, Center for Monitoring the Impact of Peace (CMIP), Berg International, 2004, and the report in English: http://www.hudson.org/files/pdf_upload/textbooks_final_for_pdf.pdf

78. Nabil Mouline, *Les Clercs de l'islam, op. cit.*, p. 306.

79. www.mitpressjournals.org/doi/pdf/10.1162/ISEC_a_00023

80. Gilles Dorronsoro, "Les Wahhabites en Afghanistan," *La Lettre d'Asie centrale*, no. 2, Autumn 1994.

81. Samir Amghar, "La Ligue islamique mondiale en Europe: un instrument de défense des intérêts stratégiques saoudiens," *Critique internationale*, Presses de Sciences Po, no. 51, 2011.

82. Reinhard Schulze, *Islamischer Internationalismus im 20. Jahrhundert: Untersuchungen zur Geschichte der islamischen Weltliga* (trans. *Islamic Internationalism in the 20thCentury: Studies in the History of the Muslim World League*), Brill, 1990.

83. Bernard Godard, Sylvie Taussig, *Les Musulmans en France. Courants, institutions, communautés: un état des lieux,* Robert Laffont, 2007.

84. US Congress, Senate, Committee on Governmental Affairs, 7/31/2003; US News and World Report, 12/15/2003.

85. The author's discussion with a MWL representative in a major European capital.

86. Glenn R. Simpson, "List of Early al-Qaeda Donors Points to Saudi Elite, Charities," www.wsj.com, March 18, 2003.

87. Steven Emerson, Testimony of Emerson Steven before the House Committee on Financial Services Subcommittee on Oversight and Investigations, "Terrorism Financing & U.S. Financial Institutions," March 2003.

88. journaldumusulman.fr/la-ligue-islamique-mondiale-a-construit -plus-de-7000-mosquees-dans-37-pays

89. *Jane's Intelligence Review,* London, January 1, 1999, quoted by Oliver Roy in op. cit., p. 45.

90. National Assembly of Quebec, Fatima Houda Pépin, Hansard, May 26, 2005.

91. François Berger, "Québec: enquête sur un tribunal islamique," *La Presse, Nouvelles générales,* February 24, 1995.

92. Denis Martin MacEoin, *The Hijacking of British Islam: How Extremist Literature is Subverting Mosques in the UK,* Policy Exchange, 2007 and https://fr.scribd.com/doc/30586814/Hijacking -of-British-islam

93. la hijra.com/comment-etudier-a-medine

94. Anouar Abdallah, *Les Oulémas et le Trône,* Al Rafed, London, 1995.

95. https://www.pri.org/stories/2011-09-06/911-forces-change
-saudis-global-religious-mission

96. Charles Allen, *God's Terrorists: The Wahhabi Cult and the Hidden Roots of Modern Jihad*, Da Capo Press, 2007.

97. Yahya Birt, an academic, director of The City Circle, a network of young British Muslims, quoted in Paul Vallely, "Wahhabism, a deadly picture," www.independent.co.uk, November 1, 2007.

98. Stanley A. Weiss and Terence Ward, "Five Saudi Imperial Projects the West has Slept Through," www.huffingtonpost.com, January 14, 2016.

99. http://www.aei.org/events/saudi-government-propaganda-in-the-united-states/

100. https://www.swissinfo.ch/fre/societe/des-vagues-%C3%A0-la-mosqu%C3%A9e-de-gen%C3%A8ve/6041156

101. Robert Lacey, *Inside the Kingdom: Kings, Clerics, Modernists, Terrorists, and the Struggle for Saudi Arabia*, Penguin Press, 2010, pp. 73 74.

102. Nabil Mouline, "Surenchères traditionalistes en terres d'islam," *Le Monde diplomatique*, March 2015.

103. Andrew Hammond, *Popular Culture In the Arab World*, American University in Cairo Press, 2007.

104. wikileaks.org/saudicables/buying-silence

105. https://weeklyworker.co.uk/worker/1064/saudi-dirty-tricks-exposed/

106. https://www.mintpressnews.com/wikileaks-exposes-secret-deal-to-get-saudi-arabia-on-un-human-rights-council/210117/

107. http://www.lefigaro.fr/international/2015/02/02/01003-20150202ARTFIG00430-ces-28-pages-qui-menacent-l-axe-washington-riyad.php

108. They have been sanitized, but are readable and are now accessible on the website: http://intelligence.house.gov/sites/intelligence.house.gov/files/documents/declasspart4.pdf

109. www.theguardian.com/world/2010/dec/05/wikileaks cables saudi terrorist funding

110. A discussion on Twitter, published by WikiLeaks, but with its translation disputed, mentions the idea of a deal between the Pope and the King with regard to the protection of the Eastern Orthodox Church in exchange of support for the fall of Assad.

111. Report by the Soufan Group, "Foreign Fighters: An Updated Assessment of the Flow of foreign fighters into Syria and Iraq," December 2015.

112. Report by Patrick Mennucci on the surveillance of jihadi networks and individuals, Assemblée nationale (National Assembly) no. 2828 of October 4, 2015 and "Victims, Perpetrators, Assets: The Narratives of Islamic State Defectors," ICSR London Report, January 2015.

113. Stéphane Lacroix, "Les nouveaux intellectuels religieux saoudiens, le wahhabisme en question," Revue des Deux Mondes, no. 123, July 2008.

114. https://www.lemonde.fr/idees/article/2013/07/10/le-salafisme-a-la-conquete-du-pouvoir_3445712_3232.html

115. International Crisis Group (ICG) Report, Asia, 2002, p. 3.

116. Op. cit.

117. Op. cit., p. 10.

118. Op. cit., p. 9.

119. www.ft.com/intl/cms/s/0/a65d2616-a78b-11e5-955c-1e1d6de94879.html#axzz3vjU4R7Zg

120. Report on "The State of Education 2002 2003," Social Policy Development Center (SPDC), 2003, p. 161.

121. International Crisis Group (ICG) Report, Asia, 2002, op. cit., p. 17.

122. "Clercs Protestation Changements," Syllabus, Aube, 20 March 2012.

123. "Khyber Pakhtunkhwa minister defends changes to islamiat syllabus," Tribune Express, March 28, 2012.

124. www.elwatan.com/recherche/recherche.php?texte=abderrahmane +moussaoui&exec=1&x=19&y=9&fco=doctrine+wahhabite &page=1

125. chroniquesdemontreal.blogspot.fr/2012/05/algerie-lemergence -dune-nouvelle.html

126. www.huffpostmaghreb.com/2016/03/08/hamadache-k-amel -daoud_n_9406512.html

127. www.izf.net/afp/des-centaines-femmes-les-rues-dalger-pour -une-course-inedite

128. Antoine Basbous, op. cit., p. 154 et seq.

129. www.rferl.org/content/Wahhabi_Group_Launches_Conversion _Campaign_In_Bosnia/2001137.html

130. www.nationalreview.com/corner/282482/wahhabism-forgotten -legacy-bosnian-war -sarah-schlesinger/

131. Thierry Mudry, *Guerre de religions dans les Balkans*, Ellipses, 2005 and http://www.qkss.org/repository/docs/Report_inquiring _ into_the_causes_and_consequences_of_Kosovo_citizens' _ involvement_as_foreign_fighters_in_Syria_and_Iraq_307708 .pdf, and https://www.ofpra.gouv.fr/sites/default/files/atoms /files/08022016_rapport_kosovo_version_flora.pdf

132. http://www.qkss.org/repository/docs/Report_inquiring_into _the_causes_and_consequences_of_Kosovo_citizens'_involvement _as_foreign_fighters_in_Syria_and_Iraq_307708.pdf

133. Petrit Collaku, "Extremists Beat Kosovo Imam in Mitrovica," *Balkan Insight*, January 22, 2010.

134. http://www.nytimes.com/2016/05/22/world/europe/how-the-saudis -turned-kosovo-into-fertile-ground-for-isis.html

135. www.novinite.com/articles/130230/ WikiLeaks%3A+islam+and+Islamic+Extremism+in+Bulgaria

136. theweek.com/articles/570297/how saudi arabia exports radical islam

137. http://www.atlantico.fr/pepites/wikileaks-reveledessous-strategie -saoudienne-pour-exporter-islamisme-partoutplanete-2253161.html

138. francais.rt.com/opinions/11976-afrique-sub-saharienne-islam -africain-islam-arabo-africain

139. *Daily Star*, May 23, 2011, and www.lecommercedulevant.com /node/18881

140. Rose Skelton, "Mali: Faith and the Fightback," theafricareport.com

141. *Le Point*, January 21, 2016.

142. "Rising Tide of Shiism" from Kazakhstan to Spain. The struggle against the Shiites, WikiLeaks cable.

143. www.marianne.net/agora-comment-salafisme-pu-prosperer-au-niger .210115.html

144. www.theatlantic.com/magazine/archive/2016/04/the-Obama -doctrine/471525/

145. www.hum.uu.nl/medewerkers/m.vanbruinessen/publications /bruinessen_genealogies_islamic_radicalism.pdf 146. *Wall Street Journal*, December 30, 2005.

147. Philippe Raggi, *Indonésie, la nouvelle donne*, L'Harmattan, 2000 and Philippe Raggi, "Les chrétiens dans le plus grand pays musulman du monde," http://asie.espace.free.fr/espace/analytiq / raggi

148. www.rabwah.net/wikileaks-saudi-cables-reveal-secret-push-to -stop-ahmadiyya-in-indonesia/

149. www.lecourrierderussie.com/2015/11/attentats-salafisme-etat -islamique-menace-russie/

150. Mikhaïl Remizov, President of the Institute of National Strategy, an excellent French speaker, often gives talks at symposia in France.

151. www.letemps.ch/monde/2015/10/07/russes-divises-campagnesyrie

152. Report entitled, "La Salafisation des Tatars: Questions de préservation de la langue de la religion, de la prédication, de la culture nationale et ethnique (The Salafization of the Tatars: Issues regarding the preservation of the language, religion, preaching and national and ethnic culture), Symposium on "International Studies by Islamic Experts in Contemporary

Russia and the CIS countries: Achievements, Problems and Prospects," March 15–16, 2011, University of Kazan.

153. www.bbc.com/news/world-europe-1.9179399

154. Habiba Fathi, "La naissance de la coopération islamique en Asie centrale," *Recherches internationales*, no. 46, Autumn 1996.

155. Anoushiravan Ehteshami, *From the Gulf to Central Asia: Players in the New Great Game*, University of Exeter Press, 1994.

156. Eva Kochan, "La 'menace islamiste' en Russie et en Asie centrale," Regards sur l'Est, January 1, 2001, can be consulted online at http://www.regard est.com/home/breve_contenu.php?id=181

157. Eva Kochan, "La 'menace islamiste' en Russie et en Asie centrale," op. cit.

158. http://www.lexpress.fr/actualite/monde/asie/le-tadjikistan-rase13 -000-barbes-dans-son-combat-contre-le-radicalisme_1755838. html

159. Ibid.

160. Eva Kochan, "La 'menace islamiste' en Russie et en Asie centrale," op. cit.

161. www.theguardian.com/world/2002/dec/05/chechnya.nickpatonwalsh

162. Khalid, Adeeb, *Islam After Communism: Religion and Politics in Central Asia*, University of California Press, 2007.

163. http://www.operationspaix.net/41835-details-actualite-syrie-25 -000-combattants-etrangers-dans-les-rangs-jihadistes-selon-l -onu.html

164. *Combating Terrorism Center*, Per Gudmundson, "The Swedish Foreign Fighter Contingent in Syria," September 24, 2013; Samar Batrawi, "The Dutch Foreign Fighter Contingent in Syria," October 24, 2013; Fernando Reinares and Carola García Calvo, "The Spanish Foreign Fighter Contingent in Syria," January 15, 2014; Aaron Y. Zelin, "The Saudi Foreign Fighter Presence in Syria," April 28, 2014; Raffaello Pantucci, "The British Foreign Fighter Contingent in Syria," May 29, 2014; Timothy Holman, "Foreign Fighters from the Western Balkans in Syria,"

June 30, 2014; Evan Kohlmann and Laith Alkhouri, "Profiles of Foreign Fighters in Syria and Iraq," September 29, 2014; Daniel H. Heinke and Jan Raudszus, "German Foreign Fighters in Syria and Iraq," January 20, 2015; Aaron Y. Zelin, "Up to 11,000 Foreign Fighters in Syria. Steep Rise among Western Europeans," *International Center for the Study of Radicalization and Political Violence*, King's College London, December 2013.

165. http://www.levif.be/actualite/belgique/comment-l-arabie-saoudite-a-impose-son-islam-rigoriste-a-la-belgique/article-normal-55639.html

166. https://www.lemonde.fr/attaques-a-paris/article/2015/11/18/radicalisation-le-cocktail-molenbeekois_4812301_4809495.html.

167. https://www.lemonde.fr/idees/article/2015/11/23/molenbeek-saint-jean-n-est-pas-un-ghetto_4815791_3232.html

168. www.bbc.com/news/uk_11799713

169. http://www.dailymail.co.uk/news/article-2020382/You-entering-Sharia-law-Britain-As-Islamic-extremists-declare-Sharia-law-zone-London-suburb-worrying-social-moral-implications.html

170. Marwan Abou Taam, *Le Salafisme en Allemagne. Un danger pour la démocratie*, Notes by CERFA, no. 110, March 2014.

171. http://www.lalibre.be/actu/international/allemagne-la-propagande-wahhabite-en-point-de-mire-5665b870357004acd0f9969a.

172. A study by the Interior Ministry (unpublished).

173. www.smh.com.au/national/wikileaks-saudi-cables-reveal-secret-saudi-government-influence-in-australia-20150620-ght4kp.html

174. www.sbs.com.au/news/article/2015/11/18/grand-mufti-interview-its-if-we-are-ones-who-are-responsible

175. https://www.smh.com.au/politics/federal/grand-mufti-controversy-the-truth-some-say-should-not-be-spoken-20151201-glcnsi.html

176. www.mcgill.ca/files/arbitration/debates.pdf

177. http://pointdebasculecanada.ca/saudis-are-exporting-terrorism -to-canada-experts-warn/

178. Gilles Kepel, *Fitna, op. cit.*, p. 220.

179. "Saudi Publications on Hate Ideology Invade American Mosques" Report, Freedom House, 2005.

180. "Le conflit aux mille visages," *Cahier du Monde*, May 15, 16, 17, 2016.

181. www.huffingtonpost.fr/2013/10/26/arabie saoudite femmes droit conduire_n_4149304.html

182. Nabil Mouline noted in *Clercs de l'islam* that Abd al Wahhab himself had never censured members of the Al Saud family who had reached out to the Ottomans during the internal war; he had only gently reprimanded them.

183. Samir Amghar, "La Ligue islamique mondiale en Europe: un instrument de défense des intérêts stratégiques saoudiens," op. cit.

184. Samir Amghar, *Le Salafisme aujourd'hui*, Michalon, 2008, p. 124 et seq.

185. Brynjar Lia, *Architect of Global Jihad: The Life of Al-Qaeda Strategist Abu Musab al-Suri*, Columbia University Press, 2008. He is a research professor at the Norwegian Defense Research Establishment.

186. Naji Abu Bakr, *Gestion de la barbarie. L'étape par laquelle l'islam devra passer pour restaurer le califat*, Éditions de Paris, 2007.

187. Stéphane Lacroix, "Saudi Islamists and the Arab Spring," London School of Economics Kuwait Program, May 2014, p. 51–52 and https://www.religion.info/2010/10/27/islamisme-en-arabie -saoudite-produit-importation/

188. religion.info/french/entretiens/article_169.html

189. https://www.lesclesdumoyenorient.com/Contestation-politique -et-pouvoir.html

190. Israel Elad-Altman, "L'islam chiite à la conquête de la majorité sunnite," *Le Monde 2*, no. 157, February 17, 2007.

191. www.nytimes.com/2015/07/17/world/middleeast/wikileaks
-saudi-arabia-iran.html

192. www.nytimes.com/2015/07/17/world/middleeast/wikileaks-saudi
-arabia-iran.html

193. https://www.cbsnews.com/news/obama-says-director-of-national
-intelligence-to-soon-complete-28-pages-review/

194. Stéphane Lacroix, "Les nouveaux intellectuels religieux saoudiens,
le wahhabisme en question," op. cit.

195. http://www.memri.org/report/en/0/0/0/0/0/0/638.htm#_edn

OTHER BOOKS IN THE "LE MONDE COMME IL VA" COLLECTION

Michel Wieviorka, *Le Printemps du politique*, 2007

Laurence Ritter, *La Longue Marche des Arméniens*, 2007

Catherine Wihtol de Wenden and Christophe Bertossi, *Les Couleurs du drapeau: Les militaires français issus de l'immigration*, 2007

Dominique Mehl, *Enfants du don*, 2008

Didier Lapeyronnie, *Ghetto urbain*, 2008

Michel Wieviorka, *Neuf leçons de sociologie*, 2008

Farhad Khosrokhavar and Amir Nikpey, *Avoir vingt ans au pays des ayatollahs*, 2009

Yvon Le Bot, *La Révolte indienne: Les mouvements d'émancipation en Amérique latine*, 2009

Patrick Berche, *L'Histoire secrète des guerres biologiques: Mensonges et crimes d'État*, 2009

Véronique Fournier, *Le Bazar bioéthique*, 2010

Samuel Ghiles eilhac, *Le CRIF–De la Résistance juive à la tentation du lobby, de 1943 à nos jours*, 2011

Michel Wieviorka, *Pour la prochaine gauche*, 2011

Pierre Conesa, *La Fabrication de l'ennemi*, 2011

Claude Juin, *Des soldats tortionnaires*, 2012

Richard Beraha (dir.), *La Chine à Paris*, 2012

Alain Touraine, *Carnets de campagne*, 2012

Michel Foucher, *Atlas de l'influence française au xxie siècle*, 2013

Maëlegzig Bigi, Olivier Cousin, Dominique Méda, Laetitia Sibaud and Michel Wievorka, *Travailler au xxie siècle*, 2014

Michel Wieviorka, *Retour au sens*, 2015

Edgar Morin, *Penser global*, 2015

Hervé Le Bras, *Anatomie sociale de la France*, 2016